School management – a case approach
Alan Paisey

Harper & Row, Publishers
London

Cambridge San Francisco
Hagerstown Mexico City
Philadelphia São Paulo
New York Sydney

British Library Cataloguing in Publication Data

Paisey, Alan
  School management
  1. School management and organisation
  I. Title
  371.2 LB2805

  ISBN 0-06-318283-1

Typeset by Saxon Typesetting, Derby
Printed by Butler & Tanner Ltd., Frome and London

The Author

Alan Paisey held a number of teaching posts in London schools before being appointed to Bulmershe College of Higher Education in 1967. As Head of Administrative Studies, he has been responsible for the development of school management studies. The college has an established master's degree and research programme and is a centre for school management training recognized by the DES.

He obtained his doctorate at Henley, The Management College, and has published numerous articles and books, including *The Behavioural Strategy of Teachers in Britain and the United States* (NFER); *Small Organizations – the Management of Primary and Middle Schools* (NFER-Nelson): *Organization and Management in Schools* (Longman) and *The Effective Teacher* (ed.) (Ward Lock). As associate editor of the journal *School Organization and Management Abstracts* he is responsible for theses and dissertations.

After teaching for a time in the United States, he became a founder member and first president of the United Kingdom chapter of Phi Delta Kappa. He is a member of the steering committee of the BEMAS Education Management Teachers' group. Since 1975 he has been involved in a variety of duties for the CNAA and is currently a member of its Educational Organization and Management Board.

CONTENTS

FOREWORD

Training in school management (or school administration as it was usually called then) began in the early 1950s with the first experimental courses organized for the College of Preceptors by W.H. Perkins, previously Chief Education Officer for Warwickshire. Ten years later the College was running half a dozen residential courses for more than 400 heads and deputies each summer, and there had been a remarkable proliferation of bodies providing courses, including university departments of education, local education authorities, the Educational Development Association and, somewhat later, the National Association of Head Teachers.

Until that time systematic training for headship was unknown. Good heads were 'born not made', and once appointed they were expected to switch from being an assistant to headship by instinct. Controlling a school was rather like controlling a car: once you had acquired the feel of it you could 'drive by the seat of your pants'. It is astonishing how many good heads managed to run well-organized schools in those days. Perhaps it is because of increased pressures for accountability, as well as larger schools, that it is less acceptable now to throw a new head in at the deep end and hope for the best, although this is still common practice.

In *Management Development for the Education Profession* (1972), Ron Glatter held that administration and management were interchangeable terms. The local authority courses as established a couple of decades ago, however, were mainly concerned with teaching heads to adminster schools within the management structures of the authority. They were usually available just after appointment or, in some cases, during the term before taking up a first headship. The mystique of school administration was not yet shared, at any rate in most authorities, with aspirants further down the scale, whether on a selective or random basis.

During this early period two distinct kinds of course developed. Those provided by local education authorities remained essentially as training in the administrative techniques of the authority concerned, and dealt with matters such as the division of functions between its departments, financial requirements, capitation procedures, etc. Some authorities gradually introduced topics of a general character, such as educational law, but usually these sessions were undertaken by a member of the authority's staff, and interpretation and illustration were both drawn from the experience of that particular County Hall. Admirably suited as it was to its limited purpose, this form of training remained essentially parochial in its approach, even in a large authority.

Several developments, however, were demanding a different approach, supplementary rather than alternative. Large comprehensive schools, in growing numbers, could not depend entirely on the head's charismatic inspiration, which might have been adequate in small schools. Education, long spurned by the media, suddenly became newsworthy and long-cherished, comfortable traditions were ruthlessly questioned. A vocabulary once confined to industry and commerce began to invade education, its most telling shock, perhaps, being the title of a book by W. Kenneth Richmond: *The Education Industry* (1969).

The non-authority courses were the first to respond to these changes, and the Preceptors quickly amended the name of their programme from 'School Administration' to 'School Management Studies'. Many local authority courses still follow the more limited approach outlined above. This is entirely proper, for an employer should ensure that senior employees understand how to administer particular procedures. Nevertheless, the heads of schools, however much they may appear to be top management to pupils, staff and parents within the context of their individual schools, are very much middle management within the totality of a local education authority's service and they must, therefore, be able to administer management decisions bound on them from above, and to make managerial decisions and establish structures within their schools. In management terminology they are branch managers working for an employer who gives them an exceptionally high degree of discretion.

The first waves of the new managerial approach began to make themselves felt in the mid-sixties, and by the end of that decade the tide was flowing at full strength. It is significant that in a nine-page bibliography in Ron Glatter's book already referred to (1972) there are very few references to any publications earlier than 1967. It was at this time that the writer visited Cheshunt College, Cambridge, then for sale at what seemed the extortionate figure of £150,000 to £200,000, and prepared a feasibility study on its use as a full-time training centre in management studies for the staff and governors of schools. Cash flow problems prevented the College of Preceptors from developing this project but the idea was taken up again a few months later in a pamphlet *The Idea of a Staff College* (1967) written for the Head Masters' Association by Parry Michael.

The use of management concepts and technology has not found universal acceptance, however. Many teachers regard education as 'different', partly because they have been conditioned to regard industry and commerce as arid areas of activity dominated by the profit motive. Some, cocooned from the world of business, would hold that even the smiling face of capitalism, concerned with worker welfare, is a mask to enable employers to squeeze more work out of their employees and to garner richer harvests for themselves. Yet the same teachers will go to endless trouble to improve working conditions in schools so that pupils have the greatest possible chance to develop, and so that they and their teachers are encouraged to work harder.

Whilst it must be admitted that some teachers will switch off if their head starts talking about line management objectives, the principles underlying the organization of schools are no different from those applicable to a commercial undertaking. The purpose of management is the organization of resources (including manpower) to produce the optimum result. It matters not whether the end product consists of consumer goods, the sale of which will produce wages and profits, or whether the 'goal' is less tangible, as in education.

Exploration in Management (1960) by Wilfred Brown illustrates this point admirably. The book is a description of the Glacier Metal Company's concepts and methods of organization, as developed during the period when Brown was its chairman and managing director. While much of the detail is clearly the application of principles to industrial organization, any head reading this book is bound to say, time and time again: 'That fits the pattern of my own structures' or, 'That could be adopted in my school'. The same kind of parallels can also be found in *Management Made Simple* (1970) by W.T. Coventry.

Books of this kind, written without a great deal of management jargon, can be of considerable value in assisting a head to formulate his managerial organization.

What is school management?

As has been hinted above, courses in school management and administration were provided for heads and, more rarely, for deputies — the members of a school staff chiefly concerned with administration. The introduction of the term 'management', however, posed another question: 'Where does management stop?' This was put in another context by Brown (1960):

Some years ago I was a member of the Education Committee of the British Institute of Management. We received a communication from the American Management Association asking: "In Britain, is the foreman a member of the management team?" The committee argued the question at great length but the discussion became not in fact an attempt to answer the question, but an examination of the meaning of the words 'foreman' and 'management team'. Clearly, no answer could possibly be found until there was agreement about the content of these words.

Where, indeed, are the boundaries to be found in an educational institution? Brown (1960) defines as a manager: 'A member who has subordinate to him authorized roles into which he can appoint members and determine their work: he is accountable for his subordinates' work in these roles.'

Brown regards the power of hiring and firing to be an essential element of management. If this is to be accepted as *sine qua non*, only a limited number of schools would have any professional managers at all, since few heads (let alone deputies or heads of departments) have this power vested in them.

Coventry (1970) prefers a more sweeping definition: 'A manager is one who is responsible for getting things done through other people, instead of doing the job himself . . . with stated objectives to achieve, i.e. to produce certain goods or services, he directs human activities, with the help of the other resources available, towards those ends. As a positive way of life, the ambitious junior clerk could well think of himself as being on a management ladder the day he delegates some of his work to a new junior clerk, keeping a watchful eye on what he is doing in the process.'

This comes much nearer to the definition already given, that management is the organization of resources to produce the optimum result. On this basis every teacher is a manager, the planning of every lesson an exercise in management by objectives. This is the underlying theme of *The Teacher as Manager* (1970), a symposium edited by George Taylor, formerly Chief Education Officer for Leeds. It began to be recognized that management decision taking was not just a matter for senior staff, but an area in which all teachers should have some training.

The final extension of management training has grown from the recommendations of the Taylor Report (1977) and the Education Act 1980. Section 17 of the Education Act 1944 had provided bodies of governors (until 1980 called 'managers' in primary schools), whose powers were defined by articles of government (rules of management in the primary sector). Under these articles or rules the governors are charged with 'the general control of the conduct and curriculum of the school'. The head has a legal duty to control the internal organization, management and discipline of the school, and to supervise the teaching and non-teaching staff.

The division of functions envisaged by articles and rules made under section 17 of the 1944 Act was reasonably clear, and was researched in detail by George Baron and D.A. Howell in *The Government and Management of Schools* (1974). The Taylor Report, *A New Partnership in Our Schools* (1977), however, proposed a number of changes, giving parents direct representation on governing bodies (the term 'managers' was to be discontinued) and, most importantly, abolishing the principle which denied a voice to those employed in the school. In particular, the head was to be a governor *ex officio* unless he chose otherwise.

The proposals were given legislative force in the 1980 Act, and for heads a third dimension of government was added to those of management and administration. The right given to heads to opt out of government was secured by the pressure of the National Association of Head Teachers. Among many heads there was a feeling that they would be in a weaker position as members of a governing body than when they were attending as officers. One seldom hears a managing director complain that he would rather be a general manager and, if he does, it is not for this reason, yet this is basically the change of status acorded to heads by the 1980 Act.

Management training has been compelled to include this new dimension, however, and it is interesting to note that the feasibility study prepared for the use of Cheshunt College, Cambridge, in the winter of 1966´967, envisaged courses for governors. Then as now, however, there were few financial resources for training teachers, and fewer still for governors.

Over the years, therefore, there have grown up two parallel lines of courses, one local and administrative and the other dealing with broader principles, often national in character. The latter group has generally recruited students on a regional or national basis, and lecturers and group leaders have not been drawn from the area of a single local education authority. The course directors generally have been people with a national reputation in their particular fields. As a result, these courses have provided all the ingredients for a free interplay of ideas from many different sources, both staff and students contributing an input of rich variety.

Enough has been said to demonstrate that both streams of development have made an essential contribution to the growth of management studies. The local authority courses have included the acquisition of a necessary body of knowledge dealing with the 'nuts and bolts' of a particular authority's systems. The courses based on wider areas have contributed a background knowledge of management principles freed from the administrative inbreeding which it is difficult for even the largest authority to avoid in its internal provision.

Case studies

In the early years of management training, courses frequently followed the study pattern first established many years previously by the Student Christian Movement at Swanwick: a lecture followed by discussion in groups of a dozen or so members, the unit being rounded off by a plenary session at which the group either asked questions or reported back. This method continues to be used for many sessions, but a new development introduced from the United States in the early 1960s.

This is a case study or simulation exercise and, as Glatter (1972) points out, the various forms which have developed are all projects in which course members are asked to respond to various typical situations which are presented to them. The idea of involving course members in this way was adopted enthusiastically by the bodies concerned with planning in this field, and was a reminder that well-established educational principles may be relevant in parts of the system other than those in which they have been developed. The Report of the Consultative Committee of the Board of Education on *The Primary School* (1931) advised: 'The curriculum is to be thought of in terms of activity and experience rather than of knowledge to be acquired and facts to be stored.'

The early case studies generally consisted of 'in tray' exercises in which a number of papers were presented as 'authentic' documents for action and the student was required to imagine himself in the role of the recipient, and make a response. One of the earliest of these was *The Prentice Affair* (1964) devised for the College of Preceptors. For five years members of the College courses derived a great deal of information and amusement from the difficulties of Reginald Prentice, whose dubious use of corporal punishment has caused considerable embarrasment to John Squeers, the headmaster of Eatanswill County Secondary School.

This particular case study, like a number of others, simulated the kind of file which a head might find on return from a period of absence. Of the 28 documents in the tray only seven dealt with the Prentice issue, and these were interleaved with various routine matters and minor problems. The unit was divided into three parts. During the first hour students were required to sort the papers individually, discarding trivia, delegating routine work and minor problems and preparing their response to the major theme. To simulate the pressure of time the papers were not distributed until the beginning of this period, which was followed by the preparation of a report in groups for the plenary session, which ended with an assessment by the lecturer responsible for the unit.

In 1965 the College organized its first advanced course, and for some years this consisted entirely of case studies, one being presented on each day of the five-day course. These included planning a new school building (introduced by experienced school architects), timetabling and a governors' meeting. *The Prentice Affair* was published in *Education Today* (1969) shortly after it was replaced by a new study.

Using case studies

It is possible to build in almost any desired degree of sophistication in order to make the working of case studies more attractive and effective. Management decisions are almost invariably made under some pressure, a pressure which is often responsible for errors of judgement. Anything which can heighten the feeling of pressure adds to the value of a case study. It is possible, for example, to arrange for the individual study to be undertaken in one room, so that a number of verbal interruptions can be arranged. Even more realistic would be the preparation of an audio or video tape which could be programmed with parental interruptions, a reminder that the school is waiting for assembly, etc. A further extension could be the provision of recording facilities so that the course member can record his reactions to these interruptions as they occur, or make 'telephone calls' or engage in conversations arising from the study itself.

In presenting 30 case studies in a single volume, Alan Paisey has made a significant contribution to the use of this technique. Although they are arranged in pairs, each pair being drawn, broadly, both from the primary and the secondary sector, teachers will find that the case which does not belong to their particular field may nevertheless have considerable relevance for them. Management is management, and efficient management frequently depends, among other things, upon skill in delegation.

The cases set out in this book are not cast in the in-tray mould, and the format in which they are presented makes them equally suitable for consideration during a course, or for private study. The introduction to each serves the same purposes as the headnote to a law report, giving a concise summary of the main features of the case. The narrative provides a great deal more detail about the background than is possible with an in-tray exercise, where students often complain that they have not been told enough about the school.

Those with experience in relevant areas of school management will probably prefer to identify their own questions for discussion to compare with those set out by the author but it is likely that everyone will value the commentaries which have been provided. It is essential in working through these exercises to remember that they are drawn from real life. They are sober accounts of the management problems which heads and senior staff have had to solve, and the commentaries have been forged on the anvil of experience.

The book can be used in a number of different ways. Aspirants to senior management appointments may well find it valuable to treat it as a personal study course to enable them to identify a variety of issues which can arise, to think purposefully about them, and to consider a wider range of decision implications than they have so far met in practice. Those already in such a post may find help in dealing with problems which have already asserted themselves.

In recent years, schools have been encouraged to undertake school-based in-service training. This has often proved ineffective because of difficulties in planning a relevant programme. Here is such a course which may well achieve two desirable ends — an understanding by all members of the staff of the problems faced by a head (and the constraints surrounding him or her) and the essential managerial functions of every teacher. Furthermore this can be done with the minimum of management jargon. The cases might also be used in training educational administrators, to give them an insight into the problems of those whose institutions they adminster.

Although there is a logical arrangement of the cases, it is by no means necessary to work through them in the order given. Indeed relevance to the job in hand, and interest (e.g. in personal relationships or curriculum development) are more important. It is interesting to note that the plan of the book is circular — starting with the opening of a real school, it ends with the closure of existing schools in a reorganization, which in effect brings the reader back to the beginning with the opening of the reorganized school.

It is also possible to use this book in conjunction with the study of specific management techniques, in order to appreciate their appropriateness in the school situation. There is perhaps hardly an avenue of organization to which management by objectives is not appropriate though Case Studies 7.1 and 7.2 may seem most appropriate in this context. Those who have some experience of the use of critical path analysis (Programme Evaluation Review Technique or PERT) in schools, know that it can save the sanity of the head faced with a complex reorganization (Case Studies 15.1 and 15.2) or even when planning the annual timetabling operation (Case Study 9.1).

A personal example may show how this book points to management techniques which have been used for years by teachers, but which are sometimes resisted because they are called by strange new names. In 1935, I joined the staff of a public elementary school on the Essex coast. The school consisted of about 240 pupils aged between 5 and 14 in six classes. Apart from religious instruction (in which the Cambridgeshire Agreed Syllabus was used) the head wrote every syllabus in every subject throughout the school. These syllabuses, written on Imperial-sized card, were comparatively brief, but gave an outline of the topics which it was expected would be covered by each class in each subject during the year. It was then the duty of the class teacher, during the summer holiday, to prepare a list of topics, called 'the scheme', showing how he proposed to complete the syllabus week by week.

In the opening paragraph of Case Study 7.1, we find:

> The senior management team had produced a document which in very broad terms itemised the general aims of the school. However, these aims had not been interpreted into practical teaching objectives, although some isolated attempts had been made to produce check lists at the 'breakdown of skills' level, by individual teachers.

Here, quite plainly, we have identical management practice, taking into account the differences in the educational setting which have evolved during half a century. The syllabuses devised by the head of the Essex school were the generalised aims of instruction for a period of a year, the class teachers' schemes were the interpretation of those aims into what the case study calls 'practical teaching objectives'.

So, in the totality of planning a school's development it is possible to fix generalized aims which perhaps it is intended should remain reasonably static, or at least recognizable for the duration of the school lives of all the pupils currently on the roll. Changes will come, but, in general, it is desirable that they should not be so radical as to alter the aims beyond recognition. In a secondary school with a sixth form, planning for a period of stability of this generalised kind would be for seven years. The school must then identify annual, possibly termly, objectives — the steps by which the school will seek to achieve these aims.

Just as teachers in the 1930s had to record the work they had done each week, and produce a forecast for the next week which would, if necessary, state how and when shortfall would be made up, so a school must evaluate its progress towards its stated aims and review the objectives in order to make achievement possible. The terminology has changed; the practice remains the same.

Those who, like myself, served their headships between about 1954 and 1977, were without doubt fortunate. Problems there were, but education was an expanding industry; financial resources were comparatively easy. Fortunate were we who knew, in those days, that next year's roll would be larger; that there would be more teachers; and that the capitation allowance would rise. Today, heads must manage for contraction: lower rolls, fewer staff, and a capitation allowance which does not pretend to keep pace with inflation. Almost invariably a reorganization will mean redundancies, with a smaller staff attempting to do the same job and with minority subjects being eliminated. These problems are dealt with in the last two case studies in this book. All the efforts made by the local education authorities to cushion redundancy by redeployment or early retirement cannot hide the fact that ultimately someone who feels they still have a contribution to make, will be out of a job.

At one time, those concerned with educational management needed to know little of the law, apart from the Education Acts (chiefly for administrators) and the common law position of the teacher in *loco parentis*. Today, he or she must be reasonably familiar with modern employment legislation, defamation, copyright, and a host of other matters. Many of these fringe areas are dealt with in the case studies, and the student working through them should always be ready to refer to the legal constraints which may often prove a limitation on otherwise acceptable solutions.

Indeed, one of the principal advantages of the simulation technique is the way in which it compels students to be aware of constraints — legal, professional and moral. The legal limitations are the most rigid of all, distinguishing between what is permitted and what is forbidden.
Managers must work within the legal framework of the society in which they are operating and any course of action which they adopt must be amenable to the law.

It is a different matter with professional and moral constraints. Professional considerations will often set the boundaries of what is or is not practicable in any situation. They will indicate to the practising manager the area which will enable him or her to use resources to the best possible advantage. Where such an area permits more than one solution of similar quality, the manager is free to choose that which seems best. Moral considerations deal with what is right; 'what ought to be done' is the final imperative. These cases provide the reader with an opportunity to distinguish these different constraints and to identify their respective influences.

The case studies in this collection place considerable emphasis on the ethical dimension, which is plainly drawn out in many of the commentaries. If this is borne in mind by the reader working through the problems, the book will have made a significant contribution to the literature of management studies in schools, by drawing attention to the need for a systematic approach to decision making in a complex network of human and administrative situations.

Geoffrey Barrell
August 1983

PREFACE

This book is offered as a contribution to the literature in educational management. It is intended to be of particular interest to teachers who manage schools or who aspire to do so, as well as to those who are not teachers but who work in or for schools.

In recent years the potential value of case material for training programmes in educational management has become evident. The growing number of short and award bearing courses in educational management has indicated a need for teaching materials of all kinds.

The cases in this book are authentic. The narrative of each is compiled from information supplied by the following staff in the education service. Apart from one member of an independent school, they are between them employed by eight local education authorities.

Frank Agness, Head

Roy Bone, Deputy Head

Jean Bull, Head

Robert Burton, Deputy Head

Dennis Fullerton, Head

Geoffrey Green, Head

Michael Green, Deputy Head

Robert Griffin, Head

Neil Hawkes, LEA Advisor

Anthony Hill, Head

John Honeybourne, LEA Assistant Director for General Services

Winifred Howard, Head

Rodney King, LEA Adviser

Michael Lusty, LEA Assistant Education Officer

Anne Mace, Head of Department

Julie Makin, Deputy Head

Ivan Marks, Head

Wendy Merwood, Head

Michael Newton, Deputy Head

Patrick Paisey, Head of Department

Richard Peppin, Head

David Picton-Jones, Head

Elizabeth Pye, Scale 1 Teacher

David Smith, Head of Department

Jenny Willcock, Head

Keith Williams, Head

John Woodock, Head

Susan Wootton, Scale III Teacher

Anne Wrighte, Deputy Head

I record my sincere thanks to them for giving their time and attention to the task in the middle of a busy school year. Without them this book would not exist.

It has been my good fortune to have the interest and support of Geoffrey Barrell, whose own endeavours in case study work in educational management have justly assumed a high reputation and whose books on legal cases have become classic in status: *Legal Cases for Teachers* (London, Methuen 1970) and *Teachers and the Law* (London, Methuen 1984). This book is enhanced by his special contributions, reflecting his immense knowledge and experience in this field.

In addition I record my thanks to my wife, Audrey Paisey, Principal Lecturer at Bulmershe College of Higher Education, whose careful perusal of this book at each stage of its development resulted in many helpful suggestions, the clarification of difficulties, and the solution of problems.

My thanks are also expressed to Pat Richards for her expert translation of manuscripts into typescript.

It is hoped that the book does justice to all these people. Any remaining shortcomings, however, are my own responsibility.

Alan Paisey

INTRODUCTION

The means for understanding and improving the management of schools are everywhere to hand. They consist of the systematic and daily exercise of professional practice in every school in the country. It is undeniably important to supplement management in practice in various ways from other sources. Nevertheless, it is actual practice which is the best teacher.

Those who seek a greater knowledge of school management and an improvement in their own personal managerial performance in the first instance need look no further than the practice of management in other schools. Here every school has something to say. An observer or visitor can learn from every school provided negative information is given equal status with positive information. Professional practice in other schools may be evaluated in four ways: it can yield what may be emulated; it can yield what should be avoided; it may reveal what is unique to the specific school and its set of circumstances; and it may reveal what might be adapted for use elsewhere.

The infinite variety of reality offers much potential for learning but learning depends, first, upon information from direct observation or from indirect sources and, secondly, upon reflection on the data so gathered in order that it becomes knowledge which may be usable.

While the richest of all sources of instruction and learning is readily available, it is not readily accessible. By definition, those who would most profit from having access to other schools for the study of educational management cannot do so by reason of their prior commitment to their own work. Heads of schools are sometimes appointed far enough in advance of the date for taking up their posts to allow a wider study of professional practice. Schools may organize staff exchange visits. Local education authorities and institutions in higher education may incorporate visits for observational purposes in short courses in educational management. Even so, the scale on which these take place is relatively small although the secondment scheme funded by the Department of Education and Science as a basic course in educational management offers opportunities to increase this scale.

The prime purpose of this book is to put varied and pertinent material from professional practice into the hands of those who are practitioners in educational management or who aspire to senior management positions in schools. It is also intended to be of interest to those who are involved in the teaching and study of school management in award bearing and short courses offered by institutions in higher education and in short courses offered by local education authorities and other bodies. It should also be of interest to school governors, parents, advisers and others whose work or field of concern is with schools or takes them into schools, who believe that managing schools is a difficult task and wish to gain greater insight into its complexities.

The 30 cases in this book represent a large range of schools — infant and first, junior, primary and middle, secondary schools for various age ranges, secondary special and special all-age schools. They range in size from a tiny village school to a large urban comprehensive school and include schools wholly maintained by local education authorities, voluntary aided and independent schools.

The assumption is made that while each kind of school has its own characteristic problems, a study of the management of schools needs to take into account all kinds of school and to demonstrate the problems characteristic of schools in general. From the point of view of a senior teacher and his or her professional development in educational management, much can be learned from practice in different kinds of schools as well as from other schools of the same kind in which he or she currently works. From the pupil's and parent's point of view, a relevant and enjoyable curriculum, which enables the pupil to have a continuously progressive and satisfying learning experience in a challenging but non-threatening social setting, is the sole expectation, irrespective of age and ability level. To provide this is as important in the smallest rural school as in the largest urban school.

Each of the 30 cases is from a different school. They are all of recent origin, representing professional practice over a period up to the date of publication. It is never possible to know quite where a case should begin and end. A somewhat arbitrary intervention must be made in the endless ebb and flow of developments in the life of any school to capture something for study in literary form. Thus, many cases are still incomplete in terms of the parameters which are indicated within them. Others appear to have been completed, but in terms of different parameters could still be shown to be ongoing. The ramifications of previous actions and circumstances can be traced over long periods of development in a school to fashion the seamless garment of total reality which makes up school life at any point in time.

Each case consists of five parts. An introduction or overview precedes the narrative. A commentary on the narrative is followed by a list of issues for further discussion and suggested items for further reading relating to the subject matter of the case. The narrative in every case derives from written material supplied by a head of school or other senior member of the teaching staff directly involved with or able to observe directly the events which are recorded in the narrative.

It may be thought that a head's account might be more complete than that of a member of the teaching staff, however senior. It is important to have accounts from members of school staffs other than heads, however, if only to remind the reader that in organizations each individual should learn how to *be* managed as well as how to manage. The two perspectives may be different but both are important.

Inevitably the accounts of events provided are partial, incomplete and possibly biased. Only one person's perspective is represented. Even if that person is a central figure to the case this does not necessarily mean that the view given is detached and objective, however much care is taken. If all parties to the events recorded were able to present their views of them, the whole might be very different. Full and impartial data are seldom available; information on which management needs to act in reality often lacks these characteristics. In practice, the manager reading these cases must ask: What else do I need to know? Is this a balanced set of data? Readers of the cases will certainly wish to ask these and other questions before coming to the most significant question: What would I do in this situation? In the narrative for each case, facts are emphasized rather than opinion and interpretation. Identification marks of all kinds have been eliminated from the cases: pseudonyms have been introduced where necessary.

All cases contain both negative and positive elements. The governing principle has been to choose a case not wholly for its negative qualities, nor as a diatribe against a person, nor in order to attack a particular practice or institution. The cases chosen are not intended to be a selection of bizarre or spectacular problems, but rather those which are commonly found but nonetheless difficult to handle. The interesting aspect to this is that every head or senior teacher asked could quite easily identify a part of recent experience or a current concern which he or she thought to be of interest to others and worthy of attention.

The selection of material has been influenced by the need to cover a spectrum of management topics. Management in action does not have neat boundary lines. Every case about management inevitably touches on many issues, but is made to emphasize and illuminate some aspects of school management to the diminution or neglect of others which are also relevant. Each case in this collection, therefore, is chosen because it may be used to highlight a particular part of managerial conduct, responsibility and experience. Fifteen important topics are covered, each by reference to two schools, one providing for the lower age range of pupils and one the upper age range. The topics covered are: Opening a New School; Restructuring the School; Management Style; Staff Management; Staff Development; Curriculum Development; Management of the Curriculum; Pupil Grouping; Timetabling and the Use of Buildings and Facilities; Teaching Methods and Techniques; Managing Materials and Equipment; Relations with Parents; Financial Management; External Relations; and School Mergers.

The format for each case is standard. This had disadvantages as well as advantages. One of the disadvantages is that two cases, each dealing with very different topics — such as a problem family and the merger of two schools — command the same amount of space. Some narratives are therefore very condensed relative to others. The purpose, however, is to introduce a piece of professional practice, inevitably incomplete, in the hope that the reader will continue his or her own analysis, using the issues for further discussion. Each case may then be used to evoke parallels from the reader's own experience or observation, so that managerial thought will be extended and practice improved.

The nature of management

In using these case studies the reader may wish to keep in mind four important principles of management and the way in which management thought has developed during the last half century. *Management* may be defined as the universal and unavoidable personal and organizational process of relating resources to objectives. *Educational management* may be defined as the particular process of relating resources to objectives required in organizations which explicitly exist to provide education. Management is, therefore, in the first instance, a recognition and understanding of the task of the organization. Secondly, to discharge the *task*, people are needed. It is their presence, their willingness and their efforts which enable the organization to discharge the task expected of it. The focus of management is very much on the *membership* of the organization. The members, however, are seldom random. They have special knowledge, skills and potential. They are selected and may be given the means to develop so that their potentialities may become actual. The membership in action — using processes, procedures and practices — displays the organization's *technology*, the determination and application of which is the concern of management since they govern the quantitative and qualitative aspects of the product or output. While working as an organization, the members inevitably come into relationships one with another. Any pattern of such interrelationships is the *structure* of the organization. The range of possible patterns, their premises, and the actual ones which are needed or which emerge, makes the fourth important element of management. There is no separate theory of management for schools in the public sector any more than there is for any other type of organization, whether industrial or commercial. Consequently the referents which the teacher uses for his or her own development and management education can and should be widely drawn. There are legal, professional and ethical constraints and issues which are particular to schools and which give those who manage them a common bond and experience. There is a whole vocabulary of school management which goes with these constraints, providing the means for a common understanding and communication. This is no more nor less than any other industry or trade possesses, however. Management in action in any type of organization takes account of and uses both the factors which are peculiar to the type of organization concerned and those which are characteristic of all organizations.

The latter are dominant. The general values and acceptable practices of the community in question are pervasive. They vary as different circumstances and conditions persuade people to apply appropriate criteria and exercise relevant expectations according to the particular set which prevails at any one period. Within living memory, the privations and exertions of the Second World War are a dramatic case in point. Voluminous public expenditure and faith in education in the quarter of a century since 1945 provide a second example. The onset of what appears to be becoming a prolonged period of contraction and reduced faith in education provides a third. These phases are not necessarily merely national. The transmission of values and derivative practices between national communities is accommodated by many media and encouraged by political, economic, ideological and social forces.

Thus the management of organizations has been exposed to different sets of critical values and emphases, which have led to the development of management thought and a stock of recorded experience upon which to draw today. There was a time when the work content was stressed. Efficiency and economy were to the fore. It was believed that if the work content of an organization were thoroughly analyzed and people were accordingly deployed, all would be well. In the pursuit of understanding materials, processes, functions and structures, however, it was possible to lose sight of the human aspect of work — the motivation, job satisfaction, health and career of the individual organization member. To compensate for such an omission it was found necessary to restore the concern for people through a variety of means. These ranged from relatively trivial ones, such as the provision of amenities, to more sophisticated ones such as decentralizing the control of work and the introduction of job enrichment.

Consideration for people has been split into a concern for human relations and a concern for human resources. It is not enough to keep people happy at their work — though that is an important achievement. People, as organization members, are there to develop. This is an educational experience and a function of organizational membership. It is a right in natural law. The development of the human potential in the organization is inevitably good for the organization and is its most important resource. The individual and his or her work has come to be viewed as an entity. The highly selective, directed and detached behaviour of a former era has been exchanged for a more inclusive, volitional and committed behaviour. This creates more uncertainty within organizations, giving rise to management in terms of micropolitics — basically the problem of consensus. It should provide, however, a greater adaptability to external conditions, giving rise to the possibility of organizational survival. Two major concomitants in management thought have arisen from a recognition of the instability and uncertainty of external events and the greater fluidity and turbulence of life within the organization. Management should proceed on a basis of facing up to *contingencies* and dealing with each in its own right. In addition, the wisdom, skills and standing needed to make decisions and to put them into practice, requires management to be conceived as a *team* rather than as a hierarchy of individuals.

Further reading

Books:

Adams, N. (1983) *Teachers and the Law Today*. London, Hutchinson.

Barrell, G. (1970) *Legal Cases for Teachers*. London, Methuen.

Barrell, G. (1984) *Teachers and the Law*. London, Methuen.

Bush, T., Goodey, J. and Riches, C. (editors) (1980) *Approaches to School Management*. London, Harper and Row.

Department of Education and Science (1978) *Primary Education in England: a survey by HM Inspectors of Schools*. London, HMSO.

Department of Education and Science (1979) *Aspects of Secondary Education in England: a survey by HM Inspectors of Schools*. London, HMSO.

Harrison, G. and Bloy, D. (1980) *Essential Law for Teachers*. London, Oyez.

Miles, R.E. (1975) *Theories of Management*. London, McGraw-Hill Kogakusha.

Open Systems Group (1981) *Systems Behaviour*. London, Harper and Row.

Paisley, A. (1984) *Trends in educational leadership thought*, in Chapter 1, *Harling P. (editor) New Directions in Educational Leadership*, Lowes, Falmer Press.

Pollard, H. (1974) *Developments in Management Thought*. London, Heinemann.

Poster, C. (1976) *School Decision-Making*. London, Heinemann.

Richardson, E. (1973) *The Teacher, the School and the Task of Management*. London, Heinimann.

Pollard, M. (1978) *Further Developments in Management Thought*, London, Heinemann.

Journals:

Bulletin of the National Association of Secondary School Principals

Comparative Education

Comparative Education Review

Education (weekly)

Educational Management and Administration

Educational Administration Quarterly

Educational Analysis

Educational Leadership

Journal of Educational Administration and History

Journal of the National Association of Inspectors and Educational Advisers

Kappan

Principal (Journal of the National Association of Elementary School Principals)

Review of the National Association of Headteachers
Review of the Secondary Heads Association
School Organization
School Organization and Management Abstracts
The Head
The Journal of Educational Administration

CHAPTER 1
OPENING A NEW SCHOOL
Case 1.1: Headship first discovered

Introduction

The head of a new primary school is appointed. The school will open on a
very small scale but will grow progressively into a large school. It is the
head's first headship. Before she tackles anything at all, she finds herself in
the middle of controversy. There is much to learn about procedures.
Decisions of many kinds must be made and extensive preparations must be
completed before the first children are admitted. The new head is evidently
confident about the major issues such as the kind of teaching organization,
pupil grouping, general nature of the curriculum to be offered, staffing
policy and the particular ethos which should characterize the school. Some
of the immediate, practical and pressing problems about procedures require
knowledge and decisions, particularly ones concerning materials and
finance. The head finds reliable allies and friends in the exploratory — and
sometimes uncertain — task of opening the new school.

Narrative

The successful applicant was pleased to obtain her first headship, especially
as she was to be head of a brand new, purpose-built primary school — an
unusual opportunity in 1983. In the job description the head had noted
three sentences in particular: 'The school is built in an open-plan design
with three major teaching areas. There is a P.E./Assembly Hall, Dining/
Work Area, Study and Tutorial Rooms. Sympathetic and friendly
cooperation with parents will be essential and a candidate is sought whose
aims and philosophy are committed to cooperative teaching and "open"
schooling.' The school was located in an area where she wanted to work and
was in character intended to be the kind of school she herself favoured and
had already experienced as a deputy head. After the initial euphoria had
diminished, the size of the task facing the new head began to be apparent,
not least the fact that decisions made in those early days would affect the
working and private lives of many people, staff and pupils for a long time.
Within hours of being appointed she was handed a suggestion which,

because of its controversial nature, led to publicity in more than one national newspaper before the school had opened. Almost every other school in the town was named after the neighbourhood in which it was situated. Following those precedents the new school would have had a most attractive name. One of the school's governors, however, put forward the suggestion that the school should be named after someone killed in the Falklands conflict. This proposal earned itself both admiration and dismay, receiving both support and opposition. It was some months before the issue was resolved by a decision of the fully constituted governing body to call the school by its neighbourhood name, following local custom.

The head found that the support of governors, advisers, county officers, friends and colleagues was indispensable as she began the task of preparing to open the new school. Without exception, everyone with any kind of useful experience offered willing help. For example, the head of another school in the vicinity, which was almost identical in design and had opened the previous year, had much useful advice to offer. There were also many ex-colleagues who were glad to discuss matters of philosophy and the pitfalls to be avoided. Their experience proved to be invaluable. Even so, the head felt isolated during the term before the school opened. It was almost half-way through the term before any further staff were appointed, by which time she was obliged to submit orders for furniture, curtains and basic equipment without being able to consult any of her future colleagues.

One of the early tasks she undertook was to produce a list of people and departments with whom it was essential to liaise. For identification and foundation purposes she obtained for the school its scheme number, establishment number and the all-important Department of Education and Science number. An early document she received was the first computer printout disclosing how much of the capital fund had already been spent on such things as fitted cupboards, cloakroom mirrors and fire-fighting equipment. She noted that the funds available to equip the school were divided into the two usual categories, capital and capitation. The capital amount was entirely for furniture and non-consumable items of equipment. She submitted a schedule of estimated expenditure. This had to be agreed by the local education authority before the first order could be placed.

All orders involving equipment for specific areas of the curriculum were to be drawn up after discussion with the advisors with responsibility for the areas concerned. Subsequently, each order involving capital had to be submitted to and authorised by a particular officer at county level. She found out that for the first two years in the life of a new school, capitation was made available at the rate of twice the amount assessed for each child on roll when the school was full. This money was available for all consumables but might also be used for non-consumables.

Initially cash flow was quite a serious problem. There were large amounts of money available on paper, but no cash to hand for stamps, a plant for the entrance hall, hooks for hanging baskets, picture hangers, fuses, batteries and the 101 things that were unexpectedly needed. On enquiry, she found that the county treasurer's department would refund money spent out of her own pocket. Once the school was opened there would be an imprest account, topped up each month. Later there would be a school fund and a cheque book, but invariably during those early weeks she found it necessary to spend money that she did not have.

The head drew on her own previous experience. She had been team leader of a purpose-built, open-plan, team-teaching school, in which post she had found that it was false economy to buy less than the best equipment and materials, and that money spent on the purchase of materials was largely wasted unless adequate storage was also provided. Some items caused unexpected anxiety. She was surprised to find herself resolute about the educational philosophy and objectives of the school but disturbed about the purchase of curtains for it. Which rooms should have curtains and of what kind? Which designs should be chosen and who should make them? Should they be lined? Was it reasonable to expect a future school association to take on that commitment? Would there be enough willing and able mothers available to do the sewing and fitting? In the end she decided that justice should be done to the work of the architect and the builders and to the children who would be using the school. The material was chosen from a selection available from the county's supplies department and was made up and eventually fitted by their contractors. The total bill was £2250.

She considered whether all the furniture should be new or whether some should be second-hand from schools with falling rolls. On investigating the situation for second-hand furniture, however, she found that no suitable second-hand items were available in the county but was not displeased to buy new items throughout. She then needed to decide whether to equip the school with its furniture as if it were at full strength or to defer the purchase of some of it until the pupil roll built up with each successive intake. Prices probably would have risen meanwhile, but she had been told that capital not spent in the current financial year would have a percentage added to it to cover inflation. Her eventual decision was based on a fundamental consideration, however. The design of the building, with its three main areas, offered a high degree of flexibility but especially favoured team teaching organization, an integrated day and vertical grouping.

Once these resource objectives had been established, other decisions could be made more easily. The head wanted the school to function as a total entity. The building itself was a major resource. Most of its facilities were to be shared by all the children and the general use of all the different areas would reflect the overall philosophy of the school. The head decided that the whole school would be used from the very first day even though only a few children were expected in the first term, so she ordered the entire stock of furniture needed for a fully recruited school.

As far as the curriculum was concerned, the new head decided to delay all decisions until at least the senior staff were appointed in the belief that it was essential to involve those who would implement the educational policy of the school through their teaching. A main consideration was that in future the organization must adapt to the needs of a growing school roll — not only at the youngest age but also, although to a lesser degree, at every age up to eleven plus, as new families moved into the area, a recently built neighbourhood in a new town. Most of the houses were provided by the council but some private estates were being added and it was possible that houses in a further new neighbourhood would also fall within the school's catchment area. Architects' plans existed to double the size of the school to Group 6 should that prove necessary. On the first day the school was expected to open with just 46 children of whom 18 would be juniors and 28 infants; 15 of the infants would be in the reception class.

It seemed advisable, therefore, to choose a basic scheme in both language and mathematics which would allow newcomers to adjust easily, minimise teacher preparation time during the arduous early months, and provide a good deal of stimulus to other areas of the curriculum. Since the head believed that the needs of every, or indeed any child could never be satisfactorily met by any one particular scheme, she realised that eventually much time and careful thought would need to be put into discussing, examining, and selecting the work schemes which the school would eventually choose.

The head gave much thought to a staffing policy for the school. She was pleased to find the governors very supportive. Within a short time she and they were working on close and friendly terms. The task of getting the school ready for opening was made easier by the working partnership she established with them. She determined that the short-listing, interviewing and appointment of both teaching and non-teaching staff should be fully shared with representatives of the school's governors.

The head made a fundamental assumption that those staff with non-teaching duties should be treated in the same manner as the teachers. The staffroom would be open to all. A full staff meeting would include everyone who worked in the school — both teaching and non-teaching staff. This would be used for matters of overall school policy. A teaching staff meeting would be called for teachers only and used exclusively for the management of the teaching programme.

To open the school with the number of children expected meant that the head could engage two teachers and a part-time general helper. It would have been possible to delay the appointment of a deputy head but she chose to make that appointment at once. It would be someone who would be deputy for the school as a whole, rather than a teacher responsible for the infant section, which was a common practice in other primary schools in the locality. The new head wanted someone whose philosophy was not in conflict with her own, who could work well under considerable pressure, who was prepared to add new skills to those he or she already had, who was prepared to deputise for the head in a very full sense, who would accept specific responsibilities and, most important, someone who would be prepared to disagree with the head and, if necessary, act as devil's advocate. When it came to the point of short-listing and interviewing for the post, there were a number of candidates who it seemed might be able to fill the post but only one who seemed likely to fill it well.

Next to the head and deputy head, the third teacher needed to be someone with experience and expertise at infant level, someone who knew how to make young children feel valued and who could provide them with situations in which they could learn, grow and experience success. The school was fortunate in being able to choose such a teacher from an impressive short list.

The head was inundated with applications for the post of general helper. Many applicant's felt that their own experience as a parent was enough to qualify them for the post. An outstanding candidate, however, was someone who had just qualified as a nursery nurse after two years at a local college, and who had spent her own junior years in an open-plan teaching school.

With only 11 hours a week allowed for secretarial work it was obvious from the start that the head would be hard pressed to keep up to date with the work involved in opening and running a school. The first contact people have with a school is often via the secretary. Certainly the post needed someone who was familiar with the work of a school, someone who could relate well to children and adults, someone of boundless energy, a model of tact and diplomacy, someone who looked upon the job of opening a new school as a welcome challenge, and someone with potential as well as experience. Such a person was found.

Finally, one of the most important appointments to be made in any school is that of the caretaker. Consequently the interviews for that post were long and searching before an appointment was successfully made.

Precisely when can a school be said to have opened? Is it really the day when the first children start their education there, or is it weeks beforehand when the first parent signs the first admission form? Is it later when a full governing body has been appointed, or when the school association starts to function, when the brochure is printed, or when the press photographers arrive, stubbornly insisting upon the re-enacting of a ribbon being cut? These were some of the questions which the head found herself asking while preparing to open a new school.

Commentary

To be appointed to a headship for the first time and to a new school is a stimulating, if challenging professional experience. The head assumes legal responsibility for the education of children and young people in a school whose curriculum and organization must be maintained in good order.

In this case the community which the school was intended to serve was itself being formed. The size and composition of the population was uncertain. There were no settled values, no articulated points of view about education, no local tradition and no precedents to act as guidelines. The previous experience of the head and teaching staff alone becomes the basis on which a new school is built in such circumstances. A school needs to be alive to its many publics, but until these can be identified and their interests made known and interpreted, educational objectives and practices must be imported. As the head herself made clear, a long period of sensitive adjustment would be necessary following the opening of the school, as it slowly adapted to the social, political and economic realities of its developing neighbourhood.

The progressive appointments by which a teacher becomes head of a school generally provide an ad hoc proving ground and learning schedule. By the time a teacher becomes a newly appointed head of school, he or she has acquired a sufficient overview of the work of schools in the sector concerned. If the teacher's previous appointment as a deputy head of school has been properly used, it should have enabled him or her to get some feeling of what it is like to be head, to learn the regulations and administrative procedures involved and to become familiar with the many aspects of the work of the head — the problems which must be tackled and the decisions which must be made.

However, deputy headship in primary schools is unfortunately not always used constructively to prepare a teacher for headship. In this particular case, the new head seems to have observed or have had personal experience of the limited access a deputy head may have to the work of the school overall and understanding of the tasks of the head. She is therefore determined to offer the deputy head in her school a genuine position. She calculates that this will provide depth of management in the school, a more convincing and credible basis for leading the staff and conducting the business of the school, the better motivation of the deputy head and the constructive preparation of the deputy head for headship in due course. For these reasons she is anxious to appoint a deputy head at the beginning.

Although a newly appointed head may thus be well prepared concerning strategic considerations and matters of principle and practice, he or she may still find confusing decisions on what to do first and what procedures to follow for doing anything. Local education authorities may provide short induction programmes to help new heads and these may include a visit to the offices to meet various people with whom a head will come into contact for administrative purposes.

In this case the staffing of the school was the subject of special concern, distinguished by two considerations. The vacancies were clearly identified and the kind of person required was specified. Moreover, a highly participative policy was advocated as being the best way to establish a new school and help it to be sensitive and adaptive to the needs of its growth and development in a newly forming neighbourhood and community.

Issues for further discussion

1. What should be the head's order of priorities on opening a new school? What methods may be used systematically to plan and fulfil the complete range of tasks?

2. The employer's responsibility for inducting new heads.

3. Establishing good relations with the governing body.

4. Local heads as a support group for new heads.

5. The importance of the physical condition and aesthetic appeal of school buildings.

6. Teaching and non-teaching staff (a) sharing the same staff room and (b) sharing in school policy making.

7. The desirable skills and qualities of:
   (a) secretary,
   (b) caretaker,
   (c) deputy head
   in either a primary or secondary school.

8. Criteria for adopting a particular curricular scheme in a primary school.

9. How to gauge the character of a new and developing neighbourhood.

10. Financial experience and expertise of those seeking headships. Should this be given higher priority?

Further reading

Jones, D. (1980) *Primary School Management*. Newton Abbott, David & Charles.

Urwick, L. (1963) *The Elements of Administration*. London, Pitman.

Whitaker, P. (1983) *The Primary Head*. London, Heinemann.

Case 1.2: Resourcefulness and versatility in action

Introduction

In spite of a few muddles and mistakes a new secondary school is successfully opened. The head and deputy head teachers and other senior teachers — appointed either well in advance of, or just before the first term began — form a united and flexible team. They adjust willingly and quickly to extremely uncertain, sometimes threatening and rapidly changing, circumstances. Versatility and improvization abound. Some of the acute difficulties they face are beyond their capacity to avoid but some are of their own making as they begin the uncharted way forward in founding a new school.

Two issues stand out. First, the function of planning and preparation is to achieve objectives and to avoid serious problems in opening the school. Secondly, the incremental growth of the school offers an opportunity to consolidate development and achievement but at the same time creates the possibility that insular values and practices will eventually prevail as the senior staff who founded the school find it difficult to adjust to new values and practices which inevitably present themselves as the staff numbers grow to their full complement.

The narrative presents the difficulties encountered over materials and equipment, the initial deployment of staff, the viability of the school's first roll and the provisional pastoral system. Soon the need to review progress is felt and so the problems of evaluation are opened up.

Narrative

The school was to be a new, mixed comprehensive school for the 11 to 16 age range, situated in a growing London overspill estate from which it was to draw half its pupils, the remainder of the intake being from private residential estates. It was to have an intake which was comprehensive in terms of environment as well as ability.

It was intended that the school should be built in three phases. The initial phase included all the facilities that a small, expanding school would need or could use to start with. Most of the facilities needed for fourth and fifth-year work were to be included in phase two. Phase three was reserved for consolidation and final completion.

The head was appointed nine months before the school was due to open. At that time the phase one buildings were incomplete. When the school opened the following September, the buildings were still not complete. The builders did not leave the site until the following February. Owing to the lack of specialized accommodation, children were changing in classrooms for physical education and games. Physical education itself was taught in the largest classroom available, drama in a room intended for history and music with folding screens as walls. The areas of the school that were in use had only been handed over two weeks before the school opened.

Prior to this the head and the deputy head worked from a hutted classroom one and a half miles from the school site. Interviews for teaching, secretarial, catering, caretaking and cleaning staff appointments were held in it. Many deliveries of equipment were also stored in it, so that the working space became restricted to a small area around the telephone. As it was necessary at this stage to obtain permission from the builder's clerk of works to visit the school site, tempers frequently became frayed and harsh words flowed.

The firm supplying furniture — desks, tables, science benches, chairs and stools — failed to deliver them on time and did not do so until after the beginning of the term. This news precipitated a crisis. Local schools were closed for the summer holiday. Most head teachers were already on vacation, as were many of the caretakers. In any event there was little likelihood that other schools would have spare furniture. A collection of tables and chairs, many very old and stained, and odd shape and size, was assembled from church halls, schools whose heads and caretakers were available, and from the local council. When the pupils arrived for the first day of term they had somewhere to sit and something to write with, some of the stationery having been delivered. Cricket bats had been delivered but since no ball of any shape or size had been received, playing games was impossible.

The planning for the organization of the school had, of course, been undertaken by the head assisted by the deputy head. It was agreed that the head would be responsible for the English teaching and the deputy head for the mathematics teaching. Eight other staff were appointed. They took charge of science, modern languages, boys' physical education and games, girls' physical education and games, boys' technical studies, girls' technical studies, drama and music. The staff responsible for the last six subject areas listed also agreed to support English, and share in teaching geography, history, religious education and art. The arrangements worked well. Everyone was prepared to try his or her hand at most things.

The anticipated roll fluctuated wildly in the weeks before the school's opening. The main reason for this was that the school was situated in an area where selection still took place. This area was served altogether by a boys' grammar school, a girls' high school and eight secondary modern schools. Parents of the academically able children within the catchment area were given the option of the comprehensive school or the selective schools.

Before the school opened, meetings were held in all the local junior schools for the parents of the children within the catchment area. The school's philosophy and aims were explained. The results were disappointing, though not unexpected. The academically able all decided to go to the selective schools, which had a proven record in public examinations. The new school, comprehensive in name, faced the prospect of a non-comprehensive intake.

It was at this point that the local bus company cancelled one of its services. While this did not affect attendance at the boys' grammar school, which was only half a mile from the comprehensive school, it did affect the girls' grammar school three miles away. The parents of the academically able girls decided almost unanimously that it was not in the girls' best interests to undertake a complicated and time-consuming journey by other means. They changed their minds in favour of the comprehensive school.

The result was an imbalance in the numbers of boys and girls and meant that there was a very significant number of extremely capable girls who had no male counterparts. A further complication was that the catchment area had been served for some years by two other schools with which many families already had ties. These families were allowed, if they wished, to send their children to these schools and several elected to do so. A total of 130 children arrived on the first morning; this was considerably fewer than even the most pessimistic estimates.

It had been decided to establish a pastoral system on a vertical basis with three houses, each of which would have a senior member of staff as housemaster. In the first year, however, there were neither the staff nor the children to justify this. An interim system of two houses was established therefore, headed by the heads of science and modern languages respectively. Each pupil was assigned to a house on a friendship basis, using information supplied by the primary schools. The academic achievements of the members of the two houses were matched as far as possible, taking cognitive ability test scores into account. Using the same criterion each house list was then further divided in three, to provide six mixed-ability registration groups for the school.

Each member of staff took each of these groups for his specialist subject so that each lesson had to be taught six times and every class had to receive the same work at school and at home. Difficulties arose when the pattern of periods for each class was not the same. Two double periods followed by a single period did not give the same work pattern as a single period followed by two doubles, nor did any of the other possible ways of arranging five periods. Consequently, keeping the six groups in step with one another became difficult. This difficulty was especially felt when arrangements were made for visiting speakers or concerts in school time, or when they were needed to cope with the illness or external activities of staff. It was also difficult to take account of the inevitable variation of pace and depth of work that appeared among six different classes, although they were well matched initially.

Meanwhile, planning the teaching programme for Year 2 needed to be related to the progress of phase two of the building programme. With the cessation of selection in the area, the second intake was expected to be better balanced and larger. Some of the emerging matters needing attention included the effect that this intake might have on the first, the need for an evaluation of the mixed-ability teaching programme, and the pressures for more complex staff structure and pupil organization.

Commentary

A new school is inevitably an experiment. If the possibility of choice exists in the locality, parents and pupils may well be torn between a tried and tested school and the novelty and potential excitement of a new school. Unless the established school has a poor performance record and reputation, therefore, exposing one's own children to the experimental conditions of a new school is not an attractive proposition to many parents. The inescapable problems of distance, time and expense, however, are likely to persuade families to choose the new school at the expense of the old, when it is built close to their homes.

It is an enviable experience for a head and staff to plan a new school, to prepare for its opening, to implement plans and to see the school develop to its full maturity. Clearly many hidden pitfalls are faced. Such an experience is demanding and presents a period of extremely concentrated learning. Many of the factors which may cause loss of interest, low motivation and poor achievement in both staff and pupils in the well-established school, however, are absent or quiescent in the new one.

The sense of mission, a heightened sense of success and failure and the excitement generated in building an institution from nothing in the face of novel and unexpected circumstances, and the vagaries of unpredicted events, bond the founder members together. Such a bond grows from a sense of collective responsibility to discharge an onerous task. Professional reputations and personal relationships are all there to be made. The very force of the factors which unite the founder members, however, may become a handicap with the passing of time. New members who join the organization because of its growth and development, have not shared in the original dedication and responsibility. If the founder members remain in the organization, there is a danger that entrenched attitudes and status differentials may create stagnation and loss of a positive attitude towards continuing development.

The process of building up the staff involves two important principles. The foundation staff are carried forward to greater seniority as further staff are added in subordinate positions. The immediate, practical, or vocational work of the organization which they have had to do needs to be surrendered to the newcomers, as they themselves devote their time more fully to administrative planning work. This implies delegation to their successors and with it the right for them to be different and to make mistakes. It is tempting to the early incumbents, however, to keep in touch or even to interfere in the work of their successors which they formerly did themselves. Senior staff do this at the expense of the more critical work which the organization needs and pays them to do, and also at the expense of the self-respect and morale of the subordinates concerned.

Issues for further discussion

1. Becoming head of a new school compared with becoming head of a well-established school. What are the likely problems of plant management before opening?

2. Techniques for interrelating and scheduling the major variables involved in opening a new school, such as the building programme, the ordering, delivery and installation of furniture and equipment, the recruitment and induction of staff, and the determination of the curriculum and organization.

3. The constraints on curriculum formed by physical properties of the school (building, facilities, equipment, materials) which are incomplete, undelivered or subject to alteration.

4. The advantages and disadvantages experienced in planning the curriculum for a new school. What different means could be tried to those adopted in this case? What are the characteristics of block timetabling?

5. Teaching staff deployment for a new school with only a first-year intake of pupils.

6. Separate academic and pastoral systems: are they viable or desirable?

7. Appointing staff to a new school compared with an established school.

8. Staff morale — its determinants and its importance. What can be done to achieve and maintain high staff morale?

9. Mixed-ability teaching and an imbalance in the numbers of boys and girls in secondary education.

10. What steps might be taken to win parents' confidence?

Further reading

Best, R.E., Jarvis, C.B., Oddy, D. and Ribbins, P.M. (1980) *Perspectives on Pastoral Care*. London, Heinemann.

Castaldi, B. (1982) *Educational Facilities — Planning, Modernization and Management*. Boston, Allyn and Bacon.

Harlen, W. (1983) 'Evaluating the Curriculum'. Chapter 7 in Paisey, A. (editor) *The Effective Teacher*. London, Ward Lock Educational.

CHAPTER 2
RESTRUCTURING THE SCHOOL
Case 2.1: Towards involvement and job satisfaction

Introduction

A primary school has been through an unsettled period in its development. It is expecting a new head, the third to be appointed in a short space of time. The turnover of teaching staff has been rather higher than usual, considering the state of the employment market for teachers. The new head is fortunate enough to be able to spend some time visiting the school before taking up his appointment. He gives a great deal of thought to the state of the organization and the education it is providing. He determines that a substantial restructuring of the teaching staff is necessary to achieve the particular list of short-term objectives which he formulates for himself and the school.

He carries through the changes which he believes to be necessary by a series of steps designed to engage the understanding and consent of the teaching staff. On completion of this he reflects on progress to date. To obtain a measure of it he refers back to the original objectives which he had laid down for himself.

Narrative

A Group 5 primary school situated on the outskirts of a market town had been open for seven years. Its catchment area was mainly council housing estates. Most of the families in them were of low socio-economic status; many were in social need. The teaching staff regarded social factors and home circumstances as a powerful obstacle to the progress of pupils at school. Among these were a high incidence of single-parent families, low parental involvement with school, an undeveloped repertoire of language and associated behavioural problems. In its short existence the school had had a high turnover of staff, in spite of the increasing difficulties for teachers in finding other posts, including two head teachers and two acting head teachers.

The building was open-plan with areas designed for curricular activities rather than class teaching, but these were being used for more traditional teacher/class-based work. There were 235 children on roll, with a teaching establishment of head and 9.3 teachers.

The promotion of the school's second head teacher to another educational organization led to the appointment of the school's deputy as acting head teacher. This created conditions in which change was expected, and the school prepared itself for the arrival of another new head.

The newly appointed head was able to visit the school several times before taking office. In discussions with the staff he formed the impression that a flat pyramidal staff structure existed. Six of the teachers held Scale II posts respectively for infant team leadership, display, mathematics and music, reading and library, audio-visual aids, and games and outdoor pursuits. He recognized that this represented a wide span of control which would give him direct access to the staff, aided by the informal atmosphere and cordial relationships which he had also noted.

Nevertheless, on taking stock of the school and its problems and considering the need for a new strategy and direction, the head concluded that a restructuring of the staff would be necessary during the first year of his headship. He was particularly concerned about three factors:

—difficulties experienced by pupils in their academic and social development

—the unusually high turnover of teaching staff

—the need to provide more formal ways for staff to relate to one another as a management team.

Before long the head tried to clarify his own thinking and formulate a set of objectives for restructuring the teaching staff. He finally decided on the following nine objectives:

1. To reallocate the duties of individuals within the school.

2. To commit job descriptions for individuals in the organization to writing.

3. To publish such descriptions so that all members of the organization would be aware of the areas of authority and responsibility of themselves and others.

4. To create a working environment in which members believed they were making a worthwhile contribution to the work of the organization, with visible evidence for doing so.

5. To create stability in the organization.

6. To decentralize decision making, and involve the organization's members in policy making.

7. To delegate duties in order to create areas of authority and status.

8. To ensure that the exercise of authority by individuals was commensurate with their responsibilities.

9. To match jobs to perceived organizational and personal needs.

The information he obtained before taking up the headship, and his own observations of the school in action during that time, provided the new head with a basis for designing a structure which could realise these objectives. In consequence, he was provisionally able to determine a new structure as follows:

Head
Deputy head
Three team leaders

    Upper school (Deputy head)
    Middle school (Scale II)
    Lower school (Scale II)

Four curriculum coordinators/team members

    Art, craft and display (Scale II)
    Language (Scale II)
    Mathematics (Scale II)
    Social studies and science (Scale II)

Two Scale I teachers/team members

The head realised that the proposed structure provided for three substructures. All teachers, in respect of their personal teaching, would be working in teams under the authority of a team leader who would be responsible for the teaching programme for the pupils concerned as a whole. This responsibility would include pastoral and academic care and the integration of all activities as a coherent and progressive educational experience for the pupil.

Four members of staff acting in an additional capacity to that of team member would each have responsibility for developing special knowledge of a major area of the curriculum. This would consist of keeping up to date in the subject content in their curriculum fields and ways of teaching it, so that they would be able to promote it in the school and accordingly advise their colleagues of developments which were taking place.

The third substructure was the creation of upper, middle and lower schools. Each became a suborganization with its own team leader at its head, exercising a great deal of discretion with regard to policy for that part of the school. The head of school would work directly with the three team leaders to exercise control over the entire school.

Having decided on the form the new staff structure should take, the head gave his attention to the steps by which it would be possible to implement the changes represented by the design. Eventually he decided on the following course of action:

Informal, individual and group discussions to take place.

Each teacher above Scale I to be invited to submit a written impression of his or her current job to the new head.

The papers to be used as a basis for more formal preliminary individual discussions with the new head during which a brief indication of the direction of proposed change would be outlined.

The papers to be used by the head as a basis for further individual discussions to produce detailed mutually agreed job descriptions.

Such descriptions to include curricular, organizational, pastoral and administrative aspects of work.

The pattern of weekly staff meetings established by the previous head to be continued but divided into fortnightly curriculum meetings to be alternated with organizational meetings.

The duties of team leaders to include: leadership of a department; liaison; reporting concerns to the head; requisitioning for the department; taking team assemblies; pupil records; special educational needs.

The duties of coordinators to include: preparation and presentation of discussion papers for staff meetings; consultancy throughout the school; purchasing materials and equipment; advising on standardised and diagnostic testing materials; discussion with head teacher on curriculum policies.

The deputy head's work to include responsibilities for senior management in close association with the head.

These steps were taken systematically over a period of one year. Several weeks elapsed before the staff had identified all the elements of the reorganization being planned and were able to understand them as a whole. Among the notable reactions to the initiatives taken by the head were the following:

Genuine appreciation of opportunities to discuss curricular matters replaced the teachers' initial bewilderment.

Individuals became more aware of their own professional shortcomings and were prompted to do something about them.

The staff said they felt part of a professionally cohesive group.

The school appeared to become a more coherent organization.

There was more openness, a willingness to share ideas and to seek professional help from colleagues.

Staff willingly undertook an evaluation of the staff/curriculum developments.

The head was naturally anxious to know if the innovation was carrying the convictions of the staff, but above all whether it was leading to the increased effectiveness of the school. One way in which he charted the progress being made was to review what had been achieved in the light of the nine objectives he had disciplined himself to formulate at the outset. He resolved to use these as measures of the developments which had taken place to date, and in so doing to review his own part and future responsibilities, as follows:

Objective 1
The duties of individual staff had been reallocated on a rational basis through consultation. This had led to greater effectiveness in terms of task performance.

Objective 2
Written job descriptions had been prepared by mutual agreement between the head and each post holder. These appear to have created a sense of status, and clarified the areas of authority for post holders.

Objective 3
The publication of the job descriptions had also made these areas of responsibility clear to role partners. These had, in turn, created professional standing for post holders which had been recognised by colleagues.

Objective 4
During discussions teachers said they felt their contributions to be valued. They pointed to formal and subsequently informal staff discussions, improved self-image, and ability to initiate changes as evidence of this.

Objective 5
The inflow and outflow of staff had been much the same as before. Greater organizational stability remained an important objective, and it might be that demographic factors would themselves create less mobility, and enable the school to enjoy a period with few staff changes.

Objective 6
Decision making had been decentralized, and Scale II post holders shared the management of the school with the head and deputy. All staff were involved in the creation, monitoring and statements of policy for the school. They had also jointly agreed the principles of establishing a curriculum suited to the perceived needs of pupils at the school.

Objective 7
Duties had been delegated. Staff had obtained areas of real responsibility and opportunities for achievement.

Objective 8
The exercise of authority so that it was commensurate with responsibility needed continuous review by the head. Where authority had been overexercised, confrontation had been necessary. The underexercising of authority had been similarly problematic. However, it was believed that the attempted balance had created a tension which, taken as a whole, had been healthy for the organisation.

Objective 9
The needs of the school organization and its members were changing. Part of the responsibility of headship was to assess the nature of such change and to adjust the structure accordingly. This was a matter for continuous review by the head.

Commentary

In this case there is a deliberate attempt to make the organizational structure of the school more — rather than less — complex. An additional layer of middle management is introduced from the point of view of the teachers who are not team leaders. Under the previous structure, each teacher was subject to the specialisms of a variety of colleagues. Under the new structure, apart from the three team leaders themselves, each teacher is subject to a team leader.

At the same time, the more complex structure reduces the span of control — the number of subordinates reporting to a superordinate — which is intended to lead to better operational control and the better working of the school as a whole. The main operational difficulty with this structure may well be to reconcile the work of curriculum coordinators and that of team leaders. The potential clash is one between a specialist management function — the work of the curriculum coordinator — and the general management function — the work of the team leader. They are all Scale II posts but the team leader may have formal power — through controlling many variables — to block and frustrate the work of a particular curriculum coordinator, whose realm of work depends entirely on persuasion, influence and example.

The structure offers the staff the opportunity to grow in professional competence. Both job enlargement and job enrichment principles are exemplified in the new structure. The former is concerned with having opportunities for making one's expertise and knowledge more widely available, the latter with an increase in policy making and so governing the job one is doing itself.

Management training stresses the vital role played by objectives. In a school, objectives are of three kinds. Individuals have their own personal objectives. Educational objectives are those which the school has regarding the pupils. There are also resource objectives — those which the school's management has with respect to the use of the resources available. In this case the head clearly formulates objectives for the use of the most valuable resource of all — the teaching staff. He clearly wants to raise the levels of professional performance of the staff, to enhance their development and to increase their job satisfaction. The last of these apparently is well fulfilled by making the work itself more interesting and demanding, by according the staff greater recognition, by giving advancement in terms of professional standing, by creating opportunities for achievement, and by offering promotion in terms of authority and responsibility.

Issues for further discussion

1. The value of making objectives precise and explicit.

2. The importance of (a) establishing an order of priorities among objectives and (b) attaching a timescale for the achievement of each objective.

3. Communicating organizational changes to parents.

4. Definition and dimensions of a 'healthy organization'.

5. The bases of job satisfaction for teachers in primary schools.

6. The induction and training of teachers in their new jobs as team leaders.

7. Job conflict in the primary school for
   (a) the deputy head of school when also appointed as team leader of upper school;

(b) the coordinator of a curriculum area throughout the school when also appointed as team member for one part of it.

8. Work in addition to their teaching for Scale I teachers who are neither team leaders nor curriculum coordinators.

9. Means by which curriculum coordinators
   (a) keep up to date;
   (b) appraise colleagues of development at large.

10. Unsatisfactory aspects of the Burnham Scale points system with respect to the current needs of primary and secondary schools.

Further reading

Brodie, M. and Bennett, R. (editors) (1979) *Managerial Effectiveness*. Slough, Thames Valley Regional Management Centre.

Randell, G., Shaw, R., Packard, P. and Slater, J. (1979) *Staff Appraisal*. London, Institute of Personnel Management.

Woodward, S. (1982) The headteacher as Manager : A Personal View. *School Organization* 2, 2, 123–126.

Case 2.2: From closed to open organization

Introduction

A secondary school has been subject to a traditional form of government under a head whose rule was autocratic. The organizational climate of the school was formal and staff participation levels were low. The head exercised his personal right to make decisions to the full.

A new head of school seeks to introduce a more liberal form of government for the school. He does so by designing an organizational structure which includes substantial new features and involves fundamental changes in academic and pastoral organization. The way in which he implements the whole innovation is calculated to gain consensus and acceptance, encouraged by the introduction of a broader base of participation in major areas of decision making.

Narrative

The new head took up his appointment of an 11 to 16 mixed comprehensive school of 1000 pupils which had been developed from a successful secondary modern school. The catchment area was compact. None of the pupils needed to travel to school by public transport. It was made up of roughly equal proportions of private and well-established local authority housing. For largely historical reasons the school did not enjoy the best of reputations in the area though its pupils were generally polite and, very largely, in school uniform. New buildings to provide a suite of mathematics rooms, three additional laboratories, facilities for drama and music and a purpose-built remedial block were in the course of construction.

The new head found the atmosphere of the school very formal. His predecessor had never used staff first names — even to his deputies — and he took all four assemblies each week. All decisions in the school were taken by him, even the most trivial. The five heads of year met with him and the deputies once per term, as did the heads of department. There were no planned regular meetings between head and deputies. Once a month there was a full staff meeting at which the head held the floor, more or less throughout, with very little real discussion. The agendas for all these meetings were decided by the head.

The members of staff, with few exceptions, were competent but not outstanding. The average age was around 35 and some had been in the school many years. Almost no innovation was to be seen and several departments were ineffective. Overall, no one was doing any real thinking; the school was operating on a 'care and maintenance' basis.

Relationships with parents were cordial but not warm. There was a fairly active and quite recently formed parents' association; the staff were represented by two 'observers' on the committee. Parents were not really welcome at the school and their comments about teaching and the curriculum were discouraged.

Beyond some minor items and the holding of more frequent meetings with heads of year, heads of department and the deputies, the new head made no attempt to change anything radically. It was, for him, a time of assessment. Never again would he be able to look at the school with the eyes of an outsider and see, in a fairly objective way, its strengths and weaknesses. From the beginning, however, he did try to engender a more relaxed, less formal atmosphere and to project to parents and other outsiders a more welcoming approach. His other main task was to begin to build the confidence of the staff in himself as a person and as a head. Too often, in those first few months, he was aware of staff feeling that he was not being completely honest and open and of people searching for a hidden meaning in what he said that was not there.

He spent much of the autumn term planning what he would do. He believed this was his personal responsibility. Should he go for fundamental and widespread change or adopt a piecemeal approach? Ought he to tackle the somewhat moribund curriculum or first try to modify attitudes among the staff, partly by organizational and structural changes, which would stimulate discussion, thought and innovativeness?

He decided on the latter because he concluded that for curriculum changes to be successful, though the head may give the lead, the fine detail must be worked out by the staff so that there would be the commitment to see it through. To stimulate corporate thinking and innovation the process of organizational development seemed to offer the way forward.

In the early part of the spring term, he conceived a structure aimed at promoting real discussion between himself and the senior staff, and between departments. The three main proposals in this plan were:

1. Changing the staff structure for pastoral care from five year heads, all on Scale III, operating on a rotation system, to heads of lower, middle and upper school, each on Scale IV, who would not rotate. This also included a unique arrangement whereby each head of school would have responsibility for a particular year group of pupils for five terms, an idea which seemed to offer distinct advantages.

2. Grouping subject departments into three faculties, each with a head of faculty on Scale IV.

3. Setting up a body, to be known as the policy group, consisting of the head and two deputy heads, the heads of lower, middle and upper school and the three heads of faculty to determine future school policy in all areas, including the allocation of finance.

A number of other proposals were included, such as a complete review of the distribution of points in the school to take account of the above suggestions, together with a detailed set of aims and objectives for the school.

A one-day closure, on a Friday, was arranged for a staff conference early in the summer term prior to the autumn term in which the proposals were to be implemented. During the last few weeks of the previous spring term, the head prepared a substantial document, which he discussed at length in its draft form with the two deputies, for presentation to the staff. It was turned into a booklet, with a commercially printed cover and spiral binding, and distributed to staff on the last day before the Easter holiday, together with the programme for the staff conference at which it would be discussed. As well as the various proposals for change, the document included several appendices dealing with, for example, the responsibilities and powers of the policy group, faculty heads, and the heads of lower, middle and upper school, and comparing them with existing posts. A detailed staff structure grid was also included.

Discussions at the staff conference were mainly to be in small groups to allow for the maximum degree of participation. Group chairmen were appointed and well briefed in advance. The head and both deputies stayed clear of these discussion groups. At the end of the conference, each group chairman reported briefly on the deliberations of the group in a plenary session of the staff and submitted a written report to the head a few days later.

Though there was some doubt over certain details, it was clear that there was broad support for the proposals in principle or, at least, an absence of hostility. The head had the written reports of the discussion groups printed verbatim and issued to all staff together with a further paper from himself giving his reactions to their comments. A full staff meeting followed towards the end of the summer term when the original proposals, with such minor modifications as the head considered justifiable, were formally adopted.

A meeting of the governors in mid-May had been made aware of the proposals and given copies of the document. The governors decided to hold a special evening meeting, after the views of the staff were known, to discuss the document. Copies of the staff discussion groups' reports and the head's further comments were sent to the members of the governing body before the special meeting which was held early in July. This meeting lasted for four hours and, by the end of it, the governors had given their unanimous approval to the whole plan.

The next task was to make the key appointments to the posts of heads of faculty and heads of lower, middle and upper school. As there were no staffing vacancies, any posts to be filled would be from internal appointments. The head did not anticipate too much difficulty in making the three heads of school appointments.

The posts of faculty heads were quite another matter as he could only see one suitable candidate. However, he had foreseen this difficulty and had made it clear that, if a suitable head of faculty could not be appointed at once, a head of department would be invited to act as chairman of the faculty, possibly for a fixed term, to represent the faculty on the policy group until the position could be filled. The alternative would be to postpone the setting-up of the policy group until all its members were in post, but he felt that to do this would mean losing the impetus and enthusiasm that had been generated by the staff conference in June. Consequently, all six posts were internally advertised and a closing date fixed for the receipt of formal, written applications. It was understood that all applicants would be interviewed as a matter of courtesy.

Applications were received, interviews held and four appointments made before the end of the summer term. From the publication of the document, the whole process had taken just 16 weeks.

As expected, the heads of lower, middle and upper school posts were filled without difficulty and a remaining head of year was appointed to a newly created Scale III post with responsibility for primary/secondary liaison and the induction of new pupils. Only one head of faculty was appointed — for Aesthetic & Creative Arts. Two heads of department were invited to act as chairmen of the other two faculties on a temporary basis. Thus the policy group was constituted and ready to begin work after the summer vacation at the beginning of the fifth term of the head of school's tenure.

By the end of the eighth term of his headship, the head had been able to implement the entire plan. Luck played its part in that the loss of one or two staff enabled key appointments to be made earlier than might otherwise have been possible. As a system it was soon working well but its effects on the school's curriculum and teaching methodology remained to be realised and evaluated.

Commentary

This case deals with the transition and transformation of a secondary school in respect of its organizational structure, staff deployment and management style. Organizational structure is a concept of the interpersonal relationship pattern among the members of an organization. It is undoubtedly intended to be instrumental in nature and form. The pattern chosen *is* chosen because it is judged to be the best one for getting the work of the organization accomplished. In practice, structure is a distribution or sharing of jobs, authority and positions. In a school it would be perverse to deliberately choose a pattern which was unworkable and incapable of achieving the productive work for which the school existed — the care and education of children and young people.

An organizational structure may be designed in one of two ways. It can reflect the capacities, interests and propensities of the staff members as they are, or it can reflect them as they might become.

There is the possibility, therefore, of structuring according to known, obvious qualities, or of doing so according to the potential of individuals. In other words, it is possible to structure in such a way that people have room to grow and develop in their work. The job space of each individual is just a little more than he or she can give at the moment but which he or she ultimately can give with application, encouragement and a little time.

In designing a structure it is common to think of the static or temporary aspects and forget the dynamic aspects which result from subsequent changes *in* personnel and changes *of* personnel. There may also be a concentration on the *constrained behaviour* which the organization requires — that which individuals are formally obligated to do — at the expense of the *facilitated behaviour* which the organization permits — that which it cannot prevent, especially social and political conduct. Facilitated behaviour is an important aspect of the total reality in the life of a school and may have a powerful bearing on constrained behaviour, even to the point of frustrating its intended functions.

Organizational structure may be designed and implemented in many ways. In this case the head chose not to dictate a structure which he had designed, but to win support for it on rational grounds by a process of influence and persuasion. He was willing to adapt it in detail but essentially sought consensus over the principles.

He need not have introduced the senior management team as a new means for the executive management of the school. However, in doing so, simultaneously with the new structure, he clearly showed that his general strategy for the government of the school was to increase participation levels and to create a more collegial climate among the teaching staff.

Issues for further discussion

1. Autocratic headship — its strengths and weaknesses. What alternative strategies might have been employed in this case?

2. The period a new head needs to assess the school — sources of evidence and criteria used for drawing conclusions and making judgements.

3. The efficiency and effectiveness of faculties.

4. The value and limitations of rotating pastoral heads, compared with retaining them in fixed positions.

5. Job specifications and the selection of teachers for (a) heads of faculty posts, and (b) senior pastoral posts.

6. Internal promotion — procedures, advantages and disadvantages.

7. Staff meetings — their purpose and management. How might attitudes as well as systems be changed?

8. Information through documents in schools — proposals, letters, agendas, minutes, reports, policy statements and publicity literature.

9. Relations between a senior management team and the rest of the staff.

10. The work of the deputy head(s) in a school under an autocratic head compared with a school under a senior management team.

Further reading

Lyons, G. (1976) *Heads' Tasks*. Windsor, NFER.

Secondary Heads' Association (1983) *The Selection of Secondary Heads*. Occasional Paper No. 2. London, Secondary Heads' Association.

Woolcott, L. (1983) 'Achieving Administrative Efficiency'. Chapter 8 in Paisey, A. (editor) *The Effective Teacher*. London, Ward Lock Educational.

CHAPTER 3
MANAGEMENT STYLE

Case 3.1: Revitalizing the school

Introduction

The new head of a junior school of 300 pupils takes office. The mismatch which existed between his assumptions and expectations, and those of the deputy head and staff of the school, becomes manifest. The head exercises a number of prerogatives in which he feels justified. The deputy head and other members of staff clearly prefer to see such prerogatives exercised in a different manner.

By a rapid accumulation of events involving a number of the teaching staff, the head makes his wishes and his values known. This process creates a variety of reactions among the staff and eventually leads to a confrontation between the head and the deputy head.

Narrative

The incumbent head left the teaching profession half-way through the summer term at the age of 46. Among the applicants for the vacancy was the deputy head of the school but the post went to a dynamic head of another school who had held the headship there for four years.

The task confronting the head designate was demanding. The last effort at formulating objectives and a policy for the school had been made five years previously in a series of documents distributed by the former head without discussion. Since then, teachers had relied on a series of un-documented ad hoc objectives in spite of their head's opposition to the formulation of objectives. About half of the staff were recently appointed and inexperienced.

The deputy head and the local education authority adviser in discussion with the head designate stressed the need for improved teacher morale, better relationships with parents and a remodelled curriculum. The mamagement task of the head designate generally amounted to finding a new sense of purpose and direction for the school following a period of stagnation.

The head designate invited the deputy head to the school which he was soon to leave. He explained that the school expressed his philosophy perfectly. In a tour of the school lasting 30 minutes he emphasized that during his four years as head he had worked towards team teaching throughout and had encouraged the display of children's work on a massive scale as an important factor governing the attitude of pupils towards school and the school's attitudes towards its pupils.

The head designate and the deputy head discussed the staff of the school to which he had been appointed. It was also arranged for some of the staff to visit the head designate's present school. The deputy head invited him to reciprocate the visit, expressing the wish to be able to inform the school of the day of his visit. The head designate deferred a decision, saying that he would make contact soon to arrange it.

Three weeks later, the head designate and a local education authority adviser unexpectedly appeared in the deputy head's classroom during lesson time. The news spread through the school rapidly. The deputy took the visitors round the school, introducing the head designate to every class. No conversation took place with children. The visitors departed immediately afterwards, without sharing coffee with the staff or having a discussion with anyone. This totally unexpected visit caused consternation among the staff. Two arguments were advanced by way of explanation: he had simply forgotten to communicate the date of the visit; or he had *intended* to make a surprise visit — which might be interpreted as unprofessional or at least discourteous. The deputy blamed the adviser. The teaching and secretarial staff were anxious about it, believing that the head's action was deliberate. Several talked of seeking other posts.

On the first morning of the new school year at 8.30a.m., the new head told the deputy not to take school assemblies as had been her practice for several years. She was asked to empty the filing cabinet in the room she used as deputy head's room and to remove her personal possessions from the shelves so that the room could be converted to a resources centre. She expressed a wish to continue to take assemblies but the head said that he wanted his decision to stand. Although the head had stressed that the deputy head's office should be cleared within a week, he had himself emptied the filing cabinet and shelves of the deputy's belongings by the end of that same morning, placing them on the floor.

The head took similar action elsewhere in the school. Various cupboards and other items of furniture were resited, curtains were moved and the caretaker had to resite stacked chairs, physical education and other equipment. Every cupboard moved revealed dirt and led to further cleaning-up operations. The head himself cleared out some untidy lunch trays in one classroom and rebuked the deputy for failing to notice that they had been left since the end of the previous term.

Although no teacher had been criticized personally, a sense of insecurity gripped the staff as they realized that in time each might be subject to criticism. The demoralization of the deputy head was untimely for the staff. The head invited the teaching staff to look at the school noticeboard on which he had pinned a copy of the timetable, devised by the deputy head during the previous term, with considerable modifications. Some of the changes caused clashes in the use of space but several teachers said they preferred not to draw attention to them so that when difficulties occurred in due course responsibility for them would be attributed correctly to the head.

The new head at once instituted the practice of meeting all teachers in the staff room every morning before school. This replaced the message book which his predecessor had sent round for teachers to initial. The staff had always wanted this new system but, unreasonably, seemed to expect the head always to have exceptional news or information to impart. If there was none, they complained. If the head's information took more than a minute, they complained. The idea of achieving a better relationship with the head and with each other did not seem to carry much weight. Sometimes teachers were on time but the head was not. On occasions the head rushed in asking why everyone was in the staff room when the children were already in the classrooms. Some staff then would make a point of rising to their feet at nine o' clock regardless of whether the head was talking or not, although they refrained from departing.

The head's first assembly was impressive for its clarity and strength of purpose. Teachers might have felt that they now had a head who believed in being the leader, since they had complained about the ineffectiveness of the former head.

On the second day in school assembly under the head's direction, some children depicted two different kinds and degrees of stealing. Talking to the children when the scenes were over, the head said that everyone in that hall, including all the teachers, had been guilty of stealing something during their lives. Breaktime comments among the staff were hostile, until the head arrived, but no one challenged him.

On the same day, evidence of a bold policy was demonstrated. The head visited Miss Y's classroom during class time. He promptly rearranged desks and units without a word to the teacher who was in the middle of teaching the class. No discussion occurred before the visit and no explanation was given or sought. Miss Y gave vent to her anger by discussing the matter with the deputy head, but she did not want her to raise it with the head; nor would she talk to the head about it herself.

Subsequently Miss Y was kicked by a boy in her class after she had reprimanded him; this was only the second such incident in her six years of teaching. She sent for the deputy, who found her struggling with the boy. When calm was restored, the deputy advised Miss Y to talk to the head at breaktime as she herself had been told by the head not to intervene in matters of children's behaviour. Miss Y saw the head, who promised to see the boy after play. Instead the head visited the classroom and spoke to the whole class. It was alleged that the head apologised to the boy on behalf of the teacher for using force on him: 'Miss Y did not mean to grab hold of you.' The boy had been kicking a girl. Miss Y saw the deputy again. Having had her classroom reorganised in front of the children had not made her well disposed towards the head, but the matter of the boy's behaviour seemed to her to have deprived her of professional status. Miss Y was too angry to talk to the head and indeed feared to do so. Again, she did not want the matter raised by the deputy.

The deputy, however, raised the issue of disturbed children's behaviour with the head a few days later. The head spoke in disapproving terms of teachers who could not control children, but he agreed to talk about discipline generally with the staff. Before he did so, Miss Y told her colleagues what had happened. Miss Y was a quiet and courteous teacher who rarely had difficulty in managing children. Her colleagues were sympathetic to her. In the staff meeting, the head stated that whenever children misbehaved in a classroom, the teacher was at fault. There was little discussion and the deputy failed to pursue the matter on behalf of her colleagues.

In consequence, whenever a teacher experienced difficulty with a child, the head would be approached with requests for assistance. The teachers were keen to see how he dealt with disturbed children. It became habitual for the head to take such children with him on his journeys to the bank. As a result of this action, their behaviour — according to their teachers — deteriorated. Most teachers resigned themselves to being sworn at by pupils and made resigned attempts to reduce the quarrelling and fighting in the playground. Not all teachers experienced the bad behaviour of pupils, however. The head stated several times that he was trying to make teachers more self-reliant.

After some disturbing incidents with a boy who was later taken into care, Mrs. Z asked the deputy for assistance, knowing that this had been forbidden. The head noticed this breach in his preferred procedure. A curious incident followed. He called the deputy in and claimed to have heard the children in her class discussing after school the previous night how they dreaded the deputy's cane. In fact she had no cane and had never used corporal punishment. This proved to be the forerunner of a series of events which came to a climax a few days later.

Mr. X, a light-hearted young man, was poorly organized. He often left the work area shared by four classes (including the deputy's) in disarray. The deputy frequently had to reprimand or coax him into a greater awareness of his responsibilities. Sometimes she helped Mr. X and his class to clear up at the end of the day. Talking to Mr. X in his classroom about this and other matters, the deputy was abruptly called out to the work area by the head who reprimanded her for the state of the work area. The head said that he knew who was responsible because he and the deputy had discussed ways of trying to improve Mr. X's organizing skills and attitude, but he used the occasion to rebuke the deputy. The deputy, however, did not incriminate Mr. X. Mr. X, who overheard the conversation, went to the staff room to describe the encounter to his colleagues. The head expressed his disappointment that children had to work in such conditions; the deputy expressed her concern that children had to work under such a head. The deputy failed to attend the pre-school meeting the following day, and the dispute became public knowledge.

Just before the first half-term, the head asked the deputy to see him at lunchtime. Without preamble he made the following points about the deputy's work in the school. They were delivered somewhat forcefully and were partly overheard in the adjoining staffroom and school secretary's office:

—she had wasted the half-term when she was acting head by not 'improving' the school and by 'failing to make her reputation',

—she had shown no initiative since his arrival,

—her teaching was sound but lacked variety in art and craft and she left the cooking to visiting parents,

—there was too much levity in the staff room,

—she had twice rebuked a junior colleague in the staff room for making unpleasant remarks,

—she should have had a central display area in the school to impress colleagues and to set an example,

—as upper-juniors coordinator, she had not called enough meetings,

—the lower-juniors coordinator 'made' everyone in her group work uniformly, whereas the deputy allowed too much autonomy,

—her class had not done any modelling,

—on the school's bonfire night, the deputy had left before the end,

—on the day when the staff had changed the entire reading system to one the head liked, involving the physical moving and reclassification of books all over the school, she had left early,

—it was wrong for her to be attending two in-service evening sessions every week because it meant leaving school within 30 minutes of closure,

—she was not making a sufficient contribution to the school,

—she should stop wasting her time dealing with colleagues' problems,

—finally, he would not support her in any application for promotion.

Commentary

On the face of it the school appears to have become run down. The vacancy for the headship was created by the departure of the head not only from the school but from teaching altogether. The reasons for this are not known. It may have been disillusionment; it may have been for a more lucrative alternative career. Either way, it is reasonable to suppose that the school experienced a loss of momentum before the head left. There followed an interreguum in which the deputy head could have provided dynamic leadership. She probably felt that for one term — the summer term at that — her best plan was to conduct a holding operation. The result evidently did not please the new head who ultimately accused her of laissez faire leadership.

There followed a series of direct and uncompromising interventions by the new head in a variety of practices in the school, affecting a number of teachers personally and the whole staff in one way or another. This all happened in the first half term. The object of the head's actions seems to have been calculated and based on two considerations. In the first place the head patently had no intention of tolerating untidy conditions in the school. This prompted him to conduct a general clean-up and rearrangement of the physical environment of the school and to express a concern for tidiness and general behaviour. In the second place his actions were meant to re-energize the school. He had probably been appointed on the basis that the school had lost vitality and needed a new sense of mission. As an experienced head he had the self-confidence to tackle the problem in a particular way.

However, it is to be noted that no action was taken against the existing curriculum itself, although the head's hostility to the way in which it was being taught was expressed in several forms. Half of one term is indeed little time in which to reappraise it. He may or may not have done so subsequently. The fact that he confined himself to immediate and easily adjustable matters shows a patient mind and suggests that the main target was the removal of complacency and a general revitalizing of the school in the short run.

The way in which he did this is questionable. He certainly upset the staff on many occasions. This was apparently unnecessary. If management style is *how* one characteristically goes about one's managerial work, a directive style is strongly in evidence in this case rather than a compromising or facilitative style. Style should vary according to circumstances and need. In this case a single style seems to have characterised disparate circumstances and needs.

Emerging from the work of the school for the first half-term is an unpleasant and unprofessional encounter between the head and the deputy head. There had been a build-up to this confrontation. It was not a counselling session in which the leading professional and chief executive attempts to help his immediate subordinate to assess her performance with a view to future improvement and greater job satisfaction. There is instead the suggestion of the need to dominate, to break any hold or standing which the well-established deputy had among the staff, in favour of himself.

Issues for further discussion

1. The introduction and induction of a new head.

2. Tactics for making an impact on being a newly appointed head.

3. The head's rights: legal and professional.

4. Professional counselling by the head of school.

5. Management style: when to be directive, when to be facilitative, when to be compromising.

6. Pupil discipline: the teacher's contribution in relation to the contribution of the head.

7. Relationships between head and deputy head. How can sound relationships be made between all staff?

8. The value of daily pre-school staff meetings.

9. Changing a teacher's teaching methods. Why might this be necessary, and how might it be achieved?

10. School assemblies — purpose and practical value in the management of the school.

Further reading

Knipe, H. and Maclay, G. (1973) *The Dominant Man*. London, Fontana.

Paisey, A. and Paisey, T. (1980) The Question of Style in Educational Management. *Educational Administration* 9, 1, 95–106.

Waters, D. (1983) *Responsibility and Promotion in the Primary School*. London, Heinemann.

Case 3.2: Building a management team

Introduction

A secondary school changes from having a selective to a comprehensive intake of pupils at a time when pupil rolls in secondary education in the area are falling fast. Contrary to the general trend the school, as a result, is scheduled to increase its roll by over 60 per cent. The incumbent head realises that the personally directed form of management of the school which he had always used would be inappropriate to the new circumstances. He constructs a senior management team with a limited brief. One of its first important tasks is to handle requests from the local education authority. The formation, composition and remit of the team are all subject to development. There are a variety of reactions among other members of staff as the senior management team establishes its place in the managerial fabric of the school.

Narrative

A mixed voluntary aided Church of England secondary school changed from having a two-form selective entry to a four-form comprehensive intake. This was accompanied by a readjustment of the traditional catchment area, although admission was dependent upon the family having an approved Anglican link. The school size was rising counter to local and national trends from 440 pupils to a projected maximum of 720 pupils.

This increase in the number of pupils with a wider ability range required changes in the provision of buildings and staffing. A new building was constructed and there was an increase in teaching and ancillary staff. There was also a change in the management structure of the school with the introduction of a senior management team (SMT).

During the grammar school years, the head managed the school with the help of a deputy head and a senior mistress. The head liaised with the heads of department over any issue and then addressed the members of the teaching staff at a full staff meeting. Opportunities for communication and for the free flow of ideas were limited as no formal channels existed. Contacts between staff members were irregular and changes occurred largely through ad hoc individual initiatives rather than by deliberate forward planning.

The head first delegated some of his authority in creating a teacher in charge of careers, and in giving responsibility for the pastoral care of the sixth form, GCE entries, public examinations. UCCA applications and the writing of references, to the male deputy head. The senior mistress combined the task of looking after girls' uniform and welfare with running a subject department. At this stage the formal management structure was weak. The head, deputy head and senior mistress did not work together as a team and were not recognized as such by the staff.

The creation of the SMT did not come about until some months before the school changed to being a comprehensive school. A senior master was appointed to deal specifically with timetabling and options in the curriculum, and a head of lower school was put in charge of the pastoral care of the first three years. Some rationalization of roles also took place. The head gave up timetabling. Pastoral care was wholly divided between the deputy head, the senior mistress and the head of lower school. A head of middle school was later appointed, bringing the number of senior staff up to six.

These six composed a recognizable senior management team with the head as chairman and the deputy head as deputy chairman. The team met fortnightly from approximately 4.10p.m. to about 5.30p.m. when an unofficial "guillotine" was used to end the meetings. The agenda was drawn up by the head and largely consisted of matters he wished to discuss, although members were able to ask for items to be included on the agenda and contributions to discussions were freely invited.

The formalization of the management team had the effect of pulling together the senior members of staff who had previously liaised individually with the head. It brought a rationalization of work, although some areas of overlap existed, and made greater use of staff interests and specialisms. It produced a body which the staff could identify as being concerned with the management of the school — a point considered more important by the head than the rest of the staff — and it gave the individual members of the team a group identity. This was exhibited at staff meetings as individuals defended a team decision or helped to explain a point being made by a colleague to the rest of the staff. At times this was so marked that some members of staff observed that a dichotomy had been created. Nevertheless the SMT was held by most teachers to be a constructive development.

The diagram below gives an indication of the position of the senior management team in the structure of the school.

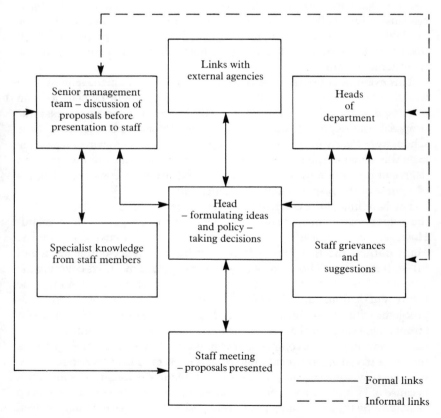

Figure 1   Senior management team in the organizational structure

The method of operation and the creative role of the senior management team could be illustrated by the school's response to requests from the local education authority for information on the school's curriculum development. The senior management team was brought into the matter some five months after the director of education had made the original contact with the school. By this time the head had completed the quantitative work required by the county's questionnaire. The departments had been alerted to the fact that a response to the question of curricular objectives would be requested. SMT met to put forward the objectives of the curriculum of the school. Each member of the team presented his or her own list of aims. Following discussion in the SMT the head then published a paper to staff for discussion and response at departmental level. These responses were collated and considered by the team before being made available in the staff room for all to read. The head prepared a final document to be presented to the governors, having discussed it with the management team.

This example supported the view of the head that the management team was able to explore significant issues so that they might be clarified and presented to the full staff meeting. It gave the head the means to examine proposals thoroughly. It was also noted that although the objectives of the school were clearly the product of the senior management team of which the head was a member, he put the paper forward to the staff as his own to give a degree of protection for senior colleagues and also to be consistent with his own view of the responsibilities of leadership.

The handling of the curriculum development report showed the work of the senior management team in responding to one particular demand. However, as noted earlier, they met frequently to discuss many topics. Many of these meetings were preludes to the appearance on the agenda of full staff meetings. The range of topics over a cycle of meetings covering the school year was very wide. It included issues of policy and planning, the future curriculum and timetable, day-to-day management — such as problems with school lunches and staff duties — and also discussion about arrangements for special events such as prize giving. Substantial matters such as staffing for the following year might well be on the same agenda as the more trivial arrangements for the end of term. This was regarded as a weakness by some because certain issues tended to recur — sometimes because of lack of time at a previous meeting. Some issues could have been dealt with by the establishment of simple procedural devices which allowed a senior staff member to act immediately without reference to other authority. However, their agendas to date have shown that the SMT has taken interest in a wide variety of school management problems. The head has kept the team abreast of recent developments in the school, thus increasing the feeling of privilege among its members and enhancing their feeling of having an exclusive status. The head nevertheless has reserved the right to act alone, with the deputy head or the chairman of governors, regarding pupil admissions and new staff appointments.

There have been criticisms of the team. Many felt that objectivity among team members has been partially obscured by their departmental interests. In the original team, that is without the head of middle school, three of the five members were also heads of department, the other two being the head and the deputy head. The number with departmental responsibility was reduced to one, however, and it was significant that the head of middle school, also a head of department, on being internally appointed, formally gave up his departmental responsibility within hours of accepting the new post. Hence the departmental constraint was transitory and was almost inevitable in a relatively small secondary school. This new detachment should improve the objectivity of the team and remove suspicions of departmental partiality.

Another area of criticism was the management style of the school. The senior management team were regarded as advisers rather than having any involvement in the implementation of policy. They were distanced from the actual decision making in the school. This meant that they were treated with a certain amount of mistrust by other members of staff, because the channel of communication from the department to the senior staff had customarily been informal.

There was some evidence however, to suggest that the team was providing greater balance to decisions made on school policy, and that the attitude of the school was changing to embrace objectives consistent with those of a comprehensive school. Some of this was due to the work of the senior management team in facilitating a devolution of control. It may be that the head had acquired greater confidence in their ability to take on larger responsibilities and so was prepared to see these changes taking place. The team gained in effectiveness as the senior staff adjusted to their new relationship with the head and accepted new roles of shared responsibility. The development of the team was largely as a support group to the head. It remained to be seen whether the team would also become an effective link with departments. Some members of staff argued that there should be greater devolution of responsibility so that team members could implement policy and thereby play a fuller part in the effective management of the school in an executive capacity.

Commentary

The larger and more complex an organization becomes, the less likely that one person alone is adequate to be its leader. An organization is vulnerable if it depends upon one person for its inspiration and judgement. Although the search is still made to find persons of superlative and inclusive qualities to head an organization, in practice this is seldom successful: the demands of organization on leadership are often too powerful for one individual to fulfil.

Where the individual fails, however, the team may succeed. In schools the sheer volume of issues clamouring for attention, problems to be solved and adjustments waiting to be made, all encourage the development of a management team. Such a team may be ad hoc, called into being whenever problems of sufficient size and importance must be dealt with, or it may be permanent as in this case. It may also confine its work to matters of policy — again as in this case — or it may be conceived as an executive team to implement the policy and decisions of the head of school. It may combine both policy and executive functions — in this case this is expressed as a possible outcome in the future.

A team may thus be justified in terms of the nature of the managerial work needing to be done. Teams vary greatly in practice according to the assumptions made about their purpose and usefulness. Three important questions about teams themselves, apart from how they are conceived by their creators, are: How are the members changed? How is the team developed? How is a team's effectiveness measured? The first and most important question of all, however, is how the team is constituted. Its members may be composed of the most intelligent people available, the most experienced or qualified, or the most representative. In this case the team consisted of the most senior staff in terms of position and the scope of their formal duties. Its members were expected to discharge a general management function for the school, leaving specialist management functions to the departments.

To be effective a team needs to possess a certain range of abilities among its members. Each contributes to the work of the team and each is necessary. Each team member needs to be able to contribute one or more of them according to the size of the team. These include the ability to turn principles and plans into practice; controlling the team's own work and bringing out the best in each member; shaping the team's objectives and driving it towards the completion of its work; advancing new ideas, insights and solutions; exploring the environment, making external contacts and reporting back information and developments taking place elsewhere; evaluating ideas and weighing evidence; exercising a supportive and pastoral role among team members themselves to create a team spirit; and protecting the team from errors of omission and commission, giving attention to detail, and maintaining a sense of urgency.

If team composition followed these lines, each member of a team would be chosen primarily because of the qualities he or she possessed and was able to offer as a vital contribution to the working of the team. These would take precedence over rank, seniority or factors which may commonly govern selection for a team such as intelligence, qualification or subject representation.

Issues for further discussion

1. When the establishment of a senior management team is appropriate and when it is inappropriate.

2. Criteria for team membership selection.

3. The best size for a senior management team — the relevant factors.

4. The unintended consequences of introducing a senior management team.

5. The frequency and conduct of senior management team meetings.

6. The origin and nature of business handled by a senior management team.

7. The work of the head in a school which has a senior management team.

8. The functions of a senior management team in relation to:
   (a) a school's goveners;
   (b) a full staff meeting;
   (c) subject departments;
   (d) pastoral care units;
   (e) curriculum;
   (f) personnel development.

9. When a team is not a team — the measurement of a team's effectiveness.

10. Job rotation and job satisfaction among members of a senior management team with executive responsibilities.

Further reading

Belbin, R.M. (1983) *Management Teams — why they succeed or fail.* London, Heinemann.

Davis, S.A. (1974) 'Building More Effective Teams'. Pages 119–133 in Gellerman, S.W. *Behavioral Science in Management.* Harmondsworth, Penguin.

Department of Education and Science (1981) *The School Curriculum.* Circular 6/81. London, HMSO.

CHAPTER 4
STAFF MANAGEMENT
Case 4.1: Relations between head and teaching staff

Introduction

In a junior school of 250 pupils, over a period of two years an established head is seen dealing with a series of very varied events, all of which involve members of the school's teaching staff in one context or another: the farewell of the deputy head; a teacher seeking support for an in-service degree course; a Scale III post becoming available; a teacher deputizing for the head in school assembly; parents withdrawing their daughter in favour of independent education; the handling of music by the staff; a safety policy for the school; changing to an integrated curriculum; and introducing examinations.

The arbitrary way in which issues are approached and commitments are relinquished is obviously disconcerting to the teaching staff. Staff morale and effort are at stake, and some unusual explanations are implied.

Narrative

A member of staff who had served in the upper school for several years and who had won the respect and admiration of all staff and children alike, was internally promoted to the post of deputy head. She remained in this position for several years until her husband's job took him to a new district and she decided to give notice.

As deputy she had acted as a filter between the head and the staff, often, on her own admission, having to divert his intentions of doing or saying something unreasonable. The staff were fully aware of this fact and were duly appreciative, which they showed by giving her an expensive gift at the end of her term of duty. They were often to be heard discussing the fact that 'Mrs. B had talked him round from that' again. The children and parents also recognized the service which she had rendered. They collected enough money to give her several beautiful gifts on leaving. She had managed to know and have dealings with every child in the school. So involved had she been with the school that she stayed in the area to complete the academic year, although her husband had been moved six months earlier.

On her last day, the staff organized farewell drinks at lunch-time, and there was to be the usual end-of-term assembly in the afternoon. The head refused to attend either the drinks or the assembly, leaving the deputy to dismiss the school, with no one to bid her farewell and good luck.

Meanwhile, a member of staff had felt motivated to apply for a long, part-time, in-service degree course at the local college. The application form required the head's signature, which he duly signed when the teacher explained the point of doing the course — to obtain a degree. The head made polite remarks with no particular show of interest. Several months later, when the course was under way, and consuming a considerable portion of the teacher's free time, she became aware that other teachers on the course from the same county were claiming 'study leave' for part of the course. Enquiries were instigated in the school office, and the teacher concerned searched through all available information in the staff room without success. The requests for information were repeated to both the secretary, and then the head, who said that he knew of no such provision. The teacher then told the head of her intention of visiting the education office to obtain the information needed. The head agreed that this would be a good idea, and that he would be glad to hear about it.

The teacher visited the office of the local education authority and discovered that 'study leave' was applicable on request from the school's governors but could get no information about supply cover, as the officials insisted that the head already had full details of the procedure. Immediately on return to school, the teacher was summoned to the head's office where she was verbally attacked, with such statements as that she had been to the office behind the head's back, no one was to go to the office from his school and that he had never signed the application form for the course.

The staff representative reported back that at the next governors' meeting some discussion had taken place. The head had suggested that teachers needed his permission for such activities even if out of school hours. In reply the governors said that this was out of the question, since a teacher's time was her own. The head finally allowed the leave, with the local education authority's permission and to the satisfaction of the governors, for the second year of the part-time degree. The head supported the application for study leave in the governors' meeting and stated how pleased he was that staff were so professionally motivated as to devote their own time to upgrading their qualifications.

On the advertisement of a Scale III post for head of year, a Scale II member of the same year group was called to the head's office. She was advised that she should apply for the post, and that, in effect, it would be hers. The teacher, Mrs. X, did so, as requested, and waited. Two weeks later, a group of young men were shown round the school and into the staff room. Mrs. X told the deputy head that, in her opinion, these were interviewees for the Scale III post. The deputy said that this could not possibly be so. She knew nothing of the interviews, and the head had every intention of appointing Mrs. X to the post. Several days later, Mrs. X reported to the deputy that she was sure that an appointment had been made from the men interviewed, but that she had not had any notification at all. Later the head sent for her and confirmed, without apology, that an appointment had been made, and that the governors had felt that a male teacher was needed (there were already three men on the staff as well as the head).

The following week, Mrs. X was called to the head's office again, to learn that the new Scale III head of year was not able to be released from his present school for the next term. Consequently the head had decided to offer her the post temporarily for one term, until it could be taken up by its new holder. Mrs. X took the post temporarily, on the grounds that she might as well have the extra salary for the position which she was already filling. One term after the arrival of the new man, she was moved to another year group, but a few months later was moved back within the year group under the same Scale III teacher.

One morning the head, not wishing to take assembly, prevailed upon a Scale III teacher, Miss Y to do it for him. Reluctantly she agreed, and produced a story and ideas at ten minutes' notice. She began the assembly and was somewhat taken aback when the head appeared and seated himself at the piano. Since it was obvious that he proposed to take no part in the occasion, she ignored his presence, whereupon he began to rattle the change in his pockets and to cough in a loud and compulsive manner. As soon as the children began to say the Lord's Prayer, he struck up, on the piano, a series of arbitrary chords. Later on the head wished to have assemblies taken by senior staff on a regular basis. Miss Y refused, on the grounds that it was not her job, but agreed that in the absence of other senior staff, she would undertake the task.

A fourth-year teacher, Mrs. Z, referred the parents of a girl in her class to the head, as they clearly wished to enter their child for selective private secondary education. The staff had been informed that they should send all such queries straight to the head. The child concerned was a most industrious and hard-working girl with a good reading age. However, her work was extremely slow, though meticulous and thorough, and she showed little of the sparkle of the intellectually precocious child. On a stndardized mathematics paper her result had been unspectacular, a good average. Her teacher would have allotted her a 'B' grade all round, with no recommendation for a grammar school, as the pressure would be likely to prove too great.

Several weeks later the head called Mrs. Z to show her a confidential report that he had written on the girl, at the request of the school which her parents hoped that she would attend. He had written that the child deserved 'A — Excellent' for all subjects, and had given her a glowing report in general, although he had neither asked the class teacher for her opinion, nor requested samples of work, nor consulted the child's teacher from the previous year.

At the beginning of the next school year, after staff had been allocated to classes, there was obviously a problem regarding music teaching. The subject had always been taught by a specialist, rather than by class teachers. Various BBC programmes were suggested and tried, but lower-school staff were still not very satisfied with the arrangements.

About a quarter of the way through the term the head assembled the lower-school staff and announced that they should produce a musical play, based on a BBC programme. The staff discussed the matter amongst themselves — they included a Scale III teacher and a Scale II teacher — and then went back to the head, pointing out that they were not sufficiently sure of themselves to teach even the songs fully, let alone produce a play with them, and that they felt that the standard of performance would be very poor in contrast with the usual efforts of the school. The head accused the Scale III teacher of sedition and instructed the others to take no further notice of anything she said, declaring that the staff would now produce the musical play as a punishment.

A few weeks later the head called an unscheduled staff meeting at lunch-time on a Friday in which he produced a document, running to some 15 pages, which he declared was the school's safety policy. He handed a copy to each member of staff and then, immediately, requested them to sign a written declaration stating that they had read, understood and accepted every item. The staff pointed out that this was not strictly true, since they had just received the document for the first time, and that they could not possibly sign such a document. The head seemed somewhat upset by their refusal, and declared forcibly that any member of staff who appeared, intending to teach in his school on the next school day, must sign the declaration before he or she would be admitted to the building. This caused a great deal of worry and work for the union representatives who sent the document to their respective headquarters, who confirmed that nothing should be signed. The staff appeared on the Monday, somewhat anxious. The head did not appear at the school for the next two days, and made no reference to the safety policy when he did return.

The school had for many years operated in a fairly formal, strictly timetabled way, with written directives from the head that all children were to be seated in straight rows facing the blackboard, and that octagonal tables were to be split up to facilitate this approach. The children were not officially allowed out of sight of the class teacher at any time when they were on the premises.

At a staff meeting before the following term began the head declared that the school had never run in the way which he wanted (he had been head since the opening of the school 12 years previously, and had appointed all the staff). The school was to operate an integrated day, therefore, with immediate effect. The children were to be split into groups, where they should all be doing different things. The timetable, except for the use of the hall and TV, could be ignored — although certain amounts of time per week were still to be spent on each subject. The desks were no longer to be in rows facing the same way. No one was to say that the head had directed them to operate in this way, but nonetheless, he would only look favourably on those who did it.

At the end of the term the head called the upper-school staff to a meeting at which he announced his intention of introducing half-yearly examinations and reports four weeks into the next term. Prior to this there had only been standardized screening tests of reading and mathematics. He stated that this would demonstrate which children and staff were succeeding and which were not. At the beginning of the next term all the staff were given a sheet of paper stating the subjects to be examined, and the marks to be allocated. There was a minor protest from the lower school staff, since they had not been informed of the intention to hold examinations at all, but the head was adamant. He proposed to set the main mathematics and English papers himself. The staff were to set the remainder and mark and record them all. For a while the staff discussed the implications of the announcement among themselves, the general opinion being that the proposed examinations were iniquitous and would only serve to reinforce the failure already felt by the poorer children, but, recalling earlier attempts to discuss the lower-school staff's problems with music, they refused to raise the matter with the head.

A staff meeting was then called to allow the head a chance 'to explain to the teachers about the standardization of marks and how to do it'. A half hour's description of 'standardization' ensued, in which all staff were issued with handy gadgets to assist their standardizing. Without this, the head explained, the marks were quite valueless. Several of the staff pointed out that, as long as raw scores were not produced, the marks would emerge as a curve, even if all the children in one class scored 50 per cent less than a parallel class.

The next few weeks saw staff carefully preparing children for the shock of practising timed exercises, setting the spellings for homework and writing staff-set papers which would enable the children to feel some success in their endeavours. The day before the examinations were to begin, the head declared at another staff meeting that the children were not to be worried, overworked or upset. Teachers could explain as much as they felt was needed, read papers with the children, help where necessary and allow as much time as they felt inclined. But the children had to get used to examination conditions — it was 'good' for them.

On completion of the examinations, the head called another meeting to explain how the reports were to be written, at which some of the staff pointed out that their results when 'standardized' were most odd. The head became a little heated when trying to explain that 100 out of 100 right is not 100 correct, nor an 'A' grade. When asked by a member of staff if they could use 'proper standardized tests' next time the head went red in the face, shouted and raged at the teacher about his ignorance, declared that the staff were attacking him and that he wanted the reports filled in as he had said, and stamped out.

Two members of staff spent four hours each putting what he had ordered on to their reports, in duplicate, only to have him declare, ten days later, that the staff had misunderstood him. The reports were only for school records and needed only scores, but no comments.

Commentary

This disparate set of incidents, when accumulated in narrative form, read like an indictment of the head's managerial capacity. In so far as these events are a representative sample of the way in which the head deals with business and professional matters, they form a picture of his managerial style. This concept may be defined as the characteristic way in which an individual goes about his or her management work, in a given organization, over a substantial period of time, as assessed by those who work with him or her.

The events in this narrative took place over a period of months in the same school. They were selected by one of the teaching staff who was subject to the head's management and are evidently meant to portray questionable behavioural patterns.

It may be that the head had always resented the intercessary role which the departing deputy head had adopted, in the first cameo presented. The head may also have been jealous of his deputy's good standing. The staff certainly felt that the deputy had given good service to the school. As an ordinary act of courtesy the head would be expected to be present at the deputy's departure on the last day.

More fundamentally, however, such occasions present the head of a school with a prime opportunity to offer praise for work well done and, either explicitly or implicitly, to reiterate the main values for which the school stands. This provides a touchstone and encouragement to other members of staff in their work. In this case the reverse happened. Staff were probably wondering if effort was worthwhile and if anyone appreciated their work for the school.

In the second cameo, the head either did not know or had forgotten the local education authority's policy over supporting teachers on part-time courses. Normally a head would be expected to welcome any steps which a member of staff took for self-improvement — particularly when taken in the teacher's own time. Clearly there may be a temptation to be less enthusiastic when membership of an external course involves disruption of the school's teaching programme because it is taken during the working day.

The head agreed that the teacher should find out the necessary information from the local education authority's office. He subsequently upbraided the teacher for doing it. As organizational gatekeeper between the school and the education authority the head is understandably sensitive about the image of the school which might be projected by others. Yet he apparently agreed the contact but either forgot that he had done so or arbitrarily changed his mind. Either way, his handling of this matter must have made a discouraging and disconcerting impression on the teacher. The head eventually seized his opportunity in the governors' meeting to show approval of teachers' initiatives in their own professional development.

In the case of the Scale III post, the teacher already holding a Scale II post in the same year group was apparently invited to apply. She herself and other colleagues, however, may have interpreted the head's invitation with more finality than was warranted. It is difficult to let an incumbent know that an external appointment for a senior post is preferred. She may have proved the best applicant in the end, anyway. Being frank and direct with staff takes courage but is an honourable way to proceed. In the event the head evidently took advantage of the governors to secure an external appointment. The treatment of the internal applicant at the time of the appointment itself and subsequent to it, however, must have had a deleterious effect on that teacher's morale and presented a negative image to the staff as a whole.

The head's conduct in asking a senior member of staff to take the school assembly at short notice, only to disport himself in an eccentric manner, almost defies rational explanation. He could have been protesting at something she had omitted to say or do which was routine and sacrosanct. The act of delegation, however, should be complete and free from surveillance. Subordinates should be free to make mistakes within defined bounds.

His conduct in sending exemplary reports of a pupil to an independent school head perhaps was well meant, if unwise. He chose to provide his own subjective judgements, ignore the assessment system of his own school and avoid consulting the pupil's teacher. The pupil's work in his school relative to her age group at large may well have been 'A — Excellent' in all fields in his judgement. Nevertheless, staff were clearly resentful of his seemingly arbitrary action without explanation, and this only added to their frustration and alienation.

It is not usual for a musical play in a primary school to be produced because of a directive from the head, but certainly not as a punishment for recalcitrant behaviour of teaching staff. Fears of incompetence were probably genuine, though if low morale and alienation among staff persist, excuses for avoiding extra work can proliferate. This cameo provides a poor image of the forward planning needed to prepare staff attitudes and skills for curricular changes or significant special events.

The head's dictatorial behaviour over the school's safety policy document was rightly resisted by the staff. In a participative school the professional integrity and commitment of at least some of the staff might have been engaged in drawing up such a document. Even if it had not, time should have been given to absorb the content to discuss it and raise any queries. The head's intemperate remarks on forbidding entry to the school to any teacher who had not signed the document might have precipitated a serious industrial dispute in any other organization. His subsequent willingness to suffer personal loss of face may have assuaged some of the disaffection caused among the staff, but must have severely damaged his credibility.

In the case of the head's attempt to change the music teaching in the lower school, it was clear that too little consideration was given to the time needed to change attitudes and to adapt a teacher's expertise and ways of teaching. How much more so is this true in trying to change the entire base of the curriculum and teaching methods by fiat, with immediate effect. There seems to have been no appreciation of the fine developments by which teachers reach a mode of working which represents a balance of their abilities, interests and personal resources. This is to say nothing of the disrupting effects on the pupils. Furthermore, a uniform teaching method in concept and practice is not consistent with the various ways in which individuals learn and teach most effectively. Such a fundamental innovation requires a pilot study within the school and a staff participation and development policy.

Some attempt at planning and preparation was made over the attempt to introduce half-yearly examinations. The staff by this time were thoroughly disaffected. Only some of the staff were given prior warning. Again, a substantial change of policy requires the active support and the technical competence of all the teaching staff were given prior warning.

Help could have been obtained from an outside consultant, on the technical aspects of what the school wanted to do. Informal soundings, discussions with senior staff, and a process of dicussion and persuasion should have preceded the formal process of implementation.

Overall, it is certainly possible that the head was suffering from stress; the degree of arbitrariness and lack of consideration shown certainly borders on the irrational. Directive management has its place, but over such pervasive and substantive issues as represented in this case, it is inappropriate, counterproductive and almost certainly a frantic, if not desperate, attempt at self-defence. The question remains why this condition had arisen.

Issues for discussion

1. Staff morale — its determinants and effects on education in the primary school.

2. Staff appointment procedures for internal candidates.

3. Participation levels of the teaching staff in discussions represented in this case. When is participation desirable? When might it be more efficient and acceptable to work without participation?

4. Educational management training and retraining for primary school heads.

5. Professional counselling for heads of schools. When should a head be judged incapable of running a school?

6. Sources of stress for school heads.

7. Medical checks in the teaching profession as a condition for continuing employment. The difficulties and benefits involved.

8. Would it be possible or useful to employ an external consultant? In what particular situations might such a consultant be useful?

9. The governors and their role in relation to the matters raised in this case.

10. The benefits and limitations of the directive style in management.

Further reading

Blake, R. and Mouton, J.S. (1978) *The New Managerial Grid*. Houston, Gulf.

Dunham, J. (1983) 'Coping with Organizational Stress'. Chapter 10 in Paisey, A. (editor) *The Effective Teacher*. London, Ward Lock Educational.

Phi Delta Kappa (1980) On Mixing and Matching of Teaching and Learning Styles. *Practical Applications of Research* Phi Delta Kappa 3, 2.

Case 4.2: The organization of science

Introduction

Although falling numbers of pupils of secondary school age in the district are forecast, a new secondary school is opened. It is an 11 to 18 comprehensive school purposely built as a social centre for the local community. Strong political pressures ensure that the school is finally completed. Once the facilities are provided, however, the main responsibility to ensure that they are well managed devolves on the school. The shortcomings of operational management are highlighted in this case by the growth and development of science in the school. The focus is on the policy of the school, the structure of the science staffing, the nature of the science curriculum and the question of leadership for science.

The head of school is persuaded by an adviser — and against his better judgement — to unify science in the school through the appointment of a new member of staff to a senior post. The newcomer's difficulties are only emerging when the head and one of the deputy heads leaves the school. This creates an increased dilemma for science and a stressful situation for the person appointed to lead the science staff.

Narrative

The school was designed and built as a neighbourhood school, the social centre for the community. Local political pressure ensured that it should be opened as planned despite the fact that the school population was forecast to fall in the near future. It was intended to be six — and occasionally seven — forms of entry, although it seemed unlikely that its catchment area would provide such an entry for long. Its community provision included a large indoor swimming-pool, sports hall and small committee rooms with social lounge. In addition to a large sports field there was an all-weather pitch with floodlighting. The headmaster was large, ebullient, extrovert and regarded by many people as a very forceful person. He exuded confidence and made his staff well aware of the direction in which he expected the school to go.

Year by year, the school grew with the addition of an intake each year until it was at full strength. During this period of development extra staffing was required every year in each curriculum area. The science staff soon numbered one part-time and three full-time teachers. Each of these four served as a head of department. It was the head's stated policy that there would be no overall head of the science department. The separate subjects of biology, chemistry and physics operated as autonomous units with their own heads of department. The school, however, was in a rural setting. The catchment area included many outlying villages, farms, nurseries and a large egg farm. The introduction of rural science into the curriculum was therefore a natural development. The exciting challenge offered by a new school had enabled the head to collect a group of enthusiastic forward-thinking teachers, who were highly committed and keen to innovate, one of whom became head of rural science, to run yet another autonomous science department.

For the school's first four years there were only three laboratories, but phase two of the building programme, due to be opened within a few months, included a science department complex. This was to contain eight laboratories, four preparation rooms, a central store, greenhouse, potting-shed, animal room and two large classrooms which were to be used by the Geography Department. Despite impending economic gloom, considerable capital expenditure had been approved to equip this new building and it was viewed as one of the local education authority's 'show-place' schools. There were two full-time laboratory technicians, one male and one female. The former, who was the senior, had a background of photography before coming to the school and he was primarily responsible for servicing chemistry and physics. The young woman technician was appointed straight from leaving school and worked in the Biology and Rural Science Departments. Two more full-time technicians were appointed on the opening of the new laboratories. The science adviser of the local education authority was a very strong personality who had fought for the increase in science provision. It was an area of the curriculum which was considered favoured. The majority of the school's ancillary help was for science. This led to a certain amount of resentment from other departments, notably Modern Languages, which could have used technical assistance in the language laboratory, and the Technical Studies Department which needed help with stock and machinery.

From the beginning the school's own modified form of Nuffield Combined Science had been used in Years 1 and 2. The science adviser favoured an integrated science approach throughout the whole 11–16 phase. He had been encouraged by the appointment of the head of rural science who at his previous school had been involved in writing rural studies contributions for national integrated science courses. The separate science departments at the school seemed to be an obstacle to a greater co-ordination of the teaching schemes. During successive meetings over the plans for the phase two building programme, the science adviser pressed the head to review the wisdom of the current organizational structure for science.

Finally the head was persuaded that an overall head of science should be the next appointment. Interviews were held for this new post which became tenable from the beginning of the following year. The successful candidate was head of physics in a neighbouring school. Apart from having taught in the 16–18 age range, he had had little more experience that either of the heads of the separate science departments. He had no experience of managing a large team, although he had shown himself capable of chairing meetings of local science teachers. He got on well with people but seemed diffident. The head of physics at the school had also been interviewed for the overall head of science post. He had been at the school since its opening and, although he was to retain the responsibility for physics, he had understandable misgivings about another physicist being appointed above him. He was well organized and highly methodical but often insular in outlook. The two men knew each other well from local science teachers' meetings. The head of biology was fiery-tempered, meticulous, very determined and conservative in his outlook. His previous appointments had been in the London area but he had wanted to find a job away from the city. The head of rural science had been an experienced horticulturist before he became a teacher. He was interested in music and painting and was highly sensitive and emotional, but lacked empathy for anything inanimate. The part-time member of the science staff was in charge of chemistry. For the rest of his time he acted as warden at the local teachers' centre. This had been a useful appointment when the school could not justify a full-time chemist but, at some stage in the future, it was seen that he would have to decide whether to become full-time at the school or at the teachers' centre.

Before taking up his appointment, the new head of science's principal preoccupation was ordering equipment for the new laboratories. Although the capital sum allocated was very generous, he was determined that the best kept housekeeping methods should be adopted. With the senior of the technicians, he drew up a system of ordering and accounting and prepared a list of basic equipment for the new laboratories. The other staff were involved in modifying these lists which were put to tender with a number of apparatus suppliers. When he arrived at the school in September, he was faced with three main tasks.

First, the organization and administration of the previously separate departments had to be formed into one structure. He felt that a unified system for basic stock, finance, ordering and equipment sharing was required. This was particularly important because the number of science staff was to be increased to nine over the next two years. Although the head of physics was satisfied with the existing systems and saw no reason for change, the others were content to have these routine chores handled by someone else. In particular, the head of rural science abhorred paper work and saw it as an unnecessary intrusion into his task of teaching young people. The new arrangement still enabled each head of subject to have a hand on the purse strings, since the new head of science sliced up the Science Department's share of the 'capitation cake' and allocated it to each of them.

Secondly, development of the curriculum was needed. The original first-year intake had now reached the fifth year and plans had to be made for sixth-form courses. There was also the issue of integration. The new head of science felt committed to this ideologically and morally as it was clear that he had been appointed with integration of science courses as part of his brief. He decided to take on the specific role of coordinating the combined science course in the lower school and, with its own separate financing, had all but created a new sub-department. In general the staff supported this. It was little different, after all, from what had been happening for four years. His attempts at further integration, however, met with resistance. The heads of the separate sciences saw such a move as an erosion of their previous autonomy. Already they had become subordinate in the departmental structure and they feared the submersion of their own curricular sections within a unified scheme. Tentative moves towards discussing integration were received in a variety of ways — disinterest, well-rehearsed objections on ideological and practical grounds, and open hostility to what was conceived as unwarranted interference. Two staff members had already made it very clear to the new head of science that, in creating a head of science post, the head of school had broken faith with them over their own job specifications as given when they were appointed. Even the head of rural science, with his experience of integrated schemes, was opposed to change. The only one in support was the part-time chemist who had less to lose. His move to the post of full-time teachers' centre warden was becoming a distinct possibility.

Thirdly, the new head of science had to create a unified team from these strong-minded colleagues. Each had strengths and weaknesses and their mutual support would be invaluable for the future. Most of all, he wished to be accepted by them. He began to feel daunted by the tasks facing him.

A further blow to his morale, however, came through a change in the senior staff. The male deputy head, who had responsibility for the school's curriculum and had been a founder member of the school, obtained promotion to headship and left. The new head of science had used him as a sounding board and confessor, and felt a profound sense of loss. Within a month the head announced that he too was leaving for another headship. These changes in the senior management team made the head of science apprehensive. The newcomers might well maintain the general direction which had been adopted for science but the emphases would probably change. His fears were partially realised. The new head of school and deputy did not fill the power vacuum left by their predecessors. The head had been openly surprised that he had been appointed. He was eager to be supportive without being too sure of the direction he wanted the school to take. He was keen to make an early impact on the curriculum by encouraging ideas that were already in train, and saw the tentative discussions on science integration as a change to which he could add strong support.

The head of science felt himself to be the focus of opposing forces. The new head was striving to establish integration, whereas most of the science staff were against it. Their arguments made him doubt the wisdom of pursuing it further. A declining pupil population meant there would be fewer opportunities for promotion. Each member of the science staff had to contemplate a long career at the school. In particular he himself had little prospect of making even a sideways move. Financially, he could only consider a move outside the area as a result of promotion. He was unlikely to be offered a sideways move locally since, as yet, he had failed to show himself competent in his present post.

Commentary

This case illustrates how critical it is to have good management and to be a good manager. Public policy may result in expensive plant being provided. There may be ambitious intentions for it. But capital expenditure and the existence of need, will not produce results if the operational management is inadequate. The reverse is true; poor resources can be made to produce exceptional results when the managerial capacity involved is high. However, in this case the teaching and learning outcomes, which are the true product of the school, are not known.

A manager at any level always faces an inescapable dilemma. On the one hand there are the interests of those who form the membership of the immediate organization and who are responsible directly for producing the goods and/or services for which it exists. On the other hand are the interests of those who provide the resources for the organization to exist, who permit it to operate and who constitute the authority which delegates its powers to the organization concerned and to which the organization is accountable.

In this boundary position, the manager may be tempted to serve the interests of the one to the exclusion of the other. He or she may yield to the claims of the external interests, at whatever cost to those of the internal interests, or vice versa. The head of school had chosen a path of action with regard to science: a cluster of areas in the natural sciences would each have its own head of department and be treated as independent, autonomous departments alongside all other subject departments in the school. We do not know if other subject clusters such as humanities or technical studies were subject to the same policy.

In the event, the head is persuaded by the adviser of the local education authority to appoint a superordinate scientist. The head yields to the external interest at the expense of the internal interest, at a cost which becomes apparant as the case unfolds. If the reasons given for the move were intrinsically compelling then, of course, there was potentially much to be gained. In that event everything depended on the effectiveness of the staff selection and interviewing procedures of the schools. The inability to appoint the right person from a group of applicants, which includes individuals who are right for the job concerned, is a serious deficiency. The leadership quality in management is nowhere better exemplified than in selecting staff who will themselves be effective leaders.

The head could have held out against the adviser. The internal interests would have been satisfied and the staff concerned would presumably have rewarded their boss with good service. However, there would have been penalties. The adviser's goodwill might have been lost and subsequently there may have been a reluctance on his part to assist in further developments for science. Either way, the head faced a choice in which losses and gains had to be balanced. The narrative hints, however, that the head was denied the chance of being objective by the personal pressures put on him by the specialist adviser.

The same principle is exemplified in the situation faced by the new head of science. He had the option of finding out and serving the interests of the head and senior staff of the school in relation to those of his subordinates as members of his department or faculty. They might have coincided. In this case they did not. His position was doubly difficult because of the conditional nature of his appointment — the need to integrate science — in relation to some of the problems he faced.

Both men as managers would have preferred to be able to reconcile both sets of interests. Indeed, the manager's skill is in relating the two, in the event that they are in contradistinction to one another.

On the substantive issue of the appointment itself, a further important principle was at stake. The proposed appointment of a head of science represented a deepening of the hierarchy. If formal relationships between teaching staff members are thought of as structure, the structure takes the form of a pyramid. There is one head of school — the apex of the pyramid — but many Scale I teachers — the base of the pyramid. In this case, the many separate heads of department in the science field, each able to report direct to the head of school and/or deputy head(s) of school, represented a 'flat' pyramid. The addition of an overall head of science interposes a level of authority between the various heads of science subjects and the senior staff of the school. The fewer levels there are the flatter the pyramid, the more levels there are, as in this case, the taller the pyramid. The Burnham arrangements for the teaching profession encourage such formal structures, although schools have discretion to regulate them towards being either 'flatter' or 'taller' by the way in which they distribute their scale points.

The significance of the matter is that in the public bureaucracies where professional men and women are employed — as distinct from military and quasi-military organizations — there is an inevitable conflict between the claims of the organization concerned and the claims of professionalism. Engineers, accountants, statisticians, doctors, scientists and the like draw their sustenance and derive their being from a wider reference group than the organization in which they currently work — that is, their profession. Teachers aspire to such status. Within teaching, scientists particularly might feel that their respective disciplines have enough identity and validity to warrant independent identity within the school. Hence, the flatter the pyramid can be made, the more congenial the structure would be, potentially, to professional people. The logic of this argument is that greater professionalism should correlate with greater autonomy in organizational structures. In practice, however, the managerial problem is how to coordinate such disparate contributions to the curriculum, as highlighted in this case.

Issues for further discussion

1. Staff selection and interview procedures.

2. The functions of local education authority advisers: relations between the adviser and the head of school. How far should a head heed their advice — especially regarding staff appointments?

3. The value of faculty structures generally.

4. The case for integrated science programmes.

5. The justification for having a head of science: his job description and financial considerations.

6. Policy continuity and a change in headship: the obligations and rights of the new head.

7. Leadership of a department: creating a team.

8. Staff performance review: the methods and instruments by which this may be accomplished.

9. Curriculum revision — the evidence upon which the need for its modification should be based and the procedures for effecting it.

10. The community school in concept and practice.

Further reading

Marland, M. (1971) *Head of Department*. London, Heinemann.

Matthew, R. and Tong, S. (1982) *The Role of the Deputy Head in the Comprehensive School*. London, Ward Lock Educational.

Poster, C. (1982) *Community Education — Its Development and Management*. London, Heinemann.

CHAPTER 5
STAFF DEVELOPMENT
Case 5.1: The problematic teacher

Introduction

Over a period of time a teacher is shown to generate more anxiety among pupils, parents and staff than generally might be expected of any individual teacher. The dislocations and actual crises which grow out of the teacher's conduct bring the unwelcome attention of various people outside the school and affect the public image of the school and its standing with the local education authority.

At first sight the case seems to be one of manifest incompetence, arising either from the teacher's lack of intellectual and behavioural ability to measure up to the requirements of the job or from a studied insistence on being different — if not a deliberate determination to cause trouble.

The school tries to accommodate this teacher in a variety of ways. Her professional performance is eventually raised, only to revert to its former level when falling rolls deny the school the room for manoeuvre that it needs.

Narrative

Mrs. X qualified as a teacher after completing a two-year training course in India. Her early teaching experiences were in schools in various parts of the world as she accompanied her husband. She completed ten years of teaching, some part-time, some full-time, but of these only two in England were considered reckonable as pensionable service.

Mrs. X took a part-time job in the local infant school soon after moving house. This was increased to full-time teaching the following year. She had very little infant experience and was restricted to the top infant group. She was neither formally interviewed nor appointed by the school governors. At the time teachers were in short supply, particularly in this school which was difficult to reach by public transport and had special problems.

Two years later the head teacher retired. She had been a wise, gentle person who had seen the school through two transfers of building but felt that the county's reorganization plans for first and middle schools would be better dealt with by a new and younger head. She tactfully warned her successor about potential problems and in particular about Mrs. X whose manner with young children was strict, formal and forbidding. She was regarded as being more suitable for teaching much older junior or secondary-age children. The head had received complaints from parents about the emotional stress experienced by children in Mrs. X's class. Mrs. X had strong allies in the part-time remedial teacher, another part-time teacher of similar age and a very domineering school helper who was older but had not yet reached retirement age.

The procedure on reorganization adopted by the local education authority was that all teachers were offered the opportunity to remain on the staff or ask for redeployment. There was no question of reselection by interview. Mrs. X therefore was offered a permanent appointment in the school and she accepted.

The new head had progressive ideas on classroom management and curriculum development and soon found the staff divided into two camps, one supportive and the other hostile, Mrs. X being in the latter group. At the end of the first term the anticipated resignation of the deputy head, whose husband had changed jobs and was leaving the area, meant advertising for a replacement. The local education authority's procedures at that time prevented heads from seeing all the application forms; only the forms of short-listed candidates were seen. It was with some surprise that the head discovered Mrs. X's name on the list. The local education authority's area inspector was equally surprised to discover that no one had told the head about it earlier. He spent a short time in Mrs. X's classroom and agreed with the head that she was totally unsuitable — his comment was that she was 'a disaster in an infant school'. Protocol demanded that the interview should proceed and fortunately a highly suitable candidate was selected. Mrs. X did not appear to be embarrassed at not being appointed but obviously did not approve of the teacher who was.

The head decided to leave Mrs. X with the older children who might be less intimidated by her aversive style, but it was an unsatisfactory arrangement from the point of view of their academic progress. There was little stimulation in the work she planned although the head tried to interest her in using new materials that were being introduced into the school. The head tried a different approach by starting work on child-centred topics with the class and leaving Mrs. X to continue — but found that she refused to let the children do 'that work' in her lessons.

As with her predecessor the head found that dealing with parental complaints about Mrs. X's attitude to the children became part of life. Each complaint that the head felt was justified was discussed with Mrs. X who invariably dismissed them as being either lies, the fault of the child in being lazy or naughty, or the fault of the parent in being too fussy or over-anxious.

In despair the head sought the advice of the local education authority's inspector who visited the school and tactfully suggested to Mrs. X that she tried new approaches and attended courses. For a time there seemed to be an improvement — the head arranged for her to attend a one-week mathematics course and encouraged her to share the new ideas with colleagues but she considered the whole week to be 'a complete waste of time'.

There were several changes of staff and one by one Mrs. X's supporters left. Three deputy heads moved on to their own headships. Each had brought his or her influence to bear on her. None achieved any change of attitude in her, but there was evidence of some change in her classroom management and the introduction of more interesting activities for the children. Instead of class teaching the emphasis changed to individually planned work in the basic subjects, and the children sat in groups instead of rows. The individual approach created new problems. Children wasted time as they waited their turn to read or to ask for help with new words or learning problems. The staff found themselves placed in a supportive role as they tried to prepare children to move into her class or pushed them on to a commensurate level after being in her class. The head had found that the strategic place for her in the school was with a middle age range class. This also allowed for flexibility in placing new children. Those who were timid, slow, or very quick learners were placed in alternative classes where their needs would be more sympathetically dealt with.

This strategy did not stop the complaints completely, but certainly reduced them. The local education authority's inspectorate was kept informed of the state of affairs and the visiting inspector usually tried to see Mrs. X, but she seemed totally unaware that her teaching was being criticized. To the casual observer she was doing a satisfactory job — she always stayed behind at the end of the day to put the next day's cards in the children's books. She put work on the wall from time to time when reminded to do so and wrote up her record books and handed them in punctually. She even began to attend out-of-school functions. She reported that the parents she saw on open days never made any complaints to her, but always said how pleased they were with their children's work. It seemed that the supportive policy was paying dividends.

However, some problems remained, one of these being Mrs. X's absentmindedness. One example of this occurred when she sent home a new child's confidential records by accident in an envelope containing books which had been sent on from the previous school. The parents contacted the head in an agitated state about remarks in the record made by a teacher in the previous school that the child's mother was unmarried, which was untrue. The grandmother called to see the head, demanding to know why such a statement was in the child's record and threatening to take the matter further. The head, with the agreement of the head of the previous school and the parents, deleted the offending statements in front of the parents. After causing so much concern to parents and annoyance to the two heads, Mrs. X was strongly advised to be extremely careful about the confidentiality of school records in future.

Two factors then played a part in precipitating the re-emergence of the earlier problems: the economic policy of the local education authority which led to subsequent cutbacks in staffing and the proposed amalgamation of the school with an adjoining school.

The policy relating to Mrs. X's school was that until the amalgamation, no permanent replacements of staff would be made if anyone left. When the deputy head moved to be head of another school she was not replaced. This reduced the staff to four full-time teachers and reduced the possibility of 'protecting' Mrs. X. She was responsible for a full-sized class and parental complaints increased.

In accordance with the county's policy concerning reorganization it was possible for each teacher to discuss his or her own position with the inspectors and administrators. Mrs. X was told, as was each member of the staff, that it was the education committee's intention wherever possible to offer continued employment to all teachers within their own part of the county, with safeguarding of salary and status. As Mrs. X did not drive and local public transport was sparse, a transfer would have been difficult for her so she considered asking for part-time employment when the schools amalgamated. She was by then within two years of retirement and so was advised that in her own best interests she should continue working full-time as long as possible to enhance what was a small pension with so few years of reckonable service. Mrs. X decided to take that advice.

Meanwhile parental complaints increased. The head was investigating problems concerning almost a quarter of the class. Most of these were emotional problems caused by fear of Mrs. X, resulting in nightmares, bed-wetting and school refusal, the rest pertaining to poor academic progress. A letter of complaint from a parent (not among those already mentioned) to the area education officer about the school in general brought the local education authority's inspector to investigate. The complaints against Mrs. X were seen as being at the root of the official complaint. The head felt that she would make one more attempt to change Mrs. X's attitudes before intervention by the inspector. This was done. All the complaints were discussed and the head insisted that a change to a sympathetic understanding of each child's needs was imperative, otherwise the inspectorate would be requested to deal with the situation.

Mrs. X was again advised to give the children work commensurate with their ability, work that was relevant and interesting. She was told to seek the advice of colleagues for support in her work and was given a list of sources of information within the school. She was still not prepared to accept that the parents' complaints were justified. The deputy head, at the head's request, followed up this talk emphasizing that everything the head had said was true and that she should change her attitude. The deputy head finally convinced Mrs. X that this time the head would take further action through the inspectorate if she continued to refuse to cooperate.

Mrs. X made a genuine attempt to follow the advice she had been given. The children were taken on local visits and their work was centred around these activities. No further complaints were received and each of the parents concerned reported great improvements in the children's attitude to school. On the second day of the following term the head received another official complaint from the parent, one whose child had just moved into Mrs. X's class. The head discussed it with Mrs. X in the presence of the deputy head and at the same time referred the matter formally to the inspectorate.

Commentary

From a management standpoint, it is interesting that no mention is made of the educational objectives of the school. Clearly the teacher concerned had her own implicit personal objectives and presumably also some educational objectives for the pupils. Similarly the parents and the teacher's own colleagues entertained educational objectives which may or may not have been consonant with those of the teacher herself. The head's and other colleagues' approaches to the teacher seem mainly to have been concerned about the choice of teaching method and materials, rather than the ends which those means were meant to serve. Had this teacher ever been invited to make explicit her educational objectives for her pupils? Had she been involved in helping to evolve a set of educational objectives for the whole school which the teaching staff could collectively defend and work towards?

There is an obligation on every teacher to reach certain standards of performance. Salaries are paid for doing so. The origin and ownership of these standards, however, are matters at issue.

There are a number of surprising features in this case. The fact that they actually happen does not remove the feeling that they ought not to happen. The teacher concerned formed an alliance with a part-time colleague and an auxiliary member of staff, a school helper who was not a member of the teaching profession. The significance of this is two-fold. In the first place, the management of coalitions is an important skill required of the head. The micro-politics of an institution constantly interact with educational policy making and govern educational outcomes via decisions that can be and are, finally, made. Secondly, the management of boundaries between occupational groups within an institution is an important skill required of the head. Notably this applies to the boundary between teaching and non-teaching staff but in turn applies to sub-groups with each of these. Practical experience in the lives of most teachers abounds with cases where non-teaching staff have been able to exceed their duties and formal authority to the point of influencing and sometimes directing what can and cannot be done in the educational activity of the school.

The teacher herself must have been satisfactory at one stage since after one year's employment on a part-time basis she was engaged as a full-time teacher. At a time when teachers were in short supply, many persons were able to enter teaching and find employment, who, in times of the oversupply of teachers, would not do so. Even so, a teacher may be acceptable and effective in terms of one particular school's values, policies and practices, but become rejected and ineffective on removal to a different school. If this happens the interviewing and selection procedures may be at fault, or they may not operate at all as in this case.

It is especially surprising that a seriously underperforming teacher could survive two reorganizations of schools with the same local education authority as employer. It is possible to speculate that performance declined. With the passage of time, a teacher may become frustrated, disappointed and even embittered at her own lack of career development. This teacher saw a succession of colleagues being promoted to deputy headships and headships. Promotion and changes of school are generally stimulating and remotivating experiences for teachers. What motivation, other than a belief in one's own values and practices, does a teacher nearing retirement have? Health and stress factors play their part, too. An elderly teacher may find it hard to sustain her work, anyway. Sudden additional demands to change pace, direction or method can be very distressful and damaging. It must also be borne in mind that the price education pays for a high measure of individual teacher autonomy is the almost total absence of routine supervision which might include progress and performance reviews, counselling and health checks, if not the formal application of such systems as management by objectives.

It is understandable that in a small school with a small staff the actions of one member can easily have an effect on the reputation of the whole school — for good or bad. The attitudes and pressures of colleagues form an immediate potential influence on a teacher's professional values and practices. When these are regarded as inappropriate and relatively damaging, however, it is not enough to tell a teacher to be different. Teaching in the end is only the product of what the teacher is able and willing to do. There is a question over how much change can be induced from outside. An 'inside' change is really needed. Without an understanding of the point and purpose of a new method or new materials or new teaching strategy there may be little hope of the successful adoption of them by any teacher.

Initial training is meant to explore various alternatives with the objective of encouraging the growth of understanding, so that real choices may be made and preferences expressed. This teacher's initial training may have been defective in regard to this.

Teaching involves team management principles, notwithstanding the fact that an individual teacher may enjoy great autonomy in her own classroom at the point of application. The teaching staff have collective responsibility for the overall experiences of the children. The deployment of teachers, like that of any other resource, requires management skill to achieve exceptional results with unexceptional resources. In this case the teacher concerned had to be accommodated somehow in the organization. There is no a priori reason why every teacher should be subject to inflexible policies for grouping children for teaching purposes. The norm was assumed to be a heterogeneous, mixed ability group. When the 'timid, slow or very quick' pupils were removed from this teacher's class, her performance rating rose. When they were eventually put back, it fell. Management may either make the job fit the individual or make the individual fit the job.

In this case it seems particularly unfortunate that the former solution involving a selected group of children, which had been tried with some success, had to be discarded in favour of the full, mixed group which had been her undoing in the first place. The fall in the number of pupils gave the school less scope to accommodate her. From the pupils' point of view the size of school needs to be such as to provide a minimum variety of teachers and teaching styles.

Issues for further discussion

1. The motivation and job satisfaction of older teachers.

2. Handling complaints from parents.

3. Introducing teachers to new methods and materials.

4. Criteria for assigning teachers to classes.

5. School records — their content and accessibility.

6. The *in loco parentis* status of teachers and the access of parents to teachers and vice versa.

7. The meaning and measures of professional performance.

8. The differences between staff supervision and staff surveillance.

9. Should each school have its own policy on in-service education and training? What factors should determine a particular policy?

10. The law of constructive dismissal and dismissal procedures against a member of the teaching staff.

Further reading

Barrell, G. (1983) 'Knowing the Law'. Chapter 2 in Paisey, A. (editor) *The Effective Teacher*. London, Ward Lock Educational.

Dear, J. (1983) *Organizing Learning in the Primary School Classroom*, London, Croom Helm.

Rushby, T. and Richards, C. (1982) Staff Development in Primary Schools. *Educational Management and Administration* 10, 3, 223–231.

Case 5.2: Appraisal experiment

Introduction

The head of a large secondary comprehensive school together with his senior staff are persuaded that a participative style of management and an open climate in the school are dependent upon a positive attitude to staff development. This in turn is felt to be reliant upon a system of staff appraisals. They realise that staff performance appraisals are controversial but feel that too much might be at stake if they are ignored. They determine, therefore, that something should be done. A pilot scheme is launched and only volunteers take part. An elaborate system is used, developed by a working party of teachers who address themselves primarily to the pastoral aspects of the teacher's work. Eventually the scheme is adopted by all staff and after three years the school tries to reach some conclusions about it.

Narrative

A mixed secondary school with a roll of 1350 pupils aged 11 to 16 had a teaching staff of 71. Academic and pastoral organizations were separate with heads of department and heads of houses. The head of school made his own management philosophy explicit to the staff. He believed in extensive participation of the staff in the management of the school. He contended that by establishing the sort of environment in which teachers worked well and were strongly motivated he could produce a happy and creative climate in the school and the best possible educational achievements of the pupils.

Making this a reality, however, depended on a continuous and inclusive programme of staff development. The critical factor for such a programme was staff appraisal, admittedly a highly sensitive issue and difficult to accomplish in practice.

The main objective of staff appraisal according to the head was to provide a tool for use in the professional development of each individual member of staff and for this in turn to lead to organizational development of benefit to the school. On the one hand such a philosophy advocated self-development while on the other it necessitated supportive back-up from others. In introducing the idea of staff appraisal to senior staff for the first time, the head listed the following items by way of a justification for it:

—to let teachers know where they stood with regard to current and past performance,

—to let teachers know where they stood with regard to current and past performance,

—to create a supportive environment in the school and help motivate the teachers,

—to identify potential for future growth and development and discuss future aspirations,

—to provide a staff counselling function within the school,

—to provide a record of the development of the teachers.

The initial response from the staff at large was predictably guarded and many issues and questions were raised. It was quickly realized that staff appraisal implied a review of the work of the school. As a result, two working parties were set up for preliminary discussions. Teachers indicated that they would prefer to tackle a review of the curriculum and pastoral aspects of school life separately as a means of examining the concept and conduct of staff appraisal.

The outcome of having two working parties was that two very different approaches to appraisal were presented. The working party concerned with the curriculum felt that any attempt to appraise the work of a teacher with regard to subject knowledge and instruction should be on a non-specific basis of general and full discussion. Their approach assumed that the object should be to provide the teacher and his or her head of department with an opportunity for a thorough discussion of areas of mutual professional concern. As a sequel to this the teacher would be invited to make a written statement arising from the discussion and the superordinate would similarly write a statement about the discussion with the teacher. It was recognized, however, that there would be difficulties in this method. Essentially the prior personal relationships between the two people concerned might hinder and frustrate the achievement of a genuine appraisal. In addition some areas of considerable importance, such as enjoyment of the job, might be too sensitive to handle by direct interpersonal means.

The pastoral working party in contrast produced a highly detailed schedule of four behavioural standards (Figures 2, 3 and 4).

The more detailed structure and format for pastoral work appraisal was intended to provide an evaluation of the teacher's performance in areas other than subject teaching. Pastoral care involved the concept of guiding, caring and counselling, and the development of the whole child within the school community, as distinct from the instructional/academic role of the school. It was argued that the whole object of systematizing pastoral care was to make the aims of pastoral care overt, to formalize activities, to allocate responsibilities, and to define relationships and curriculum patterns in order that pastoral care was carried out. It was thought possible to assess the extent to which teachers within the school were successful in realising the aims and objectives of pastoral care in the school.

The items of the four standards were held to be indicators of good practice. Each could be assessed on a six-point scale. Using the schedule, the appraiser decided which point on the scale was justified and completed the following appraisal summary form (Figure 5).

Obstacles had to be cleared before the introduction of the scheme. It was to be entirely voluntary at the outset. While completed appraisal forms would form the basis of any future references, they were not to be communicated to a third person without the consent of that teacher. The forms were to be destroyed if the head of school left.

Once these principles had been established the scheme was welcomed by the staff and although initially only 11 staff participated the experiment was successful enough to encourage more than 50 per cent to seek inclusion during the second year of its operation. The introduction of an appraisal programme into the school seems to have been facilitated by a favourable organizational climate and a general feeling of trust amongst the majority of members of staff which made innovations easier and less threatening. It was also pertinent that a number of those occupying top management positions in the school had interests in the fields of staff development, counselling and general management theory and were willing to employ their ideas in practice and to encourage others to participate.

Critical to the success of the appraisal programme was the need for concise and realistic job descriptions to be drawn up. The head teacher or another senior member of staff wrote a job description for a given teacher and that teacher was then asked independently to write his or her own job description, based on actual experience in the job. These job descriptions were then exchanged and it would be on the basis of what was mutually agreed to be the job of that teacher that any future appraisals would take place.

The actual appraisal followed much the same pattern of events as that used to determine a job description. The teacher being appraised used the schedule of standards to assess his own performance in terms of his pastoral responsibilities and filled in an appraisal form. The appraiser filled in a similar form on the teacher which was then openly compared with the teacher's self-assessment. Through discussion a compromise appraisal

Standard 1: (a) Excellent tutor group management; (b) Excellent use of tutorial time; (c) Excellent awareness, and use of vertically organised group; (d) In all aspects of the role is an excellent tutor.

X applies	Marked tendency to X	Some tendency to X	Some tendency to Y	Marked tendency to Y	Y applies
Always plans and sets objectives, ensures that these are achieved.	Plans ahead. Sets objectives that are normally achieved.	Ability to plan and set objectives is developing.	Limited ability to plan. Sets some objectives which are not always achieved.	Rarely plans. Objectives not clearly designed.	Never plans, does not set objectives.
Priorities are always identified and arranged and applied. Resources used effectively.	Normally identifies, arranges and applies priorities. Resources used effectively.	Skill is developing in establishing priorities. Is learning the effective use of resources.	Priorities are not always clearly established and resources not fully utilised.	Priorities are rarely established and the use of resources largely ineffective.	Does not establish priorities and wastes resources.
Gives clear and concise information. Achieves effective feedback.	Gives information in reasonable time. All pupils, staff usually well informed.	Improving in ability to give information where required.	Rather erratic in passing on information.	Does not easily understand the need to give information.	Fails in all respects to give information.
Sets high standards. Regularly checked these and corrects any lapse.	Standards are well defined. Has good routine for checking and recognises declining standards.	Aims towards a high standard. Methods of checking are usually effective.	Has difficulty in defining standards. Attempts to check are only mildly effective.	Makes no real effort to set standards. Attempts to check are ineffective.	Quite unaware of the need to set standards. No effort made.

Standard 1: (a) Excellent tutor group management; (b) Excellent use of tutorial time; (c) Excellent awareness, and use of vertically organised group; (d) In all aspects of the role is an excellent tutor.

X applies	Marked tendency to X	Some tendency to X	Y	Marked tendency to Y	Y applies
Effectively coordinates the work involved in the role of the tutor.	On most occasions achieves what is necessary in the role of the tutor.	Developing the ability to coordinate the work as a tutor.	Attempts to coordinate the work of a tutor but not always successfully.	Sees things in isolation. Seldom attempts to coordinate.	Recognises the need for coordination of the work of a tutor.
Effectively delegates work involved with the tutor group.	On most occasions can suitably delegate work in the tutor group.	Developing the ability to delegate and gives support.	Delegates without careful consideration of individual strengths and weaknesses.	Rarely gives any delegated responsibilities to pupils and does not support them.	Fails to recognise the need to give responsibility to pupils.

Figure 2   Staff appraisal – Standard 1

Standard 2: Excellent knowledge of pupils

X applies	Marked tendency to X	Some tendency to X	Some tendency to Y	Marked tendency to Y	Y applies
Has a personal knowledge of pupils' problems and aspirations. Converses easily and can maintain a good professional relationship. Respects confidences and is trusted.	Shows a marked interest in the welfare of pupils. Willing to listen to all points of view and respects confidence.	Makes a real attempt to get to know pupils. Is endeavouring to form good relationships.	Is making some attempt to form good pupil relationships but does not yet appreciate the importance of this aspect.	Does not appear to see the need to form good relationships. Finds difficulty in conversing at pupil level.	Makes no attempt to know pupils. Does not see the need to develop any feeling of confidence. Has a tendency to gossip and lacks tact.
Always ready to counsel and give full support.	Usually available to counsel and gives good support.	Counselling ability increasing. Gives good support.	Fair counselling ability. Lacks confidence.	Not a very effective counsellor but makes an attempt.	Evades the need to counsel and passes the buck.
Can effectively criticize and is constructive in advice.	Gives praise where due.	Developing an ability to make fair criticism.	Inconsistent in ability to give encouragement and criticism.	Criticizes unfairly and makes this known to others.	Destructively criticizes and discourages pupils.
Outstanding ability to form good relationships.	Works positively with pupils in all situations.	Fits well into the tutor group 'team'.	Tends to be ineffective in relationships with pupils.	Attitude causes resentment in pupils. Difficulty in establishing personal relationships.	Not accepted by pupils. No effective personal relationships established.

Standard 2: Excellent knowledge of pupils

X applies	Marked tendency to X	Some tendency to		Marked tendency to Y	Y applies
		X	Y		
Uses every opportunity to extend and develop pupils. Counsels wisely with regard to advancement.	Acknowledges that pupils need to achieve success. Counsels as required.	Aware of the need for development of individual pupils' potential and the need to counsel.	Recognises the need for pupils to develop but does no always provide help. Little counselling given.	Limited in understanding of pupils need for development. Seldom counsels.	Disregards totally the needs of pupils. No attempt made to counsel.

Figure 3   Staff appraisal – Standard 2

Standard 3: Excellent time-keeping

X applies	Marked tendency to X	Some tendency to X	Some tendency to Y	Marked tendency to Y	Y applies
Without fail is always punctual in all aspects of time-keeping, setting excellent standards for pupils.	Can be relied upon to maintain a good time-keeping record and ensures that known difficulties are brought to the notice of relevant staff.	Fairly reliable in keeping good time. Occasionally pupils are kept waiting when priorities are not fully appreciated.	Inconsistent and liable to look for excuses to justify lapses in time-keeping.	Unaware that poor time-keeping may have a bearing on other difficulties in relationships with pupils in the group.	Not concerned about the effects of poor time-keeping. Does not recognize the inconvenience caused to others and consequent poor personal relationships that have developed.

Standard 4: Excellent relationships with (a) house head; (b) house colleagues; (c) pupils; (d) parents.

X applies	Marked tendency to X	Some tendency to X	Some tendency to Y	Marked tendency to Y	Y applies
Invariably ensures that the needs of each group are met. Capable of adapting and coordinating these needs.	Is aware of the needs of each individual group and deals promptly with all matters which affect these needs.	Is approachable, helpful, courteous and is aware of the correct procedure for dealing with the needs as presented by any one of the	When under pressure is unsure and occasionally unapproachable. Tends to shelve responsibility in relation to the	Insensitive to the needs of each of the four groups. Is inconsistent and cannot be confidently relied upon to maintain	Intolerant and unapproachable. Ignores the needs of the varying groups and therefore creates very poor relationships which

Standard 3: Excellent time-keeping

X applies	Marked tendency to X	Some tendency to X	Y	Marked tendency to Y	Y applies
		four groups to which this standard applies.	groups and passes this to others.	effective lasting relationships.	are destructive in their effect.

Figure 4 Staff appraisal – Standards 3 and 4

Self-appraiser/Appraiser/Countersigner.
Name.................

Appraisal Form – Tutors
Date.................

	X	X applies	Marked tendency to X	Some tendency to X Y	Marked tendency to Y	Y applies	Y
1a	Excellent tutor group management						Weak tutor group management
1b	Excellent use of tutorial time						Very poor use of tutorial time.
1c	Excellent awareness and use of the vertically organised group						Very poor awareness and use of the vertically organised group.
1d	In all aspects of the role is an excellent tutor.						Very poor performance as a tutor.
2	Excellent knowledge of pupils.						Very poor knowledge of pupils.
3	Excellent time-keeping						Very poor time-keeping
4a	Excellent relationships with house head.						Very poor relationships with house head.
4b	Excellent relationships with house colleagues						Very poor relationships with house colleagues.

4c   Excellent relationships
       with pupils

4d   Excellent relationships
       with parents.

Comment:

Very poor relationships
with pupils.

Very poor relationships
with parents.

Signed .... Self-appraiser

Signed .... Appraiser

Signed .... Countersigner

Figure 5   Staff appraisal – Summary Form

would result and only when this agreement had been reached would the form be countersigned. The countersigner acted as a mediator in the appraisal interview and also facilitated an appeals procedure. The countersigner was a third person of higher status than the appraisee to whom appeals could be made. When an impasse was reached the countersigner was brought into the discussions to mediate. This increased the judgemental aspects of the appraisal, however, and left the appraisee facing two superordinate colleagues. This seemed to be an imbalanced situation, so it was decided that the appraisee should be allowed to nominate a countersigner of his or her own choosing.

It was hoped that the appraisal interview would be diagnostic in character in focusing on any problems that the appraisee might have or on the expectations of his superordinate colleagues. The results of this diagnostic stage were intended to form the basis of making an action plan, if one were required. In most cases, some help could be given either by providing in-service education within the school or by directing the staff concerned to suitable in-service courses outside the school.

The appraisal interviews ranged over a number of topics including a general assessment of the teacher's work, the constraints which might inhibit performance or job satisfaction and the career aspirations of the teacher. The teacher was also invited to suggest changes that he or she felt might aid the organizational development of his or her department or the school as a whole. It was encouraging to teachers to be given the opportunity to comment on the climate, communications and dependencies within the organization.

After three years of operation the school felt able to draw some conclusions. The exercise was found to be extremely time-consuming and required strong management control and direction. It was important that all teachers within the school were appraised, including the head. While the scheme needed to be introduced with sensitivity and therefore careful timing the temptation to extend its introduction over too long a period resulted in the initial interest and enthusiasm of staff being dissipated. The most useful aspect of the appraisal system according to the staff was the discussion itself. The opportunity to talk about their jobs in an open-ended situation was more valuable to them than any other result, especially the recorded material. It was felt that the appraisal system through the interviews had enhanced relationships between colleagues.

One criticism of the scheme was that no systematic evaluation was built into the appraisal programme and no specific person was responsible for monitoring its progress. The main difficulty appeared to be a general uncertainty about what to do with the appraisals. Some thought there should be a follow-up to ensure the continuing education and development of the teacher. One of the solutions proposed was to set up encounter groups for those people who, as a result of the appraisal procedure, perceived a need which could be met by such groups. Such meetings were subsequently held as in-service sessions within school time or even over a series of evening sessions. According to the head, the main aim of the encounter groups was to help teachers to develop themselves by removing the inhibitions which they associated with their specific roles in schools.

Staff reactions to the appraisal procedures varied considerably. Some maintained that the actual writing of a record was superfluous to the real value which was derived from the discussion generated by the interview. On the one hand, it was argued that the formality of writing a report increased people's natural fears of records set down on paper while on the other there was a need to be completely fair to the appraisee in explaining how certain assessments had been arrived at. The criteria had proved to be a useful starting point while teachers were trying out the appraisal for the first time but many had adapted these in compliance with their own ideas or dispensed with the guidelines altogether and simply conducted an appraisal discussion. Most teachers felt that the appraisal operated in the area of their present job performance but saw the appraisal interview as an excellent opportunity to express their career aspirations and gain some insight as to how senior teachers foresaw their future. The appraisal of present performance was seen by most as being inextricably linked to the appraisal of potential, especially as information gathered was to be used in writing references for those seeking promotion.

It was felt generally that the appraisal through the interviews had enhanced relationships between colleagues. It also made teachers look to their work, particularly in the period during which the appraisal took place, and helped many teachers to pinpoint areas in which they might make more effort or might effectively expand their activities in the future. Teachers were less happy with the follow-up they received, particularly the encounter group sessions. There was less enthusiasm and commitment to this aspect of the programme than to the appraisal itself.

Commentary

The logic of an appraisal system is two-fold. In the first place it is argued that staff are the most expensive and important resource in the school. It is essential to ensure that the teaching staff in particular are adequate for the job and remain adequate for the job. This implies being adaptable. If circumstances, demands, resources and values change, as they inevitably do, and the teaching staff's abilities and commitments remain static then the school soon finds itself in possession of an unattractive and ineffective curriculum. To prevent this from happening the staff should be regarded as a variable asset — capable of deterioration but also capable of improvement. The latter may be accomplished by the volitional actions of individuals — a manifestation of truly professional conduct — or by the direction of the employer or the employer's representative. It may be achieved within the school organization itself, by such means as formal instruction from colleagues, job rotation, job enlargement and job enrichment, or it may be obtained by off-the-job means such as visits to other schools, taking courses offered by institutions of higher education, HMI or others. It may concern the content of teaching and the techniques of teaching it or it may concern the management of the school as an organization.

In the second place it is argued that any concept of improving the professional performance of a member of staff — or even of maintaining it in the face of rapidly changing circumstances — equally requires a concept of measurement. There is an inescapable need to know exactly the dimensions, strengths and deficiencies of a teacher's work performance in order that ideas of direction, improvement, adaptation, retraining and development can have any meaning at all. Hence the thrust in many industrial and commercial organizations has been towards systematic staff performance appraisal. This is done by using a common measure to identify weaknesses within each individual and weak individuals in relation to others, so that corrective or compensatory opportunities may be offered. The expense incurred in doing this is regarded as a justifiable investment.

In this case the time taken was cited as an expensive item. This was incurred by devising and using the measures of performance alone, however, without any consideration of costs by way of taking action on the findings.

Inevitably any assessment scheme needs delicate and sensitive handling. Original proposals and procedures always need considerable development. The task was to develop a staff appraisal programme which could be used as a vehicle for staff development, but the emphasis was on the individual counselling rather than the judgemental aspects of appraisal. Currently this is important as teachers are unsure of their future career prospects because of the contraction that is taking place in education. Such moves may help teachers over the frustrations that many of them are bound to feel. Not least, they were able to comment on their school as a workplace. Few schemes in practice permit this. In one study of over 90 sets of appraisal documents in industry and commerce, only one asked for comment on how the organization could be made to be a better place of work.

This school and its staff tried to come to terms with a contentious yet topical issue which is likely to become more prominent in school management. The scheme provided a means to develop the organization of the school and it had the virtue that much, if not all, of what developed was school-based with a high degree of participation in decision making by the teaching staff. The scheme created an environment in which teachers could work openly together to discuss the problems and tribulations that faced them in their work. They could seek help and reassurance when the need arose. To the extent that the needs of the teachers were being met, the interests of the pupils were also being served.

Issues for further discussion

1. Problems of staff appraisal with separate academic and pastoral structures. Design a staff appraisal system and programme for an actual school.

2. The meaning of 'staff development' and whose definition should prevail.

3. Appraisal systems in relation to the micro-politics of the school.

4. 'Exact' methods of performance appraisal compared with intuition.

5. The uses and abuses of job descriptions.

6. The efficacy of encounter groups among 'known' colleagues in a static staff.

7. The value of an appraisal system without the organizational commitment and resources to provide follow-up opportunities for making use of its findings.

8. Action to be taken when an appraisal repeatedly shows the same results for a teacher.

9. Formal versus informal counselling.

10. The confidentiality and use of staff records.

Further reading

Barnes, A. (editor) (1977) *Management and Headship in the Secondary School*. London, Ward Lock.

Braddick, W.A.G. and Smith, P.J. (1977) *The Design of Appraisal Systems*. Birkhampstead, Ashridge Management College.

Marland, M. (1980) *Pastoral Care*. London, Heinemann.

CHAPTER 6
MANAGEMENT OF THE CURRICULUM
Case 6.1: Mathematics takes precedence

Introduction

A middle school has been very crowded but falling rolls ease the pressure on accommodation only to reveal a range of problems which had been neglected. Some of these had attracted the attention of parents sufficiently to lead to complaints made direct to the school, to people in public office and to selected members at county and local levels.

A new head of the middle school is appointed. He takes stock of the situation and concludes that several areas of the curriculum are badly in need of revision. He also wonders where to begin the task of tackling the substantial range of problems to restore the school's standing in the eyes of parents and public. He finally decides to focus first on the mathematics programme in the school, which he sees as one of the most important and difficult jobs to be done. There follows a slow but inexorable reform in the attitudes and practices of the staff in mathematics which involves a policy to restore public confidence in the school at the same time.

Narrative

A new head took up his appointment of a two-form entry 8 to 12 middle school of 240 pupils. The school had not been in a happy state. There had been a substantial amount of parental concern over a variety of issues. This had been mostly expressed in the pressures brought to bear on county councillors and local councillors. Some, however, had been expressed directly towards the school, leaving the staff feeling embattled and on the defensive. They anticipated the arrival of the new head with mixed feelings. There were hopes that he would tackle the problems energetically but also fears that he would disturb the working arrangements which they had established.

The major task facing the new head was to lift the confidence of the staff to a level at which they could face their difficulties together. There was a need to examine their own work critically but with sensitivity towards each other.

One of the salient matters of concern in the curriculum of the school was the mathematics programme. The new head felt that a substantial revision was needed. While other areas of the curriculum were also in need of review, he was determined to make the revision of mathematics a top priority.

The scheme being used for the teaching of mathematics involved the progressive study of modern mathematical ideas based upon the need for much practical work, followed by discussion and then practice exercises. The head found very little evidence that this method was being properly carried out. In many cases the children were simply working through the practice books individually. In discussion with the staff the head found that the scheme had been introduced three years earlier, but most of the staff felt that there had been insufficient preliminary discussion over it. Some were uneasy about its worth, some felt unhappy about the methodology required and some, along with many parents and children, were openly hostile. A senior member of the staff said to the head 'I just looked through the books and found something I could recognise, then I gave them that.' The anxieties and uncertainties the staff felt about the scheme were being transmitted to the parents and pupils, and were contributing to the mutual suspicion that appeared to exist between staff and parents, resulting in the hostility of the parents and the boredom of the pupils.

The head concluded that several things needed to be done. First, the staff needed to recognise that things had to change. Secondly, the staff needed an injection of confidence to allow them to face change and be prepared to develop a wider understanding of the scheme among parents and themselves. Thirdly, the school needed an injection of expertise to lead it in the right direction. He then wondered where and how to begin and whether or not one or all of these things could or would take place.

As recognition of the problem was the first objective, he embarked on a number of different approaches. In the unsettled climate of the time he decided that a head-on approach was inappropriate. At first he made a few casual comments here and there about the difficulties of working on so many different individual topics at once and made the suggestion that it would be better if the children were grouped according to ability within each class and if the number of topics being handled at one time within the class were limited to three or four.

The head established some credibility for himself by teaching a second-year class in mathematics on a regular basis. This served the dual purpose of being seen to put into practice what he himself was proposing, and to become familiar with the day-to-day practicalities of the scheme so that realistic improvements could be made. He produced a discussion paper which outlined the main objectives and approaches of the scheme and some suggestions for achieving the methodological approach which it really required. The ensuing staff discussion of the document was faltering and limited. One young and capable member of the staff said, 'I think it's how you would like it to be, but it's not how it is.' If the paper and subsequent discussions on it had limited effect, it had at least established how the scheme should have been approached and the staff had been made aware that there was an intention to correct the deficiencies. Most of the staff were well aware that a great deal needed to be done and there was a general feeling that extended discussions would be necessary. It was at this point that a number of fortuitous events took place which enabled the head to sustain the movement he had begun.

The school appointed a new deputy head who was an enthusiastic first-year student on a two-year award bearing course on 'The Teaching of Mathematics in the Middle School'. He was keen to get started on the mathematics scheme, and shared the head's views on the approach, objectives and methodology needed for teaching it. His arrival was the catalyst that was badly needed. In the early stage of his appointment he looked at the scheme and how it operated in the school. All the while, every attempt was made to build up the confidence of the staff wherever possible. The head also worked to develop organizational stability that would allow the school to conduct a reappraisal of the scheme and to implement necessary changes effectively.

Over the next two or three months the school set about building up the resources needed to tackle the problem. The local education authority had produced a set of guidelines for mathematics in the middle school. As well as this, the recently published Cockroft Report was in the forefront of people's minds. Further help came from another member of the staff who had registered for an in-service B.Ed. degree course, part of which enabled her to make a detailed study of the scheme which the school had adopted. She was anxious to be actively involved.

The school realized that the rationale for its particular mathematics scheme was at one with the recommendations outlined in the county guidelines, and also the major recommendations outlined in the Cockroft Report. The head was thereby able to assure the staff that their scheme was firmly supported at large and that they had every reason to feel confident. The senior staff discussed progress and concluded that there was a need to embark on a programme of regular in-service education for the staff, as well as preparations to set up a series of parents' evenings to explain the school's policy for mathematics.

A parents' evening for children in the first two years of the school was planned. Some of the staff were very keen to be involved in the whole enterprise, but there was a very fraught discussion with two teachers who, while recognising the need, were visibly anxious, and reluctant to participate. In fact their anxiety led them to ask to be excused from attending the meeting which, by then, had been arranged. The deputy head was disappointed by the withdrawal of these two members of staff, but pressed ahead with contingency plans for the evening while trying to persuade other teachers to come. On the day before the first parents' meeting was due to be held, the head and deputy head went home convinced that they had failed to persuade the remaining two members of the teaching staff to take part.

The next morning, however, they came in to find that their two colleagues had discussed the matter and had decided that they would attend the meeting after all. This, as it turned out, was to be a major breakthrough. The evening meeting went well, although the number of parents in attendance was small. The scheme was explained and presented, with three or four workshop activities laid out in the room for parents to examine. Both teachers and parents were tentative, but something of a discussion took place, and the general feeling was that it had been a successful evening. The two least enthusiastic members of staff had seen that the head and deputy head could relate effectively with parents. The head felt that as a result there was a stronger and more corporate base of expertise and goodwill in the school.

The next stage was to hold a meeting for the parents of the fourth-year children and also to provide some in-service training sessions for the staff. A date was agreed for the first staff in-service session and also for the parents' evening. There was unanimous agreement among the staff that both were a good idea. Stemming from the arguments of the more supportive staff, a general feeling grew that there was nothing to fear but everything to gain from holding such events. The fact that the two colleagues who had been reluctant to attend the first parents' evening had actually been involved in a successful venture helped. They both agreed to attend the meeting for the parents of the fourth-year pupils, even though they were under no obligation to do so. It was agreed that everyone would be involved in mounting a workshop activity and the deputy head agreed to coordinate this. Much activity then took place in preparation for the evening.

There was some dissent. One member of staff was heard to comment that 'they don't seem to realise that we've got homes to run', and there were one or two other hostile comments. However, the momentum for revision and innovation had been established. Everyone could see the need for it and everyone, even if reluctantly, was taking part in it.

A seemingly unconnected event intervened which had an important bearing on these developments. The feeder first school on the same campus had been overcrowded for several years. To ease the pressure on the accommodation the final year of first-school pupils had been taught in the middle-school building. As the number on roll fell, the accommodation pressures were relieved and a date was set for dispensing with the use of the middle-school building by the first school. This meant that the middle school would in effect have no intake for one year. The middle-school staff therefore decided to hold an open evening for the parents of the new top year of the first school as a public relations exercise for the following year when they would take up their normal places in the first year of the middle school.

The evening turned out to be a great success. It attracted other parents as well, and resulted in the recruitment of additional pupils to the school. The value of meeting parents for publicity and recruitment purposes was clearly demonstrated. The staff had finally linked their own employment with the interests and support of the parental body in the catchment area.

By the time the planned staff in-service evening came around, most of the staff had been talking about their forthcoming contribution. Everyone had agreed to do something and several pairs had formed to make joint presentations. During the session itself, the deputy head spoke about the mathematics scheme and some useful discussion took place. According to their respective interests and talents each member of staff contributed differently and with varying levels of skill and commitment to the evening. Overall, the preparations and efforts made by the staff were extremely satisfying. Everybody came and everybody contributed.

The scene was set to hold the first parents' evening for the pupils in the fourth year of the school about the mathematics scheme. The staff knew that this was to be a challenging event because of the concern parents felt about the middle school's preparation of their children for secondary school experience. The initial returns were not too encouraging, but as the day approached, with increasing publicity, the prospects looked more promising. In the event, 70 parents attended — a very high percentage response. A whole range of mathematical topics were represented, including a computer corner and a section on 'Johnny Ball's Maths Games' which proved popular. It was also valuable to have the head of the local comprehensive school in attendance. When the staff were confronted with the inevitable concerns about how their scheme fitted into the work of the secondary school, the head of the comprehensive school was able to speak of the good liaison that existed between the schools. The session was a useful one in all respects, and it was agreed that further such meetings should be held at which individual topics in mathematics could perhaps be examined in greater depth. This became the focus of plans and preparations by the staff during the following months. The school's policy and practice for its mathematics programme had become subject to continuous development on a corporate basis, and at the same time was successfully serving the wider interests of the school in its public setting.

Commentary

There is an old maxim which states that the quickest way to change an organization is to change the person at the top. This presupposes, however, that the person at the top is also the person able to give effect to the changes that are needed. A new head may easily be tempted into doing too much too quickly. Yet the passage of time can kill initiative and weaken resolve. The preservation and exercise of political will is the vital ingredient for an innovation to be successfully implemented.

Leadership and innovation are the themes in this particular case. The head, as a newcomer, sees features of the school which have become familiar to the staff, in a different light. The value of having a new head lies in his being able to bring new perspectives, wider experience and different values to bear. But there is not always an ability nor a willingness to change. Leadership is necessary and includes action to overcome any reluctance or resistance to making necessary changes. It may be noted that there is a difference between changes that are imperceptibly taking place all the time — in the people who are members of the organization and events imposed on the organization from without — and those that are deliberately designed and introduced — for which the word innovation is best reserved. Innovation is very much the province of leadership rather than coping with the welter of minor changes which constantly take place.

As this case shows, a leader must first identify the innovation which is needed. This involves a qualitative judgement that something should be better than it now is. There must follow a process of sounding out how much understanding of and sympathy towards the possible innovation exist. Attitudes take longer to change than overt behaviour, yet the latter is likely to be ineffective unless it is underpinned by an appropriate attitude. Thus, time, patience, gradualism and resolution are the key factors for the leader to bear in mind in seeking to implement an innovation. But in addition, as well as the political will and determination to innovate, the leader clearly must be able to see and take advantage of fortuitous events.

In this particular case, mathematics is the focal point. Some teachers may lack confidence in their handling of mathematics so that any change at all is threatening for them. It may be that insufficient materials and equipment existed in the school for the staff to follow the adopted scheme as it was intended to be taught. They may never have had proper training and instruction for teaching it — such as could have been provided by a course at a local teachers' centre, or in the school itself or by bringing in a consultant to train and work with teachers in the school. Generally speaking, more time needs to be allowed for the acquisition of new knowledge and the mastery of new techniques needed to maintain an adapted curriculum, than is often allowed by teachers themselves or those who are responsible for management.

Issues for further discussion

1. The qualities of leadership. How should a new head establish curriculum priorities?

2. The organization of mathematics teaching in primary and middle schools.

3. The role of subject advisory teachers in a middle school.

4. Parental involvement in school life. How far should it extend in relation to the curriculum in primary and secondary schools respectively?

5. The frequency and purpose of meetings with parents at school level.

6. Liaison policy and practices between
   (a) first/infant and middle/junior schools;
   (b) middle/junior/primary and secondary schools.

7. Trends in publicity and recruitment policy and practices in
   (a) middle, junior and primary schools;
   (b) secondary schools.

8. The job of the deputy head in middle, junior and primary schools.

9. Timescale for managing curricular innovations.

10. School-based staff development — purposes, problems and programmes.

Further reading

Cyster, R., Clift, P. S. and Battle, S. (1980) *Parental Involvement in Primary Schools.* Windsor, NFER.

Paisey, A. (1982) Change and Innovation in Educational Organization. *School Organization* 2, 2, 179–183.

Stillman, A. (1984) *School to School — LEA and Teacher Involvement in Education Continuity,* Windsor, NFER – Nelson.

Case 6.2: Coping with the new sixth

Introduction

A secondary school has become used to having a sixth form of modest proportions composed of a few pupils following a regular A level programme and a majority taking or retaking O level courses or courses for other examinations. The impact of declining employment opportunities on the school is slow but significant. The compostion of sixth-form pupils changes. The more able pupils tend to take the available jobs in the locality by leaving at 16. This denies the least able local employment. They face either unemployment or an extra period at school in the sixth form. The customary courses, however, are unsuitable for many of these pupils. The school begins to notice the difficulties the new pupils face in their studies. Steps are taken to introduce a programme which is thought to be specific to their needs. The way that this is introduced and implemented, however, gives cause for concern.

Narrative

Out of 900 girls in an 11 to 18 comprehensive school, about 60 stayed on in the sixth form each year. A very small number of these were traditional sixth-formers staying for two years and taking two or three A levels. The stock explanation for the low numbers was the creaming of the top ability band by a local grammar school. The bulk of the sixth form was usually working for O level Certificate of Extended Education (CEE) or Royal Society of Arts (RSA) examinations. The O level group would be the largest, made up of girls who either had taken O level in the fifth form and wanted a better grade, or had taken CSE in the fifth form and wanted to improve this to an O level, or who wanted a small number of subjects such as commerce and human biology offered as one-year O level courses which were not offered in the fifth form at all. CEE courses were generally offered in English, mathematics and a modular general knowledge course taken by all sixth-form girls. RSA courses in typewriting, audio typing and office practice were usually taken by girls also doing O level English and commerce.

At this time the girls coming into the sixth form were making a positive choice. They came back with sights set on the qualifications needed for the course or job they expected to get after one or two years in the sixth form and they usually obtained them. The others left the fifth form for courses at the local technical college or employment. When the numbers in the sixth form began to rise, however, the staff often grumbled about the standard of work and the motivation of some of the girls. What seemed to be happening was that, as the employment situation in the area worsened, many of the more able girls took any job that was offered and left. Some even left at Easter without taking fifth-form examinations because the chance of a job seemed more important than qualifications, given they could always attend evening or day-release classes at the technical college later if they needed a qualification in a particular subject.

Because able girls were taking jobs in local shops and factories, which their predecessors in previous years would never have considered, the less academic girls had even less chance of finding a permanent job and so had the option of either being unemployed or coming back into the sixth form. Having made the decision to come back, they had to choose from the courses on offer and many of them found themselves struggling in lessons, becoming bored and troublesome, and leaving at the end of the year still without any extra qualifications.

The school had no regular meetings specifically for the staff who taught sixth-form classes to air their views. Gradually, from casual conversations in the staff room, it became apparent to each head of department that other departments were also having problems with some sixth-formers who had chosen inappropriate courses. It was a general problem and the same names were being mentioned in many departments. The heads of department had a regular meeting with the senior management team and so the problem was put on the agenda for discussion. This confirmed that there was an important change in the composition of the sixth form, since girls from the lower bands of the fifth form, who had passed few — if any — CSEs, were now coming back 'for something to do'.

In February, during their fifth year, pupils were informed about sixth-form courses, and asked to say whether they intended to return and which courses they would wish to enter. These lists were then circulated to heads of departments for comments. At this stage there could be over 100 names on the list but everyone knew they would not all be there still in September. They could indicate, however, the suitability of girls for the courses which would probably be offered. By July the actual list of sixth-formers was still not definite. Many of the girls were waiting for the examination results in August. If these were good enough, they would get their university or college places. If not, they would come back into the sixth form to improve their pass levels. Others hoped they would find a job somewhere. If they failed they would come back and assure everyone that they really meant to work hard, and they regretted having wasted so much time in the fifth form.

In September, the decision to accept a pupil into the sixth form was made by the deputy head and the sixth-form tutor. The choice of courses was left to the girl herself, provided that what she wanted to do could be fitted into her timetable. The larger departments like English had some latitude, in that there were groups for A level, O level (retake and upgrade) and CSE. If a girl chose O level and it was subsequently decided that she would not succeed, there was the possibility of transferring to CSE. In courses which had only one group there was no similar possibility. In the commerce O level group, for example, in one year 50 per cent of its number did not take the examination. They had attended classes, undertaken as much study as they could, but had little to show for it at the end of the year.

The heads of department went away from their meeting with instructions to discuss the problem with their staffs and make suggestions for future attitudes and policy. In some subjects such as commerce, it seemed possible to run a course which could culminate in either O level or CSE. Up to this time, no sixth-form girls had been entered for CSE, but it was a possibility and seemed better than doing a year's work for nothing. This could solve the problem of girls doing O level retakes in some subjects and having to fill their timetable with new subjects.

A group of girls was left who needed a full timetable of courses at a lower level. It so happened that a City and Guilds foundation course was being advertised in the educational press, and although the school had not had any City and Guilds connections before, it seemed to be a new course which met the requirements for broad-based, integrated studies, with the opportunity to develop communication/life skills as well as some vocational training at an elementary level. It would help the less able girls to discover what aptitudes they might have for different types of job. The deputy head decided to find out more about it.

When the first literature arrived, it seemed to fit the requirements as far as the level of work was concerned, and the heads of department thought that the large coursework component would suit the type of girl expected to take it. At the same time they had reservations about the teaching style it seemed to require. There was emphasis on team teaching and integration of subject areas. None of the staff had had experience of this and, mainly because of time pressures, they doubted whether they could make it work. The deputy head was also under pressure to act quickly or lose the opportunity. He made the decision to go ahead and registered with City and Guilds in time to include the foundation course with the other courses offered at the next fifth-form meeting. The response from the girls was favourable, with over 20 opting for the two specialisms — commerce and community care. The heads of department supported this development at their next meeting.

Some details of the course arrived and these were circulated to the teachers who were most likely to be involved for comments. They all thought that the content and level were suitable and the individual topics were within the staff's experience and knowledge. They were still worried about the integration of the separate sections into the broad course it was supposed to be and how they were to find time to get the team together. No one in the team had had much experience of organizing links with local industry.

At the next heads of department meeting, therefore, some important decisions were made:

—there should be several planning sessions in the summer term before the course began,

—a coordinator should be chosen at the first meeting,

—when the course began there should be regular timetabled meetings of the staff involved,

—efforts should be made to contact other local schools running similar courses,

—materials should be obtained from City and Guilds in good time for discussion and preparation.

One meeting actually took place in the summer term. The deputy head was still acting as coordinator and reported that only one other local school was doing the same course and they were also in their first year. No materials arrived until almost the end of term, so little work could be done on the detailed course planning, and there was the usual uncertainty about the precise numbers which affected the ordering of textbooks and other materials. The work experience element of the course needed to be organized early to avoid too much time being lost in September, so this was passed over to the heads of home economics and commerce to do what they could.

When September came, the actual numbers were five for the commercial option and six for community care. Apart from specialised sections, the two groups worked together. The timetable was published without the promised period for coordination meetings. The staff concerned therefore decided to try to meet on alternate Mondays, after school. The amount of integration was minimal. One of the early meetings looked at the syllabus and the sections of it allotted to the different departments, who proceeded to teach their contributions in a more or less traditional way.

The coursework had to be evaluated all the way through and an early meeting with the examiner was requested to discuss this. He came and answered questions, but would not be drawn on what the school should do. Each individual teacher could set tests, practical exercises and homework in whatever way he chose and then grade it. At this point one member of the group designed a record sheet for coursework and a system of files for different components was organized. Integration between subject areas seemed to be limited to the occasions when casual conversation between colleagues revealed that they were about to start on related topics so that if one of them did one part and the other a second part, they would avoid duplication.

Three further meetings were held in the Christmas term and only one in the Easter term. The plan for alternate Mondays did not materialize because of conflicting demands at that time. The 11 girls who started the first course completed it. They were stretched as far as individual teachers could manage in the many small sectors of the course. They covered the syllabus unevenly, depending on each teacher's favourite topics, since it was left largely to each teacher to decide what to do thoroughly out of a very wide syllabus. They compiled adequate coursework files but were not presented with an integrated course with a wide overview of local industry.

Commentary

Whatever the dictionary definition may be, the word 'curriculum' has a wide variety of meanings in practice. Many teachers reserve the use of it for the provided and intended academic experience of the pupil during formal school hours. Some extend its meaning to include the total experience which the school enables the pupil to have. This involves both in-school and out-of-school activity — academic, practical physical and social — which are there by design. A few go so far as to include those experiences which the school does not deliberately design but inevitably arise from school life as a complex organization. These notably include interpersonal treatment between the teacher and pupil and between the pupils themselves, in short the range of experiences of a pupil at school which are often called the 'hidden curriculum'.

The concept is essentially of the *total* experience of the pupil, whether the kind of experience is conceived narrowly or inclusively. It must nearly always be the result of the work of many teachers, thus raising the need to coordinate or regulate it. If anyone thinks the total shape and substance of the curriculum requires some modification, intervention is needed and also a process by which to achieve the desired new model.

In some ways, however, curriculum in this sense is an offence to teachers. It militates against individualistic professionalism. It may be seen as the result of the vagaries of the temporary organizational realities — particularly the effects of personality among the teaching staff in special pleading and local rivalries. And lying beyond these factors again are the host of pressures being mounted on the school by all kinds of bodies — the local education authority, professional organizations, trade unions, employers, other schools, associations, parents, political parties, Her Majesty's Inspectorate, and the Department of Education and Science. Consequently, curriculum can mean what the externals want the school to provide. This may explain why one head has said that whenever she hears the word curriculum mentioned 'I reach for my gun', and why a director of education said to a head of school 'I hear you are quite keen on the curriculum'.

Thus, the curriculum as the experience of the pupil in the school represents a vast compromise to satisfy a range of professional, organizational and political interests. It requires managing to a degree which is determined by the discretion accorded or taken by the teacher and the amount of influence which the school is prepared to accept or must yield to from the external forces which influence the school and create problems for it.

In this case the school seemed to be slow in realizing that there was a problem. This partly was due to the fact that curricular adjustments may require a long lead time, particularly when external examining and validating bodies are concerned, exceptionally so when new knowledge, teaching skills, procedures and organization are also needed among the teaching staff to handle it.

Ideally curriculum review should be a constant process. What else are meetings of the senior staff in a school for? The curriculum may be the fixed factor to which the varying pupil population is adjusted — which seems to have happened for a while in this case — or the latter may be constantly monitored with a view to providing modification to the curricular programme to meet their interests and needs as specifically as possible. To do the latter needs proactive rather than reactive management. A curriculum fashioned solely by the established interests of the staff may become an isolated curriculum in contrast to the appropriate curriculum. This school tried to shift from the one to the other. The power of custom and practice, however, is strong. Old values and old provisions may be regarded as good enough long after they have ceased to be effective. But new agencies and new opportunities need to be spotted. Systematic monitoring of possibilities is better than relying upon the random chance that someone may happen to see a possible solution in the nick of time.

The adaptation of curriculum cannot proceed without internal communication. Management arrangements need to exist for a regular survey of emerging problems so that solutions can be adopted with enough time for them to be implemented according to required standards. In this case the new course involved a number of prerequisites which implied changes of attitudes and teaching practices among the staff. Sometimes solutions must be implemented in haste. The risks of breakdown are then great but justifiable if the will and determination are present to correct the deficiencies as time permits. If they are not, an innovation may be completely abortive.

Issues for further discussion

1. Education in secondary school sixth forms versus education in technical colleges, sixth form colleges and tertiary colleges.

2. The readmission of pupils to secondary school sixth forms — criteria, selection and guarantees in the process.

3. Mechanisms for monitoring the progress of sixth-form pupils.

4. The claims of award bearing courses as opposed to non-award bearing purpose-built programmes for sixth-form pupils.

5. The value of the educational press, research and professional journals in the management of the curriculum in primary and secondary schools.

6. How new knowledge and practice elsewhere may be made available and usable within the school.

7. A programme for establishing and cultivating links between a school and local business and industry where none exists.

8. The work of the course coordinator: planning, resourcing, organizing, directing, reporting, evaluating.

9. The role of the head of department: responsibilities as course designer and course provider.

10. Effective communication in schools. What is it? Is it needed? How might it be made as effective as possible?

Further reading

Goodlad, J. I. (1983) A Study of Schooling: Some Implications for School Improvement. *Phi Delta Kappan* 64, 8, April, 552–558

Morris, T. and Dennison, W. F. (1982) The Role of the Comprehensive Head of Department Analysed. *Research in Education* 28, 37–48.

St. John, W. (1983) How to Plan an Effective School Communications Program. *National Association of Secondary School Principals Bulletin* 67, 459, January, 21–27.

CHAPTER 7
CURRICULUM DEVELOPMENT
Case 7.1:School unity

Introduction

A large special school, with an inclusive age span from rising 2 to 19 plus and a wide range of mild and severe handicaps among its pupils, is disconcerted about its curricular programme and the lack of coherent purpose in the school's work. Owing to the heterogeneous nature of the ages and handicaps of the pupils, teachers had become used to compartmentalized thinking about the school and their own teaching.

The senior management team recognized the prior need to alert the teaching staff to the concepts and language of curriculum development. A programme of in-school training is established as an integral part of the school's working day for the staff. Discussions and study documents are used to achieve corporate decisions which give the school unity without uniformity. There seems to be every possibility that separation will prevail but eventually it is found that unity of the whole school can be created through a common curricular framework, working to common objectives, without loss of real professional discretion by individuals and groups of teaching staff.

Narrative

The school had been opened for six years but curriculum development in it had been muted. The senior management team had produced a document which in very broad terms itemized the general aims of the school. However, these aims had not been interpreted into practical teaching objectives, although some isolated attempts had been made to produce checklists, at the 'breakdown of skills' level, by individual teachers.

A deputy headship position became vacant and as a part of a policy of planned change this person was to be used as a change agent to revitalize the curriculum. This was advertized as the essential task of the person appointed.

The senior management team consisted of the head, two deputy heads, and two other senior staff who together represented all units of the school. The initial task, set by the new deputy, was to review the aims of the school and to produce a series of objectives for the curriculum programme. An attempt was made to fix a timetable but it was considered unrealistic and unwise to limit the process of discussions and actions which might be needed. A time span of three to five years was, therefore, preferred.

The initial step was to call a full staff meeting. Using an overhead projector and handout sheets, the head introduced the staff to the vocabulary of curriculum development to be used in the school, a broad outline of events, and a presentation of the general objectives thought suitable for five core areas of the curriculum. These core areas were presented as Language, Number, Reading, Social and Motor. Comments were invited resulting in a general discussion in which it was agreed that these five were indeed the core areas but that at different ages and levels of learning difficulty, the emphases would be different for each of the five.

Further discussion led to questioning the annual review system and the preparation of individual teaching programmes in the light of new objectives. In the past few years in the ESN(S) section, Gunzberg PAC charts for assessing pupil achievement had been used to develop teaching programmes. This had caused some despondency and frequent arguments over their relevance. Thus a decision was taken to use these only as records of development, as was intended by their designer. Unfortunately this left a gap in the guidelines for producing individual programmes and the evaluation procedures to be used in the immediate future. In answer to this, at senior management level, it was decided to allow three weeks in which the two deputies would produce guidelines in the five core curricular areas. These could then be used as an interim guide and as a discussion document to initiate a wider curriculum development policy.

Looking towards the distant future, a working document was produced with each curriculum area nominated having a respective colour. It was decided at senior management level that a colour coding would help when setting up resources. At this point there was a diversion of energies among the teachers in the senior management team, when the head announced that a sum of £2000 was to be set aside to obtain furniture for resource areas. Several meetings were used for negotiations and the purchase of these resources. It was realized that a process of working backwards from the resources to the objectives was being adopted. Once the thinking of the senior management team had returned to the development of the curriculum, however, the school was divided into four sections, each associated with a resource area. The sections were Pre-School, Primary, Intermediate and Vocational. Teachers were allotted to a section according to the age and handicap they were teaching. Leadership of each team was provided by a teacher with a post of responsibility. The deputy concerned with curriculum was to liaise between the groups and the senior management team. The document prepared by the two deputies was subheaded under the four sections and the guidelines, or objectives, were presented to each member of staff before the Easter holidays.

At the beginning of the summer term, all care conferences and weekly staff area meetings were cancelled. Instead the groups met to discuss and reorganize the objectives set out in the guideline document. Each group began by choosing any one of the five core curricular areas which had an appeal for them. They discussed it, rearranged it as they wished, and added material or reduced it where necessary. Most staff stated that they found this exercise very productive.

At this point the head announced he was to be away on secondment for a year. After several weeks' work on the document, a general staff meeting was held confirming the view that at different levels different emphases would have to be placed on the core curriculum. If a curriculum was to be developed which encompassed the entire range of ESN (M) and ESN (S) children then it would be a lengthy document and would be unused. Most subgroups at that stage had reviewed only two out of the five core areas.

The head countered this by announcing he had no intention of allowing curricula to be developed separately for mildly and severely handicapped pupils. As head of one school, he thought the curriculum should be a continuum. The head also announced to the senior management staff, amid much protest, that he wished to speed up the process and to begin the next phase when each objective could be examined in specific terms. He announced that during school hours time would be available for individual teachers to develop specific objectives. The deputies were to be used to release the staff from their classes and the head would organize it himself. By that time the sub-groups had only reviewed three out of the five core areas.

Many teachers displayed signs of anxiety at the thought of producing individual work. The deputy responsible for curriculum spent a long time discussing terminology, presenting suitable procedures, discussing content, reviewing work before it was published at large, directing people to resource materials, and encouraging them in their work. This was all at an individual level. In terms of teachers' personal development, many expressed the view that they enjoyed having the time to use books and to have someone with whom to discuss problems which related to their daily classroom tasks.

After six more weeks, lists and documents relating to specific objectives were in abundance. The head asked the two deputies to sift the material and to produce the next document which itemized the specific objectives written in a behavioural form. This document, again colour coded, was handwritten to convey the idea that nothing as yet had been determined officially as the curriculum. The specific objectives were coded, and cross-referenced where possible, so that they could be allied to resource material.

This was handed to the staff prior to the summer vacation. As a result of the curriculum study, one member of the senior management team produced an annual review paper using the five core elements as headings for review. This document, which was accompanied by a general information sheet, had the effect of speeding up procedures to create more time for curriculum development.

The new term started with a return to the previously established routine school meetings consisting of case conferences once a week, lunch-time meetings for in-service training, parents' evenings, PTA meetings, teachers' meetings, staff meetings and open evenings. In addition there was a monthly meeting on the curriculum. This was an extensive commitment of time to meetings in addition to teaching and meetings about the curriculum during the teaching day.

The head, who was about to depart for his year's secondment, expressed a view that he would like to see something in type by the time he returned.

A general staff meeting was held after the summer vacation to discuss comments on the specific objectives. Several statements were made at this meeting by staff about the documentation so far: 'it was too comprehensive and bulky'; 'it was not easy to develop an individual programme because it needed extensive cross-referencing depending on the level of handicap and emphasis'; 'the emphasis would be different in philosophy for children with severe learning difficulties'; and 'the mildly handicapped were overweighting the procedures because of the emphasis on the three Rs'.

There was heated discussion which resulted in strong statements by the group from the ESN (S) unit who wished to develop a separate curriculum. They suggested that many of the specific objectives were irrelevant and the teachers' time would be wasted on sifting through the many items to locate one of them.

The departing head commented that he would 'not contemplate separate curricula as this was one school and needed one curriculum'. He reiterated he wanted a continuum so that a child could easily cross the boundaries of his handicap and so that all teachers were aware of what was happening throughout the school.

The problem was then raised concerning individualized programming. It was stated by the teachers that only guidelines were needed at the objectives level and that after that point it was a matter for the teacher to exercise skill in developing a programme for the individual child. There was talk of 'systemised robots' and sight being lost of the facility of special education to relate to each child's own learning patterns and rates.

The head left without withdrawing or changing his statement. The staff then made their own statements such as 'it will never work', 'it's a waste of time' and 'I'll never use it'. As less time was available for the curriculum meeting it lost much of its purpose and the atmosphere of a 'think tank'.

It was then decided by the acting head and curriculum deputy to discuss the procedure with each of the sub-groups and then to call a general meeting. The teachers involved with the ESN (S) children agreed to continue and it was suggested that a return to the original guidelines to complete the exercise would be a good way to begin.

In contrast to the view held by the teachers of the ESN (S) children, the teachers of the ESN (M) children then announced that they would like to develop the guidelines but to reorganize them with the following emphasis: the intermediate section of the school should concentrate on the three Rs and the vocational section should concentrate on the social aspects — with cross-referencing of the other core curricular areas to these main themes.

The senior management team decided it would be wise to use this offer of curriculum action because it was being initiated at 'shop floor' level and the original guidelines were still operative. It was agreed that the deputy for curriculum would oversee the work and have the task of producing a document which reflected and represented a continuous curriculum. It was decided by the acting head and deputy that if the teachers produced a curriculum which they would actually use, a major achievement would have been accomplished. Future experience could be used to modify the objectives.

Documents were then produced which indicated tangible objectives, yet were concise and physically manageable. During the period of development, an atmosphere of questioning among the staff had evolved and working procedures had been established for dialogue to continue.

The acting head and the deputy responsible for the curriculum agreed that many lessons had been learnt and some tangible outcomes had been achieved. The main lessons learnt had been:

—the setting of realistic objectives by consultation at 'shop floor' level and the production of a manageable document,

—the need for in-service training,

—the use of non-teaching time — making excessive demands on teachers and the repercussions,

—the involvement of external agencies — how liaison is developed,

—the need for up-to-date information and research,

—the value of staff being able to research a topic for themselves,

—the use of small groups for the discussion of narrow topics,

—how external pressures may have affected the timing of the production of a curriculum document,

—how changes in personnel affect the system adopted.

Commentary

It is often the complaint in secondary education that different subjects in the school work against the common interests, unity of purpose and the spirit of the school as a whole. The department which usually provides political expression for subjects may so easily become a vehicle for special pleading and vested interests. This is a phenomenon which may occur in all organizations. A department or part of the organization may derive its strength, internal coherence and unity by setting its sights firmly but narrowly on making its own way at the expense of all else.

The special school in this case could have suffered from this phenomenon to an even greater degree than is generally found in mainstream schools. Its age span was across the primary and secondary age ranges. It admitted both moderately and severely mentally handicapped pupils. It also admitted physically handicapped pupils. The staff felt there was justification for separate and semi-autonomous activities within their respective specialisms. Yet they shared a common resource base, they were potentially a common community and in educational terms the pupils could process, progress and transfer within the school. There was in this school, therefore, as in every other, the need for unity which does not imply uniformity. As wide a range of discretion as possible should be accorded to sub-parts of the organization. It has been well said that 'small organization within large organizations is beautiful'.

The case illustrates the senior management team of a school in action. Its members evidently have different strengths and abilities. They undertake different work but share and interchange that work. They decide to adopt a top-down strategy to achieve consensus on a set of overall and interlocking objectives for the school, to which the teaching programme is geared. Eventually, however, a bottom-up strategy is seen to be necessary and by this means consensus prevails.

The degree of participation involved, however, represents high organization maintenance costs. The time taken within the working day and beyond can be a distraction from direct teaching work. The energy required and anxiety generated by these extra activities may even detract from it. The amount of documentation is a symbol and symptom of the dangers. Yet the exercise is intended to bring great benefit to the teaching in the long run. Clearly a balance between the investment of time and effort on the one hand, and anticipated benefits on the other, must be struck. The whole process proved to be a substantial learning experience for the staff and not least for the management team.

Issues for further discussion

1. The 1981 Education Act: its content and implications.

2. School unity compared with school uniformity.

3. The senior management team — its composition, work and way of working in a special school.

4. The range of ages and handicaps which can be handled within the same school.

5. Can children with special needs be educated effectively in 'mainstream' schools?

6. Departmental motivation in a large school. How might separatist and uncooperative attitudes and practices be avoided?

7. Bottom-up compared with top-down strategies for achieving organizational unity.

8. The costs of organizational maintenance in a school where a cost is anything other than direct teaching. Specifically, how much work on curricular guidelines and documentation can be handled by teachers without special costs?

9. In what circumstances is individualized teaching justified and workable as a school policy?

10. The use of full staff meetings.

Further reading

Paisey, A. (1981) *Organization and Management in Schools*. London, Longman.

Putnam, S. (1981) The 'Reality' of School Organization. *School Organization* 1, 3, 255–266.

Stenhouse, L. (1975) *An Introduction to Curriculum Research and Development*. London, Heinemann.

Case 7.2: Getting the objectives right

Introduction

A small secondary school for ESN(M) pupils is quickly enlarged when its catchment area becomes a rapidly expanding overspill town. New and inexperienced staff are added to a small number of teachers who have become used to working in a school of homely proportions and habituated to a curriculum and teaching methods which are in need of reform.

The case concerns a patient, determined head in a volatile situation. Something must be done to establish a credible professional performance by the school. The availability of further resources resulting from the growth in pupil numbers provides opportunities for improvement. Staff attitudes and the school's inability to find additional teachers who have the required leadership skills, however, are not conducive to the head's plans for staff development, a new staff structure, a review of the curriculum and the development of teaching methods and techniques. Several efforts to review and modify existing practices are made on an ad hoc basis with indifferent results, but following a fortuitous decision to see other schools at work a new spirit prevails and a breakthrough is achieved.

Narrative

The school consisted of 65 pupils. There were seven teaching staff of whom only the head had had previous experience of teaching in a special school. There were a deputy head, two probationary teachers, two teachers who had recently completed their probationary year in the school, and a teacher who had taught for two years in a primary school. The head provided support for these staff by way of individual and small group consultations. The school served an urban and a wide rural area. Most pupils were transported to school by coach, minibus, taxi or private car. Arrangements at the beginning and end of each school day were, therefore, greatly influenced by the demands of transportation, not least by contractual agreements between the local education authority and a variety of coach firms.

The need to review the purposes and practices of the school was first felt when a member of staff complained to the head about disciplinary problems she was encountering on Friday afternoons. In discussion with the staff the head found that a range of explanations were advanced. They had a specious quality about them. These ranged from 'the children do not want to be at home for two days with nothing to do' to 'these children are exhausted by the school pressure which makes them unable to cope with further demands'. Further inquiry into the 'Friday problem', however, revealed that most teachers experienced behavioural difficulties during the last period of every day. This discovery led to further pronouncements on the 'exhaustion theory'. Attempts were made to create by discussion a positive attitude towards last-lesson teaching. Lessons which reduced pupil interactions of a verbal and physical nature were suggested as being suitable. Despite the introduction of the suggested teaching methods the problem persisted. In an attempt to assess the generality of the situation the head introduced a monitoring system of all the final lessons of the day. Information gathering was standardized in a series of incident check-lists which evaluated what actually occurred at pre-lesson time, the start of the lessons, the type of lesson and the distribution of resources.

From the information obtained it became apparent that the general level of disruptive behaviour began at or about the time when the first pupil was allowed to leave the classroom to go home. This could mean that a pupil left a class 20 minutes or so before the official school closure time. It was decided that pupils would not in future leave a classroom before 3.25 p.m., irrespective of transport arrival time. The transport firms were instructed accordingly. The afternoon break time was changed from 2.30 — 2.45 p.m. to 2.15 — 2.30 p.m. which had the effect of making the last lesson the same length as all other teaching sessions. There was a quite dramatic change in the classrooms and teachers all expressed satisfaction at the outcome.

The exercise highlighted the need for a more analytical appraisal of what was actually happening in the classroom. The need for a fresh look at the curriculum became an issue at a staff meeting and the need for a reappraisal was agreed. An occasional closure day was taken to review the school's programme. Discussion of the school's philosophy and objectives was the basis for group meetings devoted to the content and method of current curriculum practice in the core subjects. During the summary of the day's proceedings the decision was taken that for the rest of the term individual class teachers would define what they did in each subject area with their classes. At a meeting held before the start of the following term, the class teachers' written schemes were discussed and plans made for joint curriculum projects among classes. Throughout the term, informal meetings between individual teachers and groups of teachers involved in the teaching of junior and senior school pupils were held, to maintain and develop cooperative initiatives.

A balanced educational programme was very difficult to achieve in this secondary special school because of its small size. Substantial provision had to be made for basic skills teaching and also for a wide range of specialist subjects. The allocation of pupil time was on the basis of equal proportions to each area. The staff therefore had the difficult dual task of being both class and specialist teachers.

In a short space of time the school expanded to 90 pupils and seven teaching staff plus the head. Additional accommodation was added in the form of two temporary classrooms. The opportunity was taken to reassess the situation. A major concern was the fact that a class teaching approach was almost the only form of instruction. Small group teaching was used a little but individualised teaching programmes were practically non-existent. Undoubtedly the staff were doing their best but the methods, in general, were inappropriate. The situation appeared to be that the teachers with primary school experience were using basically correct techniques but with inappropriate materials, whilst the teachers with secondary school experience were attempting to adopt primary teaching methods but invariably starting work at a point which was considerably in advance of a pupil's capability.

A major worry was the state of the teaching materials and other resources. Despite readily available finance for the purchase of resources, very little had been spent on basic subjects, but a high proportion of the school's capitation allowance was being used in specialist teaching areas. A stock-taking exercise revealed, for example, that the reading materials were entirely book-based, and even then inappropriate. There was a surfeit of commercially produced pupil workbooks. The school was very well stocked with basic audio-visual equipment but this remained unused, inside closed cupboards.

The head's visits into the classrooms, and discussions with individual teachers following such visits, were revealing. For example, it was found that the teaching of the 24-hour clock was given to a class most of whom could not tell the time to within a quarter of an hour. This indicated the shortcomings of the practical teaching. The overall situation was serious because there was no cadre of experienced teachers to give a lead in good practice.

The initiative for a more fundamental curriculum inquiry was taken by the head. The head was the coordinator of the lower school staff group; the deputy head, who taught a fifth-form class, led the senior school staff group. A formal, fortnightly, after-school group meeting pattern was adopted, interspersed with informal meetings. The programme was introduced by the presentation of papers on curriculum matters by the head and the deputy. These papers were mainly concerned with the educational purposes of the school. Group discussions on the papers were followed by a plenary meeting at which the individual groups' opinions were presented by a chosen representative. Following further discussion the identified educational purposes of the school were itemized and later distributed to all teaching staff.

The morning of an in-service staff development day was used to review what was actually happening in each classroom, the purpose being to identify good practice and advocate its adoption. Conflict occurred in the senior class group between the deputy head and Mrs. A, the most experienced teacher in the school, who was in fact a competent class teacher and an excellent practitioner in her specialist subject. Mrs. A felt that her personal competence was under attack and expressed feelings of professional inadequacy. A high level of anxiety was generated and the situation was not helped by the deputy head's attitude towards the group in general and Mrs. A in particular. The final plenary session of the morning, which had been assigned for progress reports on the morning's group sessions, was used to re-emphasize the purpose of the curriculum review.

In the afternoon an adviser for audio-visual communication led a session in which many practical suggestions concerning the establishment and development of resource material appropriate to the needs of the slow learner were made. Specific advice was given on the use of the audio-visual equipment which was already in the school. The staff's response was disappointing. Later, when considerable capital was made available for further audio-visual equipment, there was a distinct lack of interest.

The staff's resistance to change was a serious managerial problem which demanded a number of initiatives by the head. These included frequent meetings with Mrs. A to reassure her. The deputy head was advised to be less prescriptive. Individual cases of good practice were favourably commented on. Encouragement was given to the work which was being done and the schemes of work covering various skills and subject areas which were being written. A standardized procedure for recording pupils' work was devised and used. Despite these efforts, however, anxiety and resentment simmered and these attitudes became evident in the staff room.

Another day's study was arranged with the specific purpose of providing staff with the opportunity to visit other special schools. Staff made individual arrangements for visits which extended throughout the county. At a staff meeting the following morning individual teachers reported on their visits. It was apparent that the venture had been a resounding success. This view was reinforced at a governors' meeting attended by Mrs. A who was the staff's representative. The item on the agenda relating to the school visits was dealt with by her. Mrs. A's own report as well as that of her colleagues was punctuated by such remarks as ' . . . I never realised how friendly our school is . . . our children are far more cooperative and friendly towards visitors . . . the same goes for staff . . . some interesting ideas in maths . . . the staff room wasn't so relaxed as ours . . . there were some good ideas in their leavers' programme'. These visits marked a distinct change in the way the teachers viewed the school in general and their own work in particular.

The school roll increased to 120 and the teaching staff increased to ten teachers plus the head. New buildings extended the accommodation. A new deputy head was appointed and Mrs. A changed her role — she was promoted to a Scale II post, with responsibility for girls' welfare, the development of a school-based community service programme, and the school leavers' programme. Two new members of staff had had previous experience in mainstream education only. The third was a probationer. An induction programme for the new staff was needed. A day's conference on remedial education was held in the local teachers' centre. All the staff attended. The format was as before — two groups working on the aims, content and practice of the school's current teaching. As a result, programmes were modified and the pupil's record of achievement was extended and developed into a pupil profile booklet which recorded the teachers' evaluation of pupils' progress in each curriculum area.

The school's allocation of graded posts had been increased so it was decided to allocate a Scale III post for curriculum development. A specific job description was written for the post of curriculum coordinator but despite the placement of three advertisements, spread over a six-month period, no suitable candidate was recruited. No compromise was made on the requirements for the post — a detailed knowledge of and considerable experience in the application of teaching by objectives in the acquisition of basic skills. Part of the advertisement was as follows (Figure 6):

The advertised vacancy is a new post which will involve teaching basic subjects to a class and working alongside colleagues during the process of devising specific learning programmes.

Thus we are seeking to appoint a senior member of staff who has considerable theoretical knowledge of, and practical expertise in, structured teaching. The person appointed will be a part of the senior management team and will be involved in the planning and decision making of the school. Specific responsibility will be in the areas of:

(i)   Curriculum Development

(ii) School Based Staff In-Service Training.

(i)   *Curriculum Development*

The primary task of the successful candidate will be to introduce objective teaching thoughout the school. The approach will need to involve staff in collective decision making which is specifically designed to produce curriculum models for the teaching of open and closed skills.

(Initially it is felt that developments should be confined to the closed curriculum.) In-depth knowledge and wide experience in classroom assessment techniques, recording methods and evaluation scales are essential.

(ii) *School Based Staff In-Service Training*

The person appointed will be required to introduce a continuous school based in-service training programme for staff. The primary function of such a programme will be to involve staff in the construction of structured programmes for closed skills and maintain involvement and commitment to the particular curriculum design.

Thus we are seeking a person who has a high degree of professional knowledge and experience who is energetic, enthusiastic and has the ability to establish goals and introduce objectives which will help achieve the goals. It is essential that applicants have experience in and possess the qualities needed for successful consensus decision making.

Figure 6 Advertisment material for Scale III post for curriculum developer

Meanwhile, changes in the balance between the supply and demand of teachers had enabled the school to recruit a teacher with previous experience in special education to fill an additional post which was allocated to the school. This increased the teaching establishment to 11 assistant teachers plus the head. Two members of staff completed a part-time Diploma in Special Education in two years and two others had started on it, giving the school a cadre of teachers with specialist qualifications.

With no response — neither external nor internal — to the advertisements for a curriculum developer, the role of curriculum coordinator was assumed by the head. The staff were informed that two Scale II posts were available and direct verbal applications were invited. It was explained that applicants should identify areas of need in the school and indicate how the need could be met. Most Scale I teachers applied and many areas of need were identified, e.g. mathematics, the library, audio-visual resources, science and coordinated communication between classes. Two candidates were selected and interviewed individually and then jointly by the head so that roles and areas of responsibility could be established. Both teachers were given specific curricular coordination roles with responsibility for library/mathematics and audio-visual resources respectively.

This arrangement meant that there was a post of responsibility allocated to a class teacher in each of the five year groups. These teachers all had defined curricular responsibilities and were the linchpins in a network for lateral and vertical communication, directly responsible to the head.

At last the way was open for innovation based on group decision making and problem solving. The established junior and senior school groupings were the basic units of the system with an overall structure to ensure intergroup communication and personnel exchanges. The programme was introduced during a day conference at the start of the new autumn term. The need for change and the newly created staffing structure and its purpose were explained at a plenary meeting. Current teaching practices were then discussed in year groupings and then in the two junior and senior study groups. Throughout the term weekly group meetings were held to discuss the school's educational objectives. Various working methods were used and their appropriateness evaluated by the groups — discussion papers, the weighting of educational objectives by individuals and then by group consensus and nominal grouping techniques. Plenary sessions followed the group meetings to discuss conclusions and to evaluate the methods. Finally, each group produced its own list of objectives which were appropriate for the age group. The groups felt that both social and academic objectives were necessary but the priorities were, not surprisingly, different: the junior end of the school placed primacy on educational skills, whereas the senior school emphasized the need for vocational skills. The groups had clearly established their purpose and direction and a confidence to pursue their specific ends, achievement of which would improve the overall effectiveness of the school. At the end of the term a purposeful further staff conference was held with the following programme (Figure 7):

Staff Conference Day: *Thursday 18th December*

Theme: Teaching to objectives.

The sessions will take the form of plenary talks on teaching to objectives in the special school for slow learners. Also, the practical application of various techniques will be attempted on an individual and small group basis.

Programme:

Session I: 9.00 – 10.30 a.m.

   (a)   Objectives and the teaching of basic skills

   (b) Practical exercises involving the basic concepts of an Objectives Approach.

10.30 – 11.00 – Coffee

Session II: 11.00 – 12.00 p.m.

   (a) The writing of Objectives Programmes

   (b) The practical application of techniques

12.00 – 1.00 p.m. – Lunch

Session III; 1.00 – 2.00 p.m.

   (a) The Objectives approach as applied to the Open Curriculum – case study.

   (b) A practical group assignment.

Session IV: 2.00 – 3.00 p.m.

   (a) Review of day's proceedings

   (b) Discussion in a plenary session.

Figure 7   Programme for staff conference on curriculum development

During the following term each group, under the leadership of the curriculum coordinators, undertook a study of specific core subjects. The purpose of their efforts was to produce programmes which were appropriate and relevant to their daily teaching tasks.

Commentary

A number of important managerial tasks presented themselves simultaneously. New staff always need to be inducted properly and integrated into the school as soon as possible. In this case, however, such staff were lacking in the professional qualifications, experience and competence suited to their employment in this particular school. With the number of pupils rising at a proportionately swift rate, the former fabric of school life and practice was decaying. A new vision was needed, based on reformulated values, expressed in a set of objectives and made into reality by a revitalized curriculum, with adapted teaching methods and techniques.

There was a great deal to do. It must have been tempting for the head to tackle all these matters at once with energy and speed. The danger he evidently saw was to do too much too soon. The head's sense of strategy comes through in this case. Strategic planning can be conceived as being either incremental or synoptic in form. Incremental planning consists of tackling what needs to be done by taking one step at a time, starting with what can most easily and usefully be done first. Direction is not always clear at any time and, therefore, the goals are not always clear and predetermined. Retrospectively, however, in such an approach it can be seen that much has been accomplished. By a process of give and take, by seizing opportunities and by adapting to changing circumstances, a measure of performance and achievement can be applied. A summary of the progress made inevitably brings the goals to light. In contrast, synoptic planning establishes the goal and the contributory steps necessary to reach it. This introduces the notion of unswerving purpose and defined strategies to reach a clear goal, which involves sweeping changes.

In this case the head seems to have groped forward at first by an incremental process. At a later stage the vision of a school controlled by its overall objectives took hold of him. This led to the eventual establishment or organizational development on synoptic lines.

The concept of objectives is indispensable in management thought and practice. Whether at classroom level and the particular piece of work being undertaken by a teacher with pupils or at school level as a whole, having an objective and knowing clearly what it is is the key to effective action. Managing actually consists of matching resources to a given objective either by increasing the resources or decreasing the objective. A problem exists only when an obstacle stands in the way of a pursued objective.

Objectives are changes of state which are sought in people or objects. Schools seek changes of state of many kinds in their pupils. Without the work of the school it is believed that those changes would not occur. If they could occur without the existence of the school there would be no need for the school.

The need is to clarify objectives, to give them enough precision, and to express them in a form which can serve as a guide for action, as a measure of achievement, and as a basis for consensus and concerted effort to obtain the best possible results. This was evidently true for the secondary special school in this case. The principles involved, however, are applicable to all schools and need actively to be recognized.

Issues for further discussion

1. The origins of objectives (a) for schools in general and (b) for a particular school.

2. The head as innovator. What are the respective merits of incremental and synoptic curriculum development? When would one be preferable to the other?

3. The organization and purpose of staff conferences.

4. Organizational development in concept and practice. How useful is it in the management of a school?

5. Award bearing courses for teachers — supporting their studies and making use of them.

6. Data collection and use in problem solving in schools. What types of management information are needed, and what systems may be used for handling them?

7. Using outside resource persons as part of a strategy for the development of the school.

8. School investment in audio-visual hardware.

9. Measures of the effectiveness of school heads.

10. The wording of public advertisements for teaching posts.

Further reading

Clark, D. L. and McKibbin, S. (1982) From Orthodoxy to Pluralism: New Views of School Administration. *Phi Delta Kappan* 63, 10, 669–672.

Fullan, M., Miles, M. B. and Taylor, G. (1981) *Organization Development in Schools: the State of the Art.* Washington DC, National Institute of Education.

Lorenz, C. (1982) Strategic Doctrine Under Fire. *Financial Times,* Friday, October 15.

CHAPTER 8
PUPIL GROUPING
Case 8.1: Necessity is compelling

Introduction

A primary school is exercised about how to group its pupils. A number of important variables are taken into account. The school is conscious of being trapped between the demands of organizational logic and those of educational logic. Faced with uncertainty over its intake numbers, it adopts a solution to provide flexibility which commands the support of staff and parents. Steps are taken, however, to avoid a repetition of extensive regrouping and to review the curriculum in the light of different circumstances. At the same time a radical change from class to team teaching is foreshadowed.

Narrative

A primary school, with a head and nine teachers, serving a rural commuter area had a roll of 286 pupils in the following age groups:

Infants			Juniors			
Reception	Middle	Top	1st Year	2nd Year	3rd Year	4th Year
21	45	34	38	52	45	51

The pupils were allocated to nine classes for teaching purposes with partial vertical grouping:

Class 1 (32)   20 reception infants
              12 middle infants

Class 2 (34)   17 middle infants
              15 top infants
              1 first-year junior with health problems
              1 reception infant (possible gifted child)

Class 3 (35)   16 middle infants
              19 top infants

Class 4   25 first-year juniors

Class 5 (31)   12 first-year juniors
              19 second-year juniors

Class 6   33 second-year juniors

Class 7   35 third-year juniors

Class 8 (28)   10 third-year juniors
               18 fourth-year juniors

Class 9   33 fourth-year juniors

In September when this pupil grouping was established, the acting head — who was normally the deputy head of the school — agreed with the teacher who had responsibility for the infants to leave Class 4 with a significantly lower number of children. This was to enable a transfer of top infants to Class 4 to take place if additional reception children entering Class 1 made other transfers necessary between Classes 1 to 3. The acting head did not want to move infants into junior classes too freely because of the very different ways of working involved in such a move. It was generally the wishes and experience of the staff to have longer periods of relative stability in pupil grouping so that the younger children especially would experience more constant relationships, teaching methods and classroom environment.

By the following January when a new head was appointed, it had become obvious that a regrouping of children would be needed for the beginning of the summer term. The numbers in the infant classes had reached the maximum permitted by the authority (35 children : 1 teacher) or were very close to the maximum. A process of consultation with local playgroups, school governors, school meals staff and parents about the possible size of the reception intake after Easter was undertaken. The head and the deputy head decided to reorganize classes for the following term on the basis of information obtained about the size of the intake. The best estimate for the number of children eligible for entering the reception class was fixed at 16.

There was, however, a further question of several children who might leave and others who might wish to join the school from other schools or from abroad. The head spent several hours interviewing prospective parents while being unable to commit himself as to exactly where a child might be placed after Easter in any of Classes 1 to 5. Those classes could be reorganized to the 35 limit which was the maximum pupil/teacher ratio. The head was conscious that once maximum numbers were attained in any class there would be a subsequent lack of flexibility if new entrants arrived during the term. The head wanted to avoid the difficulties that would arise with the teaching staff if a class exceeded the maximum number of children. Nevertheless, he considered the possibility of allowing a class to rise above 35 while maintaining slightly lower numbers elsewhere in the school, such as in the reception class.

The consensus of opinion between the head, deputy head and two Scale III teachers, who constituted the senior management team was that only Classes 1–5 should be considered for alteration after Easter. A change to Class 8, however, was also contemplated. Class 8 was the smallest class in the school. It had been deliberately kept small by the acting head to cater for pupils who had special needs and learning problems. There was no element of streaming in the grouping of children, but the head reflected that once in the juniors, classes tended to develop their own identities. Any attempt to extend the changes after Easter up to Class 8 would have entailed alterations to the whole school. It was also borne in mind that once the fourth-year juniors left in the following July from Classes 8 and 9, new arrangements would need to be made for September. A reason for not making a change to Class 8 was that during the first term of the previous academic year under the acting head, Class 8 had a temporary teacher. When the new head came the temporary teacher left and the deputy head, on relinquishing her post as acting head, had taken responsibility for that class. Already they had had two teachers in two terms, therefore another change would have been far too disruptive, especially to fourth-year leavers already identified as a group in need of stability.

Consequently, in the second half of the spring term the head suggested the following movements: 14 from Class 1 to be divided between Classes 2 and 3, and seven children from each of Classes 2 and 3 to be sent to Class 4. The names of these children were drawn up after consultations with the staff concerned. The teacher for Class 4 was asked to choose six of her first-year juniors to go to Class 5 which had dropped to 29 during the term when two children left.

During the last week of the spring term, the news that several other families were possibly arriving in the locality led to speculation that the newly formulated plans would have to be changed. The head advised the staff that now they had settled on a reasonable course of action there was no point in trying to anticipate any possible complications until they actually occurred. Letters were sent to the parents of all the children who were to move classes with information about their new classes and a full explanation for the moves that were necessary. Parents were invited to consult the head if they had any concerns. As a result of this, three parents visited the school. In the event, none was unhappy and it seemed that they had chosen the occasion to have a personal talk about their children with the new head. The school discovered that the moves were readily accepted by parents because they were perceived as 'promotion' or 'going up' for their children.

Once it had been established that there were to be no difficulties with the internal movements, the head and staff were able to go to a meeting of parents whose children were reception entrants after Easter. The meeting was held during school time. Parents were given full information and were shown into the classroom where their children would be taught. They were given the opportunity to ask questions, many of which were centred on the new language scheme which was being introduced. After this meeting one parent decided not to send her child to the school because, contrary to her assumptions, the girl was ineligible for free transport. Eventually only 13 reception infants were enrolled by the first day. A transferred pupil came on the second day.

At the beginning of the summer term the pupil grouping was finally modified, with an increase in vertical grouping, as follows:

Class 1 (31)   10 reception infants from September
                8 reception infants from January
                13 reception infants from April

Class 2 (34)   1 first-year junior
                8 top infants
                24 middle infants
                1 reception infant

Class 3 (32)   7 top infants
                23 middle infants
                2 reception infants

Class 4 (34)   14 top infants
                20 first-year juniors

Class 5 (35)   18 first-year juniors
                17 second-year juniors

Class 6   3 second-year juniors

Class 7   35 third-year juniors

Class 8 (29)   11 third-year juniors
                18 fourth-year juniors

Class 9   33 fourth-year juniors

At that point the problem created by the pupil grouping could be seen at its clearest. There was very little educational basis for the arrangement of the classes. The head, in consultation with the staff, wanted to rethink the grouping of pupils to avoid a repetition of movements at the same stage in the following year. They hoped that if the admissions pattern followed a similar course, movement of the proportions already experienced would not be repeated. In anticipation of this, the head asked all members of staff to indicate either verbally or in writing what their preferences, fears and considerations were concerning the age groups of children they might work with the following year.

The head also asked teachers to identify, if possible, other members of staff who they thought they might or might not be able to work with in a team. No prior conditions were set as to how any team should operate. While the head realized some teachers would work together better than others, there seemed to be few relationship difficulties and all teachers seemed to be on good terms with each other. The head wondered, however, whether the formation of teams would disturb the pattern of good relationships which had been enjoyed so far.

The head put certain suggestions to the staff about the possible improvements to future grouping arrangements which might be derived from combining age groups — first-year with second-year juniors, or top infants with first-year juniors. Taking the existing numbers as a guide, the head calculated that there would be 34 middle infants, 47 top infants, 29 first-year juniors, 39 second-year juniors, 50 third-year juniors, and 46 fourth-year juniors in the following year. The pupil grouping was governed by a pupil/teacher ratio of 35:1. It seemed likely that the infant numbers might be nearer 100 than the 81 calculated, as the September intake promised to be between 15 and 18 children. Numbers would be small at the beginning of the year but there was plenty of room for expansion during the year subject to a maximum of 140 and a team of up to four teachers. First-year and second-year juniors with a combined total of 68 would need two teachers. The third-year and fourth-year juniors with a combined total of 96 would need three.

The two junior groups would have more limited room for expansion, with a possibility of only two further pupils in the lower juniors but nine in the upper juniors. This seemed an acceptable risk, however, when all the uncertainties were weighed. The ideas and figures were put to the staff to stimulate discussion. The head felt no irrevocable commitment to any particular arrangement but he believed in the principle that any pupil grouping must be justifiable on educational grounds as well as the criteria already explained.

During the approaching summer term full staff meetings and sub-group meetings of staff took place to ensure that there was time to make all the necessary physical arrangements, including the allocation of rooms. Before the end of term and once the final staff decisions were made, an evening meeting with parents was scheduled. The parents were informed of the new arrangements and invited to give their reactions and to ask questions.

The head realised that the task of pupil grouping would be an annual matter but felt that some underlying principles were already being established. These included the need for teaching stability, for staff cooperation, and little if any intergroup movement of pupils during the year. The head appreciated that a review of the curriculum was a necessary corollary of the changes made in the pupil grouping. He approached the staff to examine the implications for the curriculum with a view to redesigning the programme for the following year.

Commentary

This case clearly illustrates the supposed dilemma for educational managers in which logistical considerations are regarded as antithetical to educational ones. The premise for such a dilemma is false, however. The education of children in formal institutions takes place in the real world and not in a social, political and economic vacuum. Financial, legal, staffing and accommodation frameworks govern what can be accomplished. The manager's choice is not simply between expediencies which do not serve educational purposes and educational activities which cannot be provided. Rather, in seeking the best educational provision for pupils in the school and the very best use of all resources, each of which is subject to alternative uses, he or she chooses the combination of resource use which is the most productive.

The school in this case works out a solution to the grouping problem but still feels it necessary to qualify a good solution by reference to an ideal. The vicissitudes and exigencies of organization are not only inescapable but perhaps desirable and may become in themselves a factor in the education of children. The alternative focus might easily be on the variety of organizational experience which each pupil may have as an element in his or her education.

The case also illustrates the opportunities a senior teacher as manager has to be either a *reactive* or *proactive* manager. The newly appointed head of school was obliged on taking office to assume a reactive stance. He faced a problem cast in a form which was not of his own choosing. He dealt with it as best he could but immediately looked ahead and *anticipated* a reappearance of the problem. His hope was clearly to be in a position to influence the form in which the problem reappeared on a future occasion. Being ready for events is of the essence of good management, signified by the use of the term 'proactive'.

A subsidiary point of special interest in this case is the move made by the head over teaching organization. There is an immediate assumption made that any change in the status quo should involve either all or none of the teaching staff. The head seemed to envisage that the mode should change from being class teaching organization to team teaching organization even though he is careful to allow for the reticence of a teacher to work with a particular colleague in a team or to work in a particular way. There is the suggestion that both class and team teaching could coexist, though this might need to be the outcome if some teachers preferred to keep class teaching organization. Compelling or even persuading a teacher to work in a way which does not carry his or her conviction may lead to a reduction of job satisfaction and may also reduce commitment. Variety is more difficult to organize than homogeneity but may be worth the extra investment of time and energy. If any change is contemplated on a significant scale it is often advisable to start with a pilot scheme which demonstrates the advantages and effectiveness of the new mode. If it works well as an experiment which is visible to all, it is likely to commend itself for adoption more widely.

Issues for further discussion

1. The projection of intake numbers — sources of evidence and information.

2. The uses and limitations of vertical grouping.

3. The optimum size of teaching groups. What criteria should be used for deciding which teaching group(s) or classes a pupil will be in?

4. The pupil's experience of different teachers.

5. Different teaching group sizes as an educational experience for the pupil.

6. Job rotation for teaching staff.

7. The formation of teaching teams: their size and composition. Who should decide team membership?

8. The initiation of curriculum changes in the primary school.

9. Should parents share in class membership and teaching group decisions?

10. Decision making in the primary school as a partnership between head and staff.

Further reading

Horton, T. and Raggatt, P. (1982) *Challenge and Change in the Curriculum*. London, Hodder and Stoughton.

Paisey, A. (1981) The Pupil's Experience of School Organization. *School Organization* 1, 3, 267–270.

Waters, D. (1979) *Management and Headship in the Primary School*. London, Ward Lock Educational.

Case 8.2: The dictates of practicalities

Introduction

A secondary school reflects on its policy for grouping its pupils for teaching and pastoral purposes. Both the school's earlier history and current practice are put in perspective. This account is suffused with implicit and explicit references to educational values and the philosophy of the comprehensive school. The nature of managing as a process of constant adjustment to varying circumstances is brought out. Changes in grouping policy and practice are explained as the school develops from its secondary modern status to become a large comprehensive school before falling rolls take their effect.

Narrative

Originally, the school had been an eight-form entry secondary modern school. For pastoral purposes the school had been divided into four houses, with two tutor groups per year allocated to each house. These groups were of mixed ability and contained pupils with strong family allegiances to their particular house. For teaching purposes the school was banded. There were three bands per year; generally the top and middle band contained three class groups and the lower band consisted of two smaller remedial groups.

A rapid growth in the development of the town had eventually forced the local education authority to utilize premises a mile from the main buildings. The school chose to use this facility to house first-year pupils and a first-year tutor had been appointed for this purpose. A group of teaching staff, a number being junior trained, and some part-time staff, became almost exclusively based at this annex.

A plan for reorganisation provided that both the secondary modern school and the existing grammar school should become a six-form entry 11 to 16 comprehensive school, feeding into a purpose-built sixth-form college. This plan involved a large-scale building programme which immediately affected both existing schools. It so happened that the last secondary modern intake was effectively increased to nine forms of entry while the first comprehensive intake was kept below the six-form entry figure. The movement through the system of two consecutive year groups — one of 280 and the other of 160 — produced its own peculiar problems. From the point of accommodation such a situation enabled the school to vacate the annex at the end of the second year of comprehensive reorganization and for the then 1040 pupils to occupy the main building.

The five-year period from the first comprehensive intake to the full comprehensive school produced many organizational problems. In retrospect it was easy to identify the pressures and to appreciate the particular problems which each created, but at the time simultaneous demands tended to prompt decisions which satisfied immediate needs at the expense of long-term objectives.

Three particular pressures which had a bearing on pupil groupings during this period were of particular note. The first was the need to be seen to be raising the standard of the school in the eyes of parents, who, quite naturally, saw the passing of a highly selective grammar school as a threat to educational standards in the community. The school's response to this pressure was reflected partly in curricular terms but also it contributed to a reluctance on the part of staff to modify the banded structure of the school which had for so long ensured good examination results.

The second pressure point came from a three-year building programme which particularly affected the science, technical studies, and homecraft departments although the general effects on the day-to-day life of the school went far beyond specific subject boundaries. The amount of time spent by the head and deputy heads on contingency plans that could, and should, have been spent on long-term policy was inordinate. Endeavouring to maintain a comprehensive curriculum with one home economics room and, at times, no more than two laboratories — not to mention many week-by-week losses of accommodation — became impossible, and the examination results of the second comprehensive year group bore evidence of the damage, in educational terms, of this programme.

The third set of problems concerned staff recruitment. There was a need to recruit staff experienced and keen to be involved in the development of an emerging comprehensive school but this had to be achieved against the background of declining numbers and a lower staff establishment. The importance of every vacancy forced long-term objectives to be carefully considered to ensure the right replacement.

The two main structures, pastoral and academic, affecting pupil groupings remained unchanged during this transitional period. With a declining establishment, however, it became increasingly difficult to staff eight tutor groups per year. With an intake of between 170 and 180, tutor groups of between 21 and 23 pupils each were ideal for tutorial purposes but with fewer teachers, compromises, such as the sharing of groups by part-time teachers and the reorganization of the fifth year, challenged some of the fundamental tenets of a pastoral system. A reappraisal and restructuring of the role of the tutor, followed by similar discussions on the role of the pastoral head were important predeterminates in the ultimate discussion on pastoral reorganization.

The school had prided itself that its good relationship with its feeder schools had enabled it to allocate pupils to bands without any precondition regarding the number of teaching groups in any one band. The reduction in the number of feeder schools, as a result of comprehensive reorganization, together with the introduction of uniform standardized testing in all primary schools by the local education authority, made this procedure even more effective, the school thought.

During this developmental period each six-form comprehensive intake could be divided into seven teaching groups, thus enabling-top band classes to operate with 28 or 29 pupils, middle-band classes with 25 or 26 pupils and, where necessary, a remedial group of approximately 20 pupils. The careful screening of each intake clearly identified 55 or so pupils of good, all-round, above average ability. The abilities of the next 30 pupils determined whether or not there were three top-band classes. Where two classes only were identified the second band tended to carry a wider ability range and this, coupled with good progress by well-motivated pupils, led to a demand from staff to create a top second-band class in the second year. Generally speaking, however, there were three top-band classes.

At the other end of the ability range, where there were felt to be sufficient children to justify a small group of pupils with specific learning difficulties, a separate class was created but only once did this function as a remedial class with one specialist teacher taking a large proportion of that group's timetable. Withdrawal from normal lessons became usual for children needing special help.

In the secondary modern school the banding structure had applied across Years 1 to 5 and the option system for the senior school had allowed for specific courses for particular vocational interests. With 230 pupils per year it was possible to offer realistic choices, either across the whole year group or across two bands. An attempt was made for the first comprehensive intake to offer a similar banded option scheme. In that year group of 160 pupils, with approximately 80 in each band, it was unrealistic and ended with compromises which were contrary to basic comprehensive principles. Even allowing for a more generous staffing ratio, each pool could not carry more than three teaching groups per band for ordinary classroom subjects. Some subject departments were keen to create groups with clear objectives, either to GCE *or* CSE examinations, and pupils were made aware of their examination potential in each lower-school subject as part of the third-year guidance procedure. The combination of these factors seriously restricted choices and this led to urgent discussions about future procedures. It was only after the school had become fully comprehensive and a more consistent curriculum policy for the lower school had evolved, that a satisfactory package emerged.

A number of aspects of the curriculum came under review during this period in an attempt to provide a comprehensive programme but some outcomes proved expensive and ultimately unacceptable. The development in the technical and homecraft areas to provide courses for all boys and girls of all ability levels, proved most satisfactory. Dividing any year group into groups of approximately 20 pupils and providing a range of experience with a set group of teachers did not present major difficulties. Problems did arise, however, when parts of the year group were denied some part of this experience to satisfy another demand. This happened with the attempts to introduce a second language.

As the school became comprehensive attempts were made, quite rightly, to strengthen the language provision. All pupils were given the opportunity to study French for at least two years. Pupils in the top band (nearly 90) were initially compelled to follow the course for five years. Latin was introduced into the first-year programme (and continued into the second year), and German, again for all upper-band pupils, was introduced at the second-year stage. Clearly this policy caused an imbalance in the lower-school curriculum, as well as a rapid growth in the language department. Neither of those trends was allowed to continue but although the availability of a second language for a large number of pupils ceased, its introduction for approximately 30 pupils still demanded a compromise timetable for those pupils. Within a comprehensive curriculum the establishment of an élitist group forced choices at an early stage and posed organizational problems.

Once the difficult years of differing size year groups, building works, declining staff establishment, and curriculum teething problems, were passed, it was possible to build upon the obvious strengths and concentrate upon the elimination of evident weaknesses. The school at this point had declined to its expected level of approximately 900 pupils with five year groups of between 170 and 180 pupils in each.

The first major change in the full comprehensive school was in the pastoral system, where a move to a totally horizontal structure was introduced. This move not only followed a great deal of open discussion at all levels within the school but was coupled with debate on the most effective means of introducing active tutorial work. It not only satisfied organizational needs, enabling each mixed-ability tutor group to be tutored by one person over the five years, but had a significant impact on the role of the tutor and the involvement of tutor and year head in the academic side of a pupil's development.

The development of a viable option package was greatly helped, first, by national publications on the curriculum which stimulated discussion on the philosophy of the fourth and fifth-year curriculum, and, secondly by the availability of the microcomputer which enabled greater flexibility in the options programme to be utilized to the benefit of pupils. A core of subjects had to be chosen by pupils — recreation, mathematics, English, life skills, one practical/creative subject, one humanity/language, one science subject. Three other choices were available by which pupils were able to capitalize on their strengths and introduce a career bias in their programmes. Certain difficulties arose in grouping pupils for mathematics and English, which had implications lower down the school. Because of a larger staff, the early comprehensive pupils were set across the whole year group in these two subjects in Years 3to5. At that stage there were sufficient specialists to timetable eight staff together and thereby create eight sets in these two basic subjects. Once the school was fully comprehensive there were no more than five specialists in either of these areas and as a result a form of banding, with setting in each band, was reintroduced. Mathematics and English were timetabled together for alternate bands. Since the bands must remain the same for both subjects, uncomfortable decisions were sometimes made.

In order to maintain a broad common curriculum in the lower school, which provided necessary areas of experience for each pupil, an element of choice in respect of crafts and second languages was introduced at the end of the second year. For three double periods pupils had a choice from nine subjects. These were mainly practical and creative with two languages included.

The school maintained a banded structure which, in keeping with its tradition, allocated different numbers of pupils each year to a band according to their abilities. Problems always arose, however, over pupils with special learning difficulties. Since the onset of staffing cuts, it had not been possible to staff each year group by creating seven groups. The effect of this had been to create six classes of more or less equal size, that is, approximately 28 pupils, leaving no opportunity for a small remedial group.

The school was moving into an era of moderate decline. Annual intakes of 150–155 proved to be difficult to group. If they were staffed as five classes they formed large groups and any flexibility to provide for remedial or gifted pupils would be lost. If, on the other hand, they were divided into six groups they would become expensive in staffing and after one, or at most two years, they could not be afforded.

The school soon concluded that it would have to look at different forms of pupil grouping in order to maintain a viable curriculum. Mixed age groups, particularly in set situations, where standardized testing could provide reliable criteria, would need to be introduced and modular teaching, which would enable fourth and fifth years to follow certain subjects in realistically sized groups would need to be tested.

Commentary

A commentator from outside the school may easily be led into making demands on the organization of pupils for learning purposes which are difficult to realize in practice. Not least is this so when contradictory demands are made such as: 'Why not put all the bright pupils together in the same class?' and 'It is better for pupils to be together irrespective of their academic abilities.' The school's many publics — parents, politicians and other professionals included — are constantly arguing a vast range of issues which bear on the pupil grouping policy of the school and allegedly on the individual fortunes of each pupil.

Behind the issues of pupil grouping lies the fundamental factor: the deployment of the school's total resources and the access and share which each pupil is able to have. The grouping policy is a synonym for stating the use of scarce plant, equipment and materials, such as a science laboratory or a lathe in a workshop. It is also a synonym for the share of the best and worst teachers' attention and the range of teaching expertise which is available to each pupil.

Size of class or teaching group has long been a subject of controversy in the teaching profession and sometimes one of acrimony. Local education authorities now make assumptions about the teacher/pupil ratio which are intended to limit the size of teaching groups. In some cases maxima are actually specified.

Some research data (see *Further Reading*) show that, on average, pupil achievement increases as class size is reduced. Reductions in size from say 28 to 25 are likely to make little difference in average achievement, but the advantage rises sharply for a class size of 15 and below. It appears that these general findings are true of both secondary and primary school groupings and irrespective of subject matter. The latter point is particularly surprising since it is often argued that the more structured subjects such as foreign languages, mathematics and the natural sciences would benefit more from smaller groupings than less well-structured subjects.

Many conflicting factors need to be reconciled to produce a school's pupil grouping policy. This case represents a particular pattern of choices at a particular time by a particular staff. A different set of staff in the same school may have chosen differently. Each school is faced by a total set of different constraints — notably the physical characteristics of the buildings and facilities and the qualities and number of staff. It would be interesting to know the magnitude of difficulty each constraint presented and of the relative importance which the school attached to each. Altogether, however, a formidable list of variables was introduced, some more avoidable than others, some more tangible than others, as follows:

—overall size of roll,

—a split site school,

—the assumption of mixed ability classes,

—standards and achievement expected by parents,

—building extensions and modernization,

—staff competence, interest and motivation,

—pastoral care,

—academic interests,

—cooperation of feeder schools,

—a pupil's learning styles,

—pupils with learning difficulties,

—gifted children,

—vocational education interests,

—public examinations,

—equal opportunity for boys and girls,

—age range of pupils,

—special claims of different subjects,

—addition of extra subjects to the curriculum,

—variable sized intakes of pupils,

—curricular mix for each pupil,

—access to new technology,

—availability of reliable data for grouping.

These items divide into those which can more easily be accommodated in the short term and those which can only be accommodated, if at all, in the longer term. Among the latter are clearly unavoidable features of the school such as a split site, total numbers of pupils, and staff numbers and levels of competence. These are the fundamentals which dictate the general parameters within which options for pupil grouping may be varied.

Issues for further discussion

1. The influence of the accommodation available on
   (a) the curriculum;
   (b) pupil grouping.

2. Ways of increasing the flexibility of spaces
   (a) for teaching different subjects;
   (b) for teaching groups of differing sizes.

3. Ensuring the maximum use of all accommodation and facilities: criteria for deciding on the use of extra space which becomes available for teaching purposes.

4. The idea of a pupil's 'entitlement' in the curriculum which a school offers.

5. The organization of pupils with special learning difficulties in a secondary school.

6. The integration of handicapped pupils in secondary schools.

7. The case for departmental autonomy in pupil grouping.

8. Staffing costs of different option schemes in secondary schools.

9. The distribution of non-teaching time in secondary schools.

10. The use of generalist teachers in secondary schools.

Further reading

Cahen, L.S. and Filby, N.N. (1979) The Class Size/Achievement Issue — New Evidence and a Research Plan. *Phi Delta Kappan* 60, 7, 492–495, 538.

Dunkin, M.J. and Biddle, B.J. (1974) *The Study of Teaching*. New York, Holt Rinehart and Winston.

Glass, G.V. (1982) *School Class Size: Research and Policy*. London, Sage.

CHAPTER 9
TIMETABLING AND USE OF BUILDINGS AND FACILITIES
Case 9.1: Learning to timetable and be timetabled

Introduction

A junior school becomes a 9 to 13 middle school and inherits the whole of a building which it had formerly shared with a secondary school.

Many organizational practices and ways of teaching to which the staff had grown accustomed were suddenly thrown into question by the dual need to provide a school for a wider age range, and to manage larger and more differentiated specialist accommodation.

It takes time for the teaching staff to absorb the problems and the potential of their new situation. It is a process of learning about inescapable realities. The need for a more sophisticated timetable for regulating the work of the school and rationing the use of the building and facilities in an orderly fashion becomes clear but is accepted reluctantly.

In a large junior school the teaching staff had been used to teaching in traditional classrooms with a timetable consisting of neat 30-minute periods. The timetable did not include physical education (PE) or art for many classes. The children were usually well adapted, however, when they transferred to the local grammar or secondary schools, having a sound grounding in reading, writing, arithmetic and hymn singing. But this junior school had had to develop in two years to become a 9 to 13 middle school. This meant that there was little time to adapt to such a change. It was a traumatic experience for the staff who had to face the idea of a new pattern of working, both with regard to the curriculum and the different use of physical resources.

The school building had stood for well over 100 years, housing a junior school on the upper storey and a secondary boys' school on the ground floor. A fairly amicable relationship existed between the two incumbent head teachers. That amicability, however, did not extend to the use of the gym by the junior children because it was argued that they could always 'run about at playtime' obviating the need for PE. When there seemed to be an opportunity to use the playground for games, however, the staff always said the weather was unsuitable.

The whole building became available for the use of the junior school when the secondary boys moved to a new school. That enabled the third and fourth-year 'A' classes and third and fourth-year remedial class to move downstairs. No specialist rooms were established but an ESN 'special class' moved into one room to the minor annoyance of the head teacher. The staff managed to ignore the presence of this 'special class' so the equilibrium of the school remained undisturbed. In establishing a 9 to 13 middle school the curriculum had to expand to include unexpected subjects like science and French and the former timetable had to be remodelled to accommodate double or even treble periods for practical subjects. These changes had to be undertaken by the new head teacher.

The local education authority was faced with the task of altering the building to meet the needs of the new age group. An imaginative remodelling of the downstairs area to produce a library and practical areas took place. The practical areas were open-plan to include science, art and craft, and home economics. The building alterations were designed to aid curriculum innovation in the school by seeking to develop progressive primary school practices, but some teachers viewed it cynically as a means of cutting down building costs. Others were clearly worried about the effects of the new design on teachers and pupils. 'If you take the doors off and remove some of the partitions, chaos will ensue. You can't have groups of children being taught different things with no wall between them. It's not fair to the staff,' the deputy head said at the first staff meeting with the new headteacher. Teachers thought that the outcome would be considerable stress for themselves and the pupils. They argued that woodwork could not take place at the same time as a 'quiet' didactically taught science lesson, so the areas would be unused for long periods of time.

The initial response to such allegations was to establish class bases in the traditional primary school pattern and to introduce the staff and children gradually to the specialised areas in order that they might become accustomed to working in the open-plan environment. It soon became apparent that if the curriculum objectives were to be met then the areas would have to be in continuous use and greater teacher cooperation would have to be developed. This in itself was an innovation, but staff quickly learned that both they and the children benefited through lesson planning which enabled 'noisy' crafts to take place at the same time as 'practical' science and that quieter aspects of the respective subjects could be accommodated in a similar manner. It was also apparent that with several staff using one area, it was essential for one teacher to have responsibility for that area if resources were to be maintained in order and quantity. This in itself led to greater cooperation and an awareness of the needs of colleagues.

The open-plan design did not aid the teaching of French or music because, as one teacher asserted, 'no one could concentrate on creative writing or mental arithmetic with those dreadful recorders squeaking all the time.' But where could such teaching take place? The initial music centre had to be the gymnasium/hall — a separate building where the piano was housed — but the transportation of musical instruments from one building to another was not desirable because of difficulties of supervision and the vagaries of the weather; it also limited physical education activities. The answer was to find a room which could be shut off from the rest of the open-plan building and which would double for the use of both subjects. This was achieved and it was possible to concentrate equipment such as cassette recorders, record players and slide projectors where they would be both useful and essential to the teaching methods involved. It soon became apparent however that one room was very limiting and needed careful timetabling so that it could be used to its full potential. Thus all the special areas were established to the partial satisfaction of the staff and as time passed both staff and pupils became used to a greater degree of movement around the school, and became more aware of the need for cooperation.

These arrangements were achieved during the expansion of the school but as numbers fell the opportunities of contraction became attractively apparent with the result that there were separate music and French rooms; this further increased teacher and pupil satisfaction. In addition there was the opportunity for remedial teaching for small groups in either the French or music rooms enabling both teacher and pupil to enjoy the lack of interruption which 'open' class bases had to tolerate.

Years one and two had a total of 89 pupils, year three had 76 pupils and year four had 57 pupils. The imbalance in numbers was due to parental choice, and produced added difficulties in timetabling. The resultant pattern of classes was one first-year class; one vertically grouped first/second-year class and one second-year class; three third-year classes and two fourth-year classes. Each class group was of mixed ability and each class teacher was responsible for the teaching of mathematics and English to his or her own class. Through this mode of practice the children were able to relate to one teacher for a proportion of each day, which maintained the primary school approach to pastoral care.

The two younger age groups spent more time on communication studies than the two older age groups but the latter had more time allocated to practical subjects such as science and home economics and French. This arrangement took account of the child's developmental stage and indicated how the child's needs changed in curriculum terms from the general to the specific — from general scientific topics to the separate sciences, from environmental studies to history and geography — and how the curriculum broadened to encompass new subjects such as a second language.

In some subject areas the amount of time allocated to each subject was constant over the four years. These included religious education, music and physical education/games which could be developed in other ways both through the formal curriculum and through out of school activities. The head thought that if a policy of setting were adopted, the timetabling of the school would become more complicated, but it was found possible to circumvent the difficulty by 'matching' setted subjects against non-setted subjects. In the top year of the school 'setted' French worked in a three-way arrangement with physical education and music or religious education for two sessions per week and was matched against music and physical education for another two sessions. That particular arrangement allowed for the planned four French lessons, two music lessons, two physical education lessons and one religious education lesson.

Setting was adopted in the school for French only in the top year, but it was considered desirable that the children mixed with their peer group in other ways in order to develop their social awareness. Thus for the practical subjects of home economics, science and art/craft the year group was divided into three mixed ability groups and for games into three different groupings. By adopting this method the children not only had the opportunity of working with different friends but also of working with teachers other than their own class teacher, thereby preparing them for the upper-school methods of teaching.

The school found that the task of constructing the timetable was not as formidable as in secondary schools where the core curriculum was supplemented by options. Nevertheless, it discovered that there were still the same basic problems of resource allocation to be solved. These problems were not made easier by the need to observe the Health and Safety at Work Act. It was found necessary to have relatively small groups of pupils working with a teacher in subjects such as science and home economics —

which could mean proportionally larger groups working with other teachers.

Having discovered the constraints, and prior to the formulation of the timetable, there was a period of consultation with the staff when preferences were noted. With these in mind, the deputy head and head teacher designed the timetable and presented it to the staff for comment and alteration as necessary.

Once the final form was established, the first stage of planning was completed and the staff were then able to embark on the more detailed planning necessary for the approaching new school year.

Commentary

A timetable in a school — as in public transportation — provides order and predictability. It cannot please everyone all the time. In a classteacher based programme a teacher may be happy to take mathematics at a certain time but not all the pupils may be so. In an integrated day programme the relative freedom of the pupil to manage as much of his or her own time as possible provides individuals with the opportunity to schedule and prioritize subjects and assignments at their own discretion.

The chief constraint on such freedom does not spring from size of school nor necessarily from the age range of the pupils involved. The critical factor is the school's policy for its curriculum — particularly and notably the distribution of resources in terms of the share which each pupil receives. In practical terms this means that the timetable operates as a rationing device. Thus, pupils in groups of a certain size and composition have access to a succession of general or special rooms, equipment and materials, teacher time and expertise, and the use of a variety of facilities. The less resources are shared the less need there is for a timetable. If a single teacher can provide a complete curriculum for a class in the same room all the time, there is no need for a school-based timetable, though there may be need for one to regulate activities within the class and room.

In this case the head first set out to establish the educational objectives of the new middle school to be accomplished through its curriculum. This entailed the identification of a wider range of subjects to be taught than existed in the previous junior school.

Where the primary school philosophy extends into the middle years of schooling, the integration of subjects is found to be accepted practice in many schools. The only formal timetabling needed involves the allocation of specialised practical areas for the use of particular groups of staff and children. The remainder of the timetable may be left blank for teachers working individually or in teams to centre their work around their class bases. This type of organisation may be typified by one group of staff working with the same group of children for much of the week.

This philosophy is more readily adopted by the 8 to 12 middle school, but it is less easily maintained in the 9 to 13 middle school where separate subjects make their appearance, adding to the complexities of timetabling. In addition, there is often a greater degree of specialisation but by maintaining the primary school philosophy it is possible to arrange teams of teachers for each age band of children to include those necessary specialisms, provided that versatility in the staffing is available.

The timetable should be seen as the servant of the curriculum and not its master. It is desirable that flexibility and not rigidity of pupil and staff groupings is obtained. Such flexibility may be used to reflect the needs of, and the differences in children, in their capabilities, their rates and modes of learning and their varying levels of interest and motivation.

The head saw the timetable as the means to achieve the best possible outcomes for the pupils at different stages in their development. One principle at stake is that of balance in the curriculum. Such balance may need to be conceived in terms of the entire length of time that the pupil is in the school — in this instance for four years. Variable-sized intakes, staff changes and many other circumstances may impose constraints on what and how much can be offered at any one time. Thus compensations must be operated over the longer period.

In a period of contraction, those middle schools which have appointed staff who are primary school orientated and generalist teachers with one or two specialist subjects, but who are interested in and able to extend their curriculum responsibilities, find themselves in a more favourable position than those schools which have exclusively selected specialist teachers.

Issues for further discussion

1. Adapting old buildings to modern educational practice. What criteria should be used to determine a successful adaptation?

2. The use of timetabling in primary education. Is this necessarily a breach of liberal educational philosophy?

3. Career prospects for generalist teachers in primary and secondary schools in future.

4. Converting teaching organization from class teaching to team teaching.

5. Staff retraining for working in open areas.

6. Convincing parents that changing from a junior school basis to that of a 9 to 13 middle school is educationally sound. What are the changing curricular needs of a pupil over the four-year period 7 to 11, 8 to 12 or 9 to 13?

7. A policy for helping parents to understand open-plan and team teaching organization.

8. Coping with falling rolls in a 9 to 13 middle school on a 50 per cent specialist timetable.

9. Financial management in a school with four teaching teams.

10. Liaison between 9 to 13 middle schools and their related upper schools.

Further reading

Garland, R. (editor) (1982) *Microcomputers and Children in the Primary School*. Lewes, Falmer Press.

OECD (1975) *Programme on Educational Building: School Building and Educational Change*. Paris, OECD.

Shipman, M. (1983) *Assessment in Primary and Middle Schools*. London, Croom Helm.

Case 9.2: Managing space

Introduction

A large secondary school awaits the completion of a building programme which has been in progress and characterized the life of the school for nearly ten years. The sixth and final building phase still remains to be undertaken. One of the by-products of this experience is that the school staff themselves have accumulated a considerable knowledge of school building policy and techniques from their constant interaction with officials and contractors over such a long period. They become emboldened to make demands for modification to parts of the previously completed plant on the basis of actually using it. The staff develop skills in design and negotiation. With flair and determination significant building changes are made to the benefit of the school and at agreeable financial costs.

Narrative

A Group 11 comprehensive secondary school was under construction throughout the later 1970s. By 1980 Phase 5 of the building programme had been completed but the site still contained seven 'terrapin' buildings. These were evidence of yet another building phase. The development of the school had therefore been accomplished over a period of time which had never been free from the dislocations and inconveniences of being a building site. Financial cuts had from time to time complicated matters still further and heightened the anxieties and frustrations of the staff.

Nevertheless, the period had been one of adaptation and managerial achievement. The school had learnt a great deal about the work of the local education authority, its architects and the building industry. The senior staff felt informed and competent enough to intervene with a view to solving operational problems which had arisen from earlier phases of the building programme already completed and in use.

Over a period of five years the school was able to achieve a number of modifications to the building. A working agreement was made with the local education authority which helped with the cost of materials if the school supplied the labour. Among the schemes brought to a successful conclusion by this method were the following:

—the school office enlarged,

—a room built as an office for the design technology department, with a storage room for wood above it,

—a sixth-form library created out of one wing of the school library,

—two small rooms for the sixth-form teaching by subdividing a large room,

—a covered way between changing rooms and the sports hall,

—an office for the head of the upper school,

—extra car-parking space and outdoor seating around the school by removing cycle sheds and using the material salvaged.

With this record of achievement to its credit, the school felt encouraged to tackle some larger problems raised by other parts of the building. One of the most unsatisfactory features of the building completed during phase one is represented by Plan A (Figure 8).

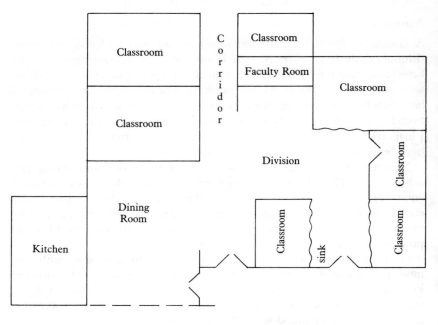

Figure 8   Secondary school plant: Plan A

The design was open-plan to allow for flexibility so that groups could overflow from the classrooms into the division area. The folding doors were installed to enable this to happen. In theory it should have given flexibility to teaching groups and the possibility of team teaching, but in reality it proved impossible to keep the division area empty; it was floor space which had to be used for 40 periods of teaching each week. The folding doors were never designed to be opened and closed eight times a day. Given so much use, they were constantly in need of repair. However, the major fault was that the division area as a teaching space was too open. It was subject to constant interruptions as pupils passed through the area to enter the surrounding classrooms. Those using the staircase were also seen and heard by the class in the division area. From 11 o'clock until 2 o'clock each day noise and distractions from the kitchen and dining room added to the problems. Even without these constant interruptions the division area could not be used for lead lessons as its L-shape made seating the pupils an impossible task.

In another part of the school buildings a two-storey block had been built during Phase 4 of the building programme, which had survived a series of financial cuts. The upper storey was designed as a specialist English area together with sixth-form accommodation. The ground floor was for home economics, art, needlework and light crafts, completed as represented by Plan B in Figure 9.

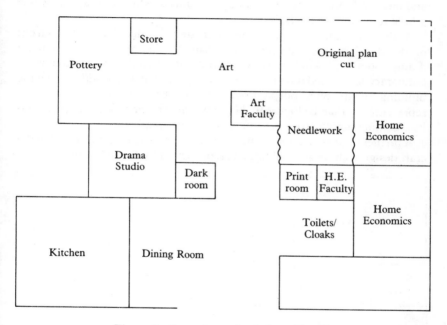

Figure 9 Secondary school plant: Plan B

It may been seen from Figure 9 that a dining-room and kitchen are provided together with an open-plan design similar to that represented by Plan A in Figure 8. With the completion of the building in Figure 9 the school took stock of developments to date. As a result of the cumulative building completions, the school was very short of teaching space but oversupplied with dining and catering facilities. In phase two of the building programme a dining-room and kitchen had also been included in a block designed to house the Lower School. Furthermore, the latest dining and catering accommodation represented by Plan B in Figure 9 needed capital outlay on equipment and expenditure to staff it.

The school raised the problem with the architect's department and those concerned with minor works expenditure of the local education authority. The outcome was a result which took into account a number of different problems caused by the buildings and offered a solution which satisfied the more pressing needs of the school.

The dining and catering facilities in the lower school block were extended and modified. A cafeteria system was introduced, which enabled the whole school to use the single facility.

At the same time walls were added to create a corridor and a classroom out of the division area represented in Plan A (Figure 8). The adjoining dining-room and kitchen were altered into two large classrooms as temporary accommodation for the music department which still awaited the building of its own purpose-built block. The kitchen in the area, represented as Plan B (Figure 9), became a third home economics room and its adjoining dining space became a light craft area.

A further scheme was started to solve a number of problems located in the craft design technology building, as represented by Plan C in Figure 10.

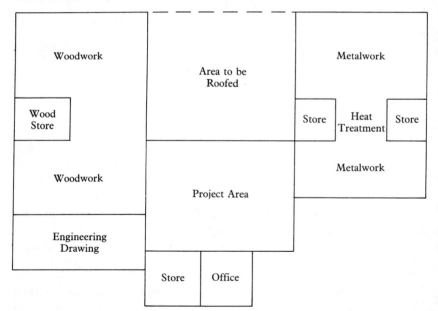

Figure 10   Secondary school plant: Plan C

As can be seen from Figure 10, the original idea was to build two metal workshops, two woodwork shops, an engineering drawing-room and an open area for project work. In discussion with the staff of the department the problems were identified as follows:

—access to the area; and safety, particularly between the two metal workshops through the heat treatment room,

—lack of storage for materials,

—need for space for car maintenance,

—overcrowding.

The head of the design technology department drew up a plan to provide a solution for all these problems. The head of school then contacted the adviser for craft design technology and the governors. With their support, he approached the director of education with the plan. This involved roofing the area shown in Figure 10. The craft design technology department itself was unable to build the new roof but if the roof could be provided by the local education authority they were prepared to tackle the rest of the adaptation. Initially the school was informed that the roofing would be too expensive and therefore not possible. As it was a question of costing, however, the head asked that they should debate detailed figures. When the costings were prepared by the architect's department the head asked for them to be itemized. The entire adaptation would have cost more than the local education authority was prepared to find. The cost for the roofing alone accounted for two-fifths of the total. The authority was willing to find this sum and, on the school's offer and proven record of self-help over the years, was persuaded to support the scheme as a whole.

Throughout the period it was invaluable for the school to have a technician appointed to do on-site jobs to a high standard. Jobs completed with his help meant that the school was able to avoid delays, cutbacks and bureaucratic procedures. It also meant that costs were cut and precise solutions to problems were obtained. The expert advice and work of the craft design technology staff were indispensable. At all times the school kept in touch with the county architects and learnt all it could about planning permission, building regulations and standards.

The school's buildings were made into a better resource than was originally planned through the enthusiasm and applied knowledge of many staff and by negotiating and winning the support of the local education authority.

Commentary

Problem solving is a characteristic task of management in schools as in every other type of organization. It is an ongoing task with respect to both immediate and longer-term interests. In the search for solutions to problems people commonly assume the boundaries within which they may be found as they attempt to obtain exceptional results from unexceptional resources. This does not imply, however, that the quantity and quality of resources available should be regarded as invariable, or that managerial action cannot improve them.

Buildings and facilities in particular are resources which are commonly taken as given. Strenuous efforts are made to adapt to them as they are. It may not occur to the school that by adapting the buildings and facilities themselves, disproportionate benefits may be obtained. The physical properties of the school have a considerable bearing on both the curriculum which can be offered and the discipline and morale of the entire school. Changes which are contemplated, however, need to be properly researched by way of feasibility studies, since benefits may be more imaginary than real.

In this case the disadvantages of particular parts of the building were experienced daily. The school was fortunate to have a senior management team with the organizational capacity to mount a campaign to get permission and support for the modifications required, and the political will and practical skills to carry them out. The school was aided in its purpose by its own knowledge of building policy and techniques. Teachers commonly deplore the extent of building space taken for use as cloakrooms, corridors and storage. This can be as high as 35 per cent. Some schools — notably in the primary sector — have been ingenious in adapting old buildings, converting unlikely spaces into useful and flexible teaching areas, and generally bringing as much non-teaching space as possible into use for teaching purposes. However, as they did in this case, pupil movement and noise levels may create problems as the proportion of space used for teaching purposes increases.

Issues for discussion

1. How does one detect that a problem exists in school management?
2. How to measure the efficiency of accommodation and facilities.
3. Ways of creating flexible teaching spaces.
4. Sound-proofing devices in flexible teaching areas.

5. The advantages and disadvantages of using unorthodox spaces for teaching purposes.

6. The use of open-plan for teaching in secondary schools compared with primary schools.

7. The need for feasibility and pilot studies in school management.

8. Using the work of parents and voluntary labour in modifying school buildings.

9. Teacher involvement in the building of a school.

10. Alternative catering schemes.

Further reading

Bennett, N. (editor) (1980) *Open Plan Schools : Teaching, Curriculum, Design*. Slough, NFER.

Davis, J. and Loveless, E.E. (1981) *The Administrator and Educational Facilities*. Washington DC, University of America.

Ward, C. (editor) (1976) *British School Buildings: Designs and Appraisals 1964–1974*. London, Architectural Press.

CHAPTER 10
TEACHING METHODS AND TECHNIQUES
Case 10.1: Encounter with open plan

Introduction

This account reveals the innermost feelings and reactions of a mature student teacher on having her first encounter with open-plan teaching. Against the background of her own ideological disposition and set of expectations of open-plan teaching, she rapidly identifies the professional skills needed to be an effective teacher in an open-plan setting. She readily sees them exemplified in the resident teacher, only to realize her own inadequacies about which she becomes highly sensitive. The teaching practice for the student teacher proves to be a process of self-realisation. She falls far short of her own expectations of herself and uncovers a need for wider and more sophisticated behavioural patterns than she had anticipated. Disappointment with her own performance makes her disillusioned with open-plan teaching. She evokes the virtues of traditional classroom teaching in self-defence but finally recognizes that the shortcomings are her own and expresses a determination to correct them.

Narrative

It was hard for the student teacher to analyze the place of this first block teaching practice in her development as a teacher when still feeling overwhelmed by a sense of lack of achievement and total demoralisation. In considering the curriculum content, and the response of the pupils, some areas which could be improved became clearer, but the central problem seemed to be her negative feelings throughout the practice. How much they derived from external circumstances and how much from personal difficulties had to be analysed to point the way towards more positive development, if possible.

Although this was her first experience of an open-plan school, she had expected to find there a lively and exciting atmosphere which could provide a sense of adventure and discovery in which many children could thrive. In theory, open-plan seemed to agree with her personal set of educational values. The layout and teaching methods encouraged independence and an awareness of the interrelationship of subjects across the curriculum. The school fostered a relaxed, non-paternalistic relationship between children and teachers. Children were genuinely enthusiastic about learning (she heard a few groans when work was handed out by the class teacher, and many enthusiastic noises). They had been taught a wide range of skills and approaches to subjects and were capable of concentrated periods of undirected independent work, and of responsibly taking over the running of some lessons such as games or 'reporting back' sessions. The class teacher's enthusiasm for the children's energy and individuality led to a close and good working relationship which had been built up over several years. Although the system was termed 'team teaching', in fact the children in this part of the school worked mostly with the class teacher.

The organizational and educational structure of the school and the resulting happy and fruitful learning environment seemed very desirable to her on her preliminary visits, but somewhat hard to assimilate. Her initial reaction was perhaps the first mistake: she recognized the high and enviable standards but gained little insight as to how they were achieved and began to feel that she could not meet such a challenge. She could *see* that ultimately, in the open-plan school, as in any other school, standards depended entirely on the enthusiasm, knowledge and expertise of the teachers and the learning environment which they provided. She *felt* inadequate, instead of regarding it as a part of a larger learning experience. It would have been more fruitful if she had tried to be more outward-looking and to gain greater insight into the children's needs and enthusiasms. Instead, she concentrated on providing herself with a well-planned scheme of work, which was adequate as far as many of the objectives and the organization were concerned, but did not solve the central problem of the relationship between her as a teacher and the class, or take sufficiently into account the high expectations of the children that there would be a varied and flexible approach.

The experience and ability of the class teacher during the time he had been with the class had built up a complex relationship in which the expectations and limitations on both sides were clear. The children expected and received a high level of stimulation from a wide variety of teaching techniques, but knew that they could not step beyond certain boundaries of behaviour without incurring displeasure. Their behaviour with other teachers was noticeably different, and changed markedly according to whether or not the class teacher was in sight. The effect of her obvious nervousness, often inappropriate approach and ineffective efforts at discipline were electric from almost the first lesson with the class. If she had entered into the situation with more dynamism and more positive attitudes — working for the children instead of regarding their lack of discipline as a threat (conscious of the comparison with the class teacher's control) — perhaps they would have begun to feel that she was worth listening to, or at least expected to be listened to.

She became more nervous as the situation deteriorated, feeling that she was turning a previously orderly situation into anarchy. This made her less able to relax and develop a sense of humour which might have rescued the class situations which rapidly became an ordeal. Some initial confidence and motivation was essential in going into an untried situation like that. It proved too late to build a better relationship after the first two or three weeks in this instance, though a class teacher would have to develop one during a whole year's contact.

The small group work was much better managed on all levels. She felt free to deal with fewer problems of discipline and free to develop relationships which she felt were being destroyed in class lessons. The inability to put down problems quickly resulted in nagging in class lessons and led to a feeling of total frustration at having to adopt tactics and drop schemes in a way which went against how she had hoped to teach. In groups this was, on the whole, different. She gained personal satisfaction and the children responded well, or felt that she cared how they responded, because she showed a variety of responses to them and a larger ratio of encouragement to reprimand.

Feeling that she had to strive desperately to maintain control a good deal of the time, it was difficult for her to show enough encouragement at times. She felt that moving around individuals and talking about their work redressed this to a certain extent, but her general tone was too humourless. Partly nervousness, and partly lack of projection led to a monotonous voice, which some children could not hear easily. This she tried to work on, but with limited success.

As a working environment the physical space gave her many opportunities for a variety of work of different types and in different numbers, though it was disconcerting for her at first to be uncertain *where* to set up a science experiment. She found it interesting to observe where the children chose to set to work on their assignments: the size, position and composition of their working groups gave an indication of their attitudes to work or how they felt on that day or about that particular piece of work. However, she often found herself having to move children around to stop disruption — a strategy she did not like using. She found that perhaps because of the size of the space, the children were often careless about furniture, equipment and the standard of the completed work she had set them. Repeated efforts at tidying up were rather unsuccessful, and she determined to try in future to establish a better routine.

She found that some features of the open-plan space were taxing in unexpected ways. The feeling of exposure and the problem of establishing a 'presence' when she was not within four walls and behind a closed door in a traditional classroom were at first hard to cope with. Much as she liked the results of open-plan teaching in seeing the children moving about and learning relatively freely, she found that the range of techniques needed to cope with distractions and the lack of automatic 'authority from the desk' came very slowly, if at all. Discussing it with the class teacher, she was given some suggestions but never solved the problem created by the lack of the inner feeling of 'presence', as she afterwards described it.

Partly because she felt overwhelmed by these problems, and partly because the practice was so short, the level of concern and insight into children's interests and abilities, and the amount of work accomplished fell far short of what she had hoped to achieve. The results as shown in written work only slowly improved across the four weeks, but part of this was due to the fact that she frequently did not get through the exposition before she had to move the children rapidly on to written work for disciplinary reasons. Partly too, she had overassessed their rate of assimilating new ideas and approaches. An improvement set in once the children saw from marked work that she appreciated what they did. Displayed work added to this.

She felt she had learned to begin teaching more slowly and cautiously, to mesh with attitudes and methods the children were used to, giving them confidence that they could achieve good work for her *before* attempting to go on to something unfamiliar. In presenting them with an uncertain, unfamiliar and not very encouraging approach, she found that many children lost interest early on. Some children, however, responded consistently well and were frustrated if other children's behaviour did not allow the planned work to develop. In future she was determined to try to develop strategies to hold the interest of the majority of children more successfully, adopting a more flexible and humourous approach if possible.

She observed that it was difficult not to be aware of the effect she was having upon the carefully built structure of the class, and upon the class teacher and even upon the behaviour of individual children. This became an inhibiting factor which created barriers between her and experiences which could have been used as useful learning opportunities. Falling so far short of her aims in class work could have been regarded partly as a natural feature of teaching practice from which she could have learned a great deal with the advice of other teachers. She felt that in not having a particularly resilient attitude or a positive approach, these difficulties developed into an attack on her personality, which got between her and the interest and satisfaction she had hoped to get from whole class work as she had from group work and from working with children individually.

Commentary

Individuals seek to enter the teaching profession with preconceived or assumed ideas about the nature of teaching and the skills required by the teacher. Pupils, parents and other adults who have the opportunity to see teachers at work probably seldom, if ever, reflect on the range of skills required. They are quick, however, to identify deficiencies in a teacher. In this case the student teacher was a highly successful university graduate and a parent herself. Being in the position of teacher proved to be a powerful experience. Her thoughts about herself, children at school, the nature and transmission of knowledge, the expertise of teachers and how teaching should be organized were all thrown into temporary disarray by the teaching practice in an open-plan school.

The pupils, of course, found themselves exposed to a teacher who was not only new to them but a stranger to the school. It is the experience of pupils generally to have a variety of teachers during their stay in a school. These might include a new teacher to the school. A student teacher, however, is both new and inexperienced. Furthermore, student teachers may take over classes in the middle of a term and cause disruption in the established flow of work under the regular teacher. Training, however, is a necessary function and all pupils must be given a fair share of any disadvantages which student teachers incur, as well as the advantages.

The case highlights the school as a place of work. Varied working conditions exist as a result of different architectural characteristics and features, as well as the ideological and educational preferences of teachers. *What* should be taught has increasingly become subject to public scrutiny and external pressures on the school. *How* it should be taught remains the prerogative of the school. The exercise of this perrogative may be to maximize the motivation and job satisfaction of the teaching staff or the reverse. Teachers feel keenly about the way they can and want to work. In so far as occupational mobility permits, teachers can take posts in schools where they are comfortable in the professional sense. With reduced job vacancies and compulsory redeployment, however, teachers may not always have the opportunity to work in ways which they prefer.

It would remain to be seen whether the student teacher in this case could come to terms with the particular ways of working in this school. If she were permanently appointed to such a school she might remain uneasy or even disaffected, becoming subject to stress and ineffective as a teacher, unless the benefits of further training and opportunity for personal development could be obtained.

Careful counselling of the teacher is thereby implied. This extends to making plain to applicants how they are expected to work or the degree of freedom they have in choosing their teaching methods and techniques. It extends to the teacher training programme. A close and constructive relationship between the school and the training institution should exist. This should be characterized by the deliberate placement of student teachers to gain a variety of experience, a thorough briefing and induction into the school once chosen, and a systematic support service in both the school and the training institution, which offers the opportunity to talk problems through and provides incremental training targets for the individual student teacher to realize his or her full potential.

The management of time, space, materials, relationships and work in progress is a skilled task. Student teachers cannot expect to be able to match the professional performance of an experienced teacher. If this could be readily done there would be no justification for training. It must be remembered that such training takes place at the initial stage to enable a teacher to be acceptable as a member of a school staff, and also during employment as a teacher in response to new developments and needs.

Issues for further discussion

1. Should recruitment to teaching in primary schools be limited to those in their early twenties?

2. How does the stability of the social composition and structure of the teaching group affect the educational progress of the pupil?

3. The architecture of the school as a determinant of teaching organization.

4. Open-plan teaching compared with classroom teaching from the pupil's and the teacher's point of view.

5. The school as partner in the initial training of teachers with particular reference to the contribution of the head of school.

6. The work of the teacher as student teacher's supervisor.

7. The main sources of poor morale for the student teacher during practice teaching and how to deal with those which lie within the purview of the school.

8. Is it possible for the pupil to be involved in a more conscious part during the student teacher's practice teaching?

9. How far is teaching subject to systematic and incremental improvement?

10. What practical difficulties lie in the path of improving teaching practice by matching more closely the student teacher's readiness for a specific experience and the opportunity to have it?

Further reading

Bennett, N., Andreae, J., Hegarty, P. and Wade, B. (1980) *Open Plan Schools*. Windsor, NFER.

Napier, R.W. and Gershenfeld, M.K. (1973) *Groups: Theory and Experience*. New York, Houghton Mifflin.

Paisey, T. (1983) 'Adjusting to Work, Pupils and Colleagues'. Chapter 6 in Paisey, A. (editor) *The Effective Teacher*. London, Ward Lock Educational.

Case 10.2: Diagnosis and treatment

Introduction

An area is served by grammar and secondary modern schools. One of the secondary modern schools has accommodated itself to the local system over a period of many years under the same head until his retirement. The new head of school reviews many aspects of school life. His attention is particularly drawn to the general state of teaching methods and techniques employed by the staff. He feels that while there may be much to commend there is good cause to encourage the staff to look afresh at the ways in which they teach. The educational needs of the pupils are not being met, in his judgement. A change in educational objectives implies a change in the means to achieve them. Teaching methods and techniques are seen to be critical. The head's first approaches to the staff to induce a willingness to change, however, produce defensive attitudes. Eventually a revision of the educational objectives on a participative basis leads to a more receptive response. The head makes some organizational changes in support of the staff. He finds that changing teaching methods and techniques is a more extensive task than expected. To obtain effective changes in the teaching requires more time and a more inclusive strategy than he at first realized.

Narrative

A secondary school with a 12 to 16 age range was part of a local system which included selective schools catering for about 25 per cent of the most academically able pupils. The school had grown so accustomed to this arrangement over a period of many years that a certain amount of apathy had set in. The staff felt that there was little prestige to be gained by continually striving for public examination results, particularly at GCE O level. They thought that the effort needed would be at the expense of other commitments which might be of greater value to the pupils. Apart from this, however, there was the question of feasibility. As one senior member of staff frequently said, there was 'no point in trying to turn geese into swans'.

A new head was appointed. One of the many issues which he considered were in need of attention was teaching methods and techniques. His first attempt to confront the staff about a need for an improvement was rebuffed with references to the local selective system and the disabilities which the school consequently suffered. His second attempt was to stress the positive achievements of the school and the ways in which the skills and enthusiasm of the staff had been brought together for the benefit of pupils. He focused on the need for confidence in learning so that the school would see itself as making a contribution to the education system rather than being a victim of it.

The new head evoked some of the references to teaching methods and techniques in *Aspects of Secondary Education in England* by HM Inspectorate, which had been published for over five years but which seemed to be unfamiliar to many members of the teaching staff. At this point the teachers declared that they were perfectly well aware of what pupils needed. They said that the problem was not in identifying the needs of the pupils, but in finding the administrative and classroom answers to them.

The head inferred that staff fully expected him to take steps himself which would have a bearing on the issue he had raised. At the same time he realized that it was not a difficult task to convince members of the teaching staff that teaching methods and techniques were in need of improvement. Most teachers he found were only too skilled at knowing their inadequacies, if less ready to admit to them and to remedy them. Public pronouncements and references to them, however, seemed to generate despair, cynicism or the irrational direction of blame towards others, notably various authorities within the education service.

Nonetheless, the staff responded positively to the head's invitation to look at the objectives of the school. To do so had been in any case an obligation laid on the school by the local education authority.

A series of meetings of various sub-groups of staff, a specially convened group to consider the curriculum, and the whole staff were held. It was finally agreed that the school would focus its work on four sets of considerations.

1. The identification and encouragement of pupils' talents
    — standards of achievement
    — examinations and certification
    — competition as a principle
    — public recognition and performance

2. The development of pupils' personal qualities
    — imagination, vitality, individuality
    — cooperation, confidence, self-respect

3. The pupils' experience of a broad curriculum
    — various traditional cultures
    — various subject disciplines

4. The preparation of pupils for later responsibilities
    — in the family
    — in employment
    — in the community
    — in further and higher education

The head asked each department and curriculum group in the school to discuss these items and to draw up a list of ways in which each contributed to them. They were also asked to identify how they could contribute more towards them in the future. It was pointed out that expressions of willingness to do more did not constitute a commitment. The head's third request was for the identification of work being done which was not fairly reflected in these items in any way. A very important fourth request was to identify ways in which the approach to the teaching might be inhibiting the achievement of these items in the school's objectives. The head thought fit to point out that teaching methods and techniques were a major factor in the curriculum — even to the extent of being more important than subject content. It was emphasized that the teaching methods and techniques of every member of staff formed a contribution to the curriculum as a whole.

To reinforce this the head visited classrooms for complete class periods in every department. Each visit was followed by a debriefing session in which the teacher was invited to reflect on the lesson. This included a discussion on his or her intentions measured against actual performance in the light of the declared objectives of the school and the overall curriculum which the pupil was receiving.

Very soon it was realised that the next step would have to be the provision of practical help by the head, if a change of teaching methods and techniques was to take place. The main organizational issues to emerge from the process so far were that the size of teaching groups was too large — with an average level of 27 — and the inability to set pupils into homogeneous groups in the fourth and fifth years. The main issues which related to the pupils themselves were their lack of confidence, poor oral ability, their willingness to be totally directed and their lack of social skills which discouraged them from taking initiatives.

The head and his senior colleagues reasoned that if the level of oral ability was to be raised, contact between teacher and pupil should be increased. If setting for examination subjects in years four and five were to take place, options would have to be replaced by courses. A selection from lists of subjects on the 'educational supermarket' principle would have to be replaced by courses recommended by the school on the basis of the pupil's ability and the school's judgement of what was educationally desirable. Teaching groups in years four and five would have to be small to accommodate the variety of courses needed to respond to individual pupil needs as perceived by the school. Groups as small as 20 would have to be created in years two and three with a maximum of 27 in contrast to previous practice in which only 3 out of 38 teaching groups in the fourth year contained more than 20 pupils.

These organizational changes were consequently made so that conditions would be right to begin a process of review and change of the teaching methods employed in the school. A further stimulus to this process was given by asking those heads of department who were rewriting syllabuses to lay them out under four headings: Content; Teaching Method; Pupil Activity; and Assessment. Heads of department were asked to reconsider the second and third of these each year. It was stressed that the process of exploring teaching methods and the range of pupil activity was more important than registering them in the minds of teachers as fixed and unchangeable.

It became apparent at this point that further progress would be impaired by two considerations which had been overlooked. First, a number of teachers had received a narrow initial training with an emphasis on teacher instruction. Secondly, a number of examination syllabuses reinforced this approach and actually militated against alternatives.

These matters were brought to the fore in the head's dealings with the teaching staff in design, craft and technology. The pressures on teaching staff in craft and technology had been to add the word 'design' to the title of their teaching area in the curriculum. The reason for this had been understood in concept but not carried through into practical teaching. In part this was due to the fact that the head of the department and several colleagues had been trained with an emphasis on pure craftmanship rather than with child-centred learning in view. The demonstrable expertise of the teacher was to be imitated by the pupil under instruction from the teacher.

The preferred examination syllabus for woodwork at O level was restrictive. Pupils were not required to submit a design or a drawing, much less discuss their practical project or provide evidence of such discussion and initiatives in their own learning process. Pupils took a theoretical paper which involved such questions as 'Draw a marking gauge and name its parts' which demanded an ability in recall rather than an understanding of theories underpinning practical work, comparisons between intention and actual product and the process of design and technology employed. An alternative syllabus made it possible to study such issues but the preference among the teachers was for the syllabus which gave pride of place to craftmanship itself.

Teachers, when asked, defined bad teaching in their subject as a sequence of 'instruction and demonstration without the possibility of setting any problem which can use the instruction given and learning received.' Staff readily confessed that large parts of the courses leading to examinations were characterized by such teaching — rather than good teaching which they defined as 'making the ordinary extraordinary and involving the mental and physical activity of the pupil in a product which requires the pupil to move back and forth between the abstract and the concrete.'

The head's efforts to date left him more convinced than ever of the significance of teaching method and technique as a variable in the education process and its power to realize or frustrate the objectives of the school. The review undertaken clearly pointed to the need for styles of teaching which encouraged vitality, hard work, imagination and discussion among pupils rather than imitation, acquiescence and silence. Smaller classes would undoubtedly help in making the change. The introduction of different programmes would also help. The staff agreed to try out a City and Guilds Foundation Course in engineering and a teacher interested in pupils with special needs undertook the teaching and assessment of language through pottery. The head and senior staff also agreed to study profile assessment work by City and Guilds vocational preparation examiners with a view to adopting new techniques in the school. With these initial moves, however, came the realization that strategic thinking, planning and persistence over a period of time would be necessary to effect substantial improvements in teaching methods and techniques throughout the school as a whole. Furthermore, it was recognized that this attempt to create changes was based upon relatively simple premises. The more sophisticated premises and processes advocated by Her Majesty's Inspectorate in connection with the concept of the 'entitlement curriculum' seemed comparatively daunting.

Commentary

Many people in and out of the teaching profession probably make two basic assumptions when they think about pupils at school: learning can be fun and learning can be effective. Some people do not make these assumptions. A parent wrote to the head of a secondary special school protesting that his son was 'enjoying school too much' — therefore 'it could not be doing him much good.' Likewise the occasional teacher despairs of learning — 'whatever you do for them seems to make little difference — they try to forget it all as soon as they can.'

Teaching is a major vehicle for learning in schools. There are many alternative strategies for teaching, however, and within each of these there are myriads of options over detail. Thus there is endless scope for the teacher to vary the way in which he or she tackles any particular teaching assignment. Initial and in-service training indeed should have alerted the teacher to some of the possibilities — at least to the fact that many possibilities exist. Apart from how teachers actually teach at any given time, it is safe to say that every one of them either knows the alternatives which are to be preferred but does not adopt them or does not know of such alternatives but would adopt them if he or she did know about them. It is the business of in-service training to ensure that teachers are well informed.

Superordinates such as heads of department and heads of schools may also regard it as part of their jobs to keep teachers well informed about alternatives and developments in teaching methods and techniques. A few years ago the position of professional tutor was created in some secondary schools to formalize the process of keeping teachers informed and inducting or training them into new methods and techniques.

As in all jobs habituation and the line of least resistance may prevail to the detriment of continuous experiment and development. The chances of promotion or the pressures of colleagues encourage many teachers to avoid stagnation. Most teachers respond to encouragement and praise. They persevere if their efforts are shown to be worthwhile by the head or other senior colleagues, parents, and above all by the pupils themselves. Appreciation and achievement are usually strong motivators. The professional teacher, usually has, in addition, the motivation which springs from a sense of vocation. Characteristic of such teachers are internalized standards of professional practice through training and continuous application to professional development.

In this case it is implied that judgements are made on the basis of brief samples of a teacher's teaching. Over a longer period of time in the teacher's working year, however, there may be more variety and greater effectiveness than brief observations and discussion can ever convey. Knowing what a teacher should change from being and doing is difficult to establish. Pupils provide a constant source of informal information to the teacher on the effectiveness and enjoyableness of the teaching. This source may be neglected or underused. At the other extreme it may be used more formally and systematically.

Differences in sheer technicalities in the classroom may be an important variable, as assumed in this case. But behind the procedures, features and programmes which may be variously adopted, lies the impact which the teacher makes as a person on the pupil and the pupil's learning. By all the means at his or her command the teacher can make an impact on the pupil in terms of a concern for work to be done and concern for the pupil as a person. The impact made may veer strongly towards one or the other or be weak in both. The best result is when the teacher is perceived by the pupil to be strongly and simultaneously concerned for both. There is evidence that learning results and school achievement correlate highly with this.

The assumption is widely and justifiably made that a teacher has been trained to teach and maintains and improves his or her competence to do so. This is achieved mostly by voluntary effort — through the membership of academic and professional associations, private study, attending courses, dialogue with colleagues, and the constant experimentation and adjustment of teaching methods and techniques. Interventionism is generally repugnant whether from a senior colleague, the head of school, an adviser or member of HM Inspectorate. The price of this freedom, however, is volitional commitment, vigilance and adaptation.

Issues for further discussion

1. The relative importance of teaching methods and techniques to subject content in the pupil's learning.

2. Public examinations and teacher morale in secondary schools with intakes restricted to lower ability levels.

3. Alternative qualitative bases for the composition of teaching groups.

4. The interrelations between class size, teaching methods and techniques, and developments in pupils' oracy.

5. The observation of lessons by heads of school: practical and professional implications.

6. The involvement of pupils in an evaluation of teaching methods and techniques.

7. The determinants of a teacher's personal teaching style and the possibilities for changes in it by imposed and volitional means.

8. School-based training programmes to modify and improve teaching methods and techniques: how long should these be expected to take? What form might a programme take?

9. How should professionalism in teaching be expressed in relation to the least able pupils?

10. The entitlement curriculum — assessing the contribution of a particular subject to each of the suggested categories for analysing the secondary school curriculum.

Further reading

Bennett, N. and McNamara, D. (1979) *Focus on Teaching*. London. Longman.

Borich, G.D. and Madden, S.K. (1977) *Evaluating Classroom Instruction: A Sourcebook of Instruments*. Reading Mass., Addison-Wesley.

Paisey, A. (1975) *The Behavioural Strategy of Teachers in Britain and the United States*. Windsor, NFER.

CHAPTER 11
MANAGING MATERIALS AND EQUIPMENT
Case 11.1: Resources at the centre

Introduction

A large primary school is concerned about the management of its materials and equipment used for teaching and learning. It takes the view that such resources should be available to each teacher and accessible to each child. Trying to implement these ideas leads the school towards the establishment of a central resource area. All kinds of questions and practical difficulties are raised, however, with the attempt to make a central resource area workable in practice. It is discovered that too many unwarranted assumptions have been made. The use of the resource centre does not work out as intended. Some success is recorded but staff are not satisfied that they have been able to make it as useful for teaching purposes as they had envisaged. They are left in a state of uncertainty as to its value and the reasons for their failure to realize its full potential.

Narrative

The school was a large urban primary school, open plan in design with 12 teachers working in five teams of two or three teachers in each team, and a roll of 370 children from the ages of 5 to 12 years. History, geography and the science subjects were taught in an integrated way through topic work. Through this topic work the teachers created learning situations which allowed children to explore and develop a variety of skills and knowledge. It was essential that the resources for this work were organized in such a way as to enable easy access to information, materials and equipment for both teachers and children. Although rolls in the primary sector were falling generally, in this school the roll was actually rising, the school quickly becoming overcrowded. The design of the school incorporated a resource centre and library situated centrally within reach of all the team areas. However, as the number within the school grew it was soon realized that the resource centre had to be used as a home base area for 30 children in the junior team. When mobile classrooms were erected on the site, a reorganization of children and teaching areas enabled the school to release the resource centre as a home base area, thus making it free for development as a central learning area once again.

A teacher already holding a Scale III post as a team leader showed an interest in the resource centre and took over that responsibility in conjunction with the teacher who was responsible for coordinating topic work in the centre. This teacher also worked closely with all the staff to set up the centre. Several staff discussions took place over the need for the centre and the way it could serve the curriculum offered in the school. Many questions were posed:

— Why should the school have a centralized resource centre?

— What should be available in the resource centre?

— What should the staff hope to get from the resource centre?

— What should the children be able to get from the resource centre?

— How should the resources be organized and classified?

— What system should be used for retrieval and what system should be adopted for books and equipment?

— How accessible should the resources be to all age groups?

— Should the resource centre be manned and, if so, by whom?

Each of these questions was discussed and a strategy was designed to make the centre workable.

The staff agreed that a centralized resource centre would be more economical in space, money, books and equipment. A great variety of resources could be bought, or made and could be available to more children if they were organized in a centrally designed area, and not fragmented among the teams. It was decided that the non-fiction library should be the central feature of the resource area. Charts and pictures should be displayed in an open area along with pictures used by the children for their topic work and pictures for display and reference. Slides and filmstrips with viewers would be stored in the centre, available for constant use by the children. Work sheets and work cards would be assembled into topic kits used for reference or as the central resource of a team's topic work. Larger items of interest such as fossils, stones, stamps, coins and other objects of interest would be collected, catalogued and stored for use.

The staff expressed concern over the wastage and duplicate ordering of display paper, paints and exercise books. Each team was given an annual budget but, since much display material was used centrally, teams felt that it would be fairer and more economical if art materials and exercise books were removed from the team budget and drawn from the central resource.

The staff agreed that they could use the resource centre to get information, pictures and artefacts that could be used as the basic resources for team projects. These items would be of interest and for reference to promote further investigation on behalf of the children. Whilst the centre was being built up there would be few resources available. The staff agreed to help by donating charts, cards and kits they had collected from their work in the teams, thus enabling them to be used by other colleagues. It was hoped that each member of staff would be responsible for teaching the children in their care the necessary research skills which would allow them easy access to information and materials in the resource centre. The school library service and museum service would be used in conjunction with the centre.

It was agreed that the centre would be open to all children in the school. They should be taught how to use the centre and how to search for information in books and topic kits for their own interest. The resource centre should be a stimulating place to work, a quiet area where children could read or make notes. If children removed books they should be taught how to return them to the correct place.

It was also agreed that the equipment and books should be catalogued using both the Dewey classification and the county's own colour coding system to enable children at all stages of their learning to find information. Books and large topic kits would be stored on bookshelves for easy retrieval. The topic kits and picture kits would be stored in Lawco boxes. The large charts and pictures would be stored in drawers and chart racks. These had previously proved extremely difficult to store without damage and with easy access.

With staffing levels being so stringent and so many classrooms situated outside the main school building, the teachers felt that the centre could not be manned all the time by a member of the teaching staff. Ideas for timetabling were discussed but soon dismissed as a restriction of the freedom of access of children in the school. Finally, it was agreed to try a timetable involving parents who would work in the centre on a voluntary basis. The staff felt that children should be trusted to use the centre but needed help and guidance to avoid unnecessary waste of time. It was found, however, that many parents were at work and could not give their time freely to the school. For this reason the centre was manned by parents for three days each week only, and for the rest of the week by teaching staff.

While the system was being developed and set up the discussions continued. The area was released as a home base area. Suitable furniture was retrieved from the teams. After much discussion circular tables were used. Small display cabinets were placed in the library area. The chart rack was brought out of the quiet room into the team areas and the Lawco boxes filled with pictures for the children to use in their projects. The pictures were catalogued and put in Dewey order and colour coded. Larger boxes were assembled to take topic kits for reference only. These topic kits were made up of published material and work cards made up by the teachers. The slides and film strips were coded and placed in the area for use. A small quiet room nearby was set up as a listening area with a library of tapes and the tape recorders. Children were taught to use the machines and were allowed to use the room to listen to tapes. Teachers made tapes from the books.

After two months had elapsed the staff felt that the centre was not functioning as intended. The teacher responsible for the centre became increasingly concerned that it was underused and misused. The children had not been taught adequately how to use the centre, and, therefore, equipment and books were not returned to their correct places. One group of children tended to dominate its use mainly because they worked in the team area close by.

The staff discussed the problem and agreed that the centre was not very conducive as a learning environment. It was unfair for one teacher to be responsible for display work in the area. Staff agreed to share this responsibility and display children's work or other work of interest in the area. The staff promised to teach the children the procedures for removing and returning the books and equipment and to be responsible for making them function well. More display board was put up on the walls and the teacher in charge of the area prominently posted suggestions of activities that the children could do in it which would lead them into information searches. The area began to look attractive to the children and its use increased. Parents continued to supervise the area well on three days each week. Staff noted the improvement in the use of paint, display paper and exercise books since they had been stored centrally in the resource centre. There was much less wastage and it was easier to keep a check on the use of these materials. However, in general, the resource centre was underfunctioning and the staff had still not discovered why this was so.

As the team areas were all active and busy, staff found it difficult to give time to the resource centre. Increased pupil numbers led to the greater use of the resource area even for regular teaching activities. Displays were put up by staff, but the resource centre was still a cause of dissatisfaction to the teacher in charge and the concern of the other staff. With a further year's budget available to the school, there was a possibility that the resource centre could be developed and changed. However, many questions raised by the staff remained to be answered. The Scale III teacher in charge was also responsible for the leadership of a team of three teachers, but found difficulty in allocating his time between activities in the team, the resource centre and after-school clubs. Staff wondered if the resource centre should be run by someone who had no other responsibility. This question led to a whole staff discussion on posts of responsibility. During the discussion some teachers argued that either a smaller resource centre, or just a library area was needed. It was still an open question as to how to make it function efficiently.

Commentary

On purely financial grounds schools want to avoid waste and obtain the maximum use from materials and equipment. On educational grounds they may choose to give as much freedom of action as possible to their pupils. In this case, the school is mindful of the need to adapt to shrinking funds for expenditure on learning and teaching resources. It is not known if it sought to supplement its official income from its local education authority by private financial initiatives of its own. It certainly adopts a strong educational policy in wanting to maximize the discretion of each pupil in managing his or her own learning by being able to have access to a wide range of resources.

Therein lay the major difficulty, however, because it takes time even for young, adaptable pupils to change their own learning behaviour, to learn in fact how to take a new approach to study. It is a change for pupils from doing their schoolwork one way to doing it in another way. It is not only that new skills must be learned to use new systems and to have access to new materials. Pupils have to learn an accompanying new attitude to themselves, their teachers and to their own learning. They have to grow *into* a new management of learning system and then to grow up *with* it.

The case highlights the principle of efficiency. This is achieving a given outcome at least possible cost. Efficiency does not tell one whether the objective pursued is the right one. It is simply a measure of how well one is getting there. Normally in a school the advantages of access by all and intensive usage would need to be considered alongside the costs incurred. Materials and equipment may be used up or may wear out faster than the budget is capable of replacing them. The time factor involved is also pertinent. Pupils may take more time leaving their home base to go to a central resource centre than the net additional benefits to their work might warrant. Such travel as is involved might also provide opportunities for disturbing others by chance or by intent and, perhaps, a risk element — the greater possibility of accidents.

There was an 'opportunity cost' in having the resource centre. Scale points were allocated which could have been used for something else. Teachers' time given to the centre was at the expense of other duties. It may not be possible to use the space taken for the centre for other purposes simultaneously. An effect may also be that centralizing resources robs the respective team areas of a sense of personal possession and guardianship of resources which are peculiar to themselves, reflect their particular interests and help to provide a sense of distinctive identity.

Issues for further discussion

1. The educational arguments for and against a centralized resource centre.

2. The practical arguments for a teaching group having and managing its own teaching – learning resources.

3. The practical arguments for the centralized location and management of teaching – learning resources.

4. The management of expensive items of equipment in primary schools.

5. The use of parents as auxiliaries.

6. Alternative ways of manning a centralized resource centre.

7. Techniques for classifying, storing, retrieving and loaning equipment and returnable materials in a centralized resource centre.

8. Training the pupils in independent learning. What are the arguments for and against it? What attitudes and skills do they need?

9. Sources of funding and the supply and renewal of materials and equipment in addition to the formal budget.

10. Making use of industrial/commercial advice.

Further reading

Lavender, A.M. and Megarry, J. (1979) *Management of Resource Centres: Design and Layout*. Glasgow, Jordanhill College of Education.

OECD (1981) *Programme on Educational Building : School Furniture*. Paris, OECD.

Waters, D. (1982) *Primary School Projects*. London, Heinemann.

Case 11.2: Careers guidance package

Introduction

A secondary school decides to investigate the possibilities of introducing a careers guidance package. Enquiries lead to an investigation of the merits of a particular computer assisted system. As a sophisticated system, it requires a thorough evaluation of its potential. The staff examine the likely difficulties they would encounter in trying to introduce it into the school, by way of a feasibility study. Many problems are anticipated but overcome and the system is successfully installed.

Narrative

A secondary school decided to introduce a careers guidance package for the use of its pupils. It found that there had been several different testing and selection aids available for some years in the field of careers guidance, one of the better known and more widely used being an interest test — the APV Occupational Interests Guide, developed by the Department of Business Studies, Edinburgh University. In conjunction with the Educational Computer Centre, the London Borough of Havering had developed its Computer Assisted Learning (CAL) programme. Further research at both centres had subsequently produced the JIIG-CAL System (Job Ideas and Information Generator/Computer Aided Learning).

The system is intended to act as a resource for careers offices, careers teachers and others concerned with the careers education and guidance of young people. It is designed to help pupils of all levels and ability make realistic assessments about themselves, and it generates ideas and information about careers which may be suited to an individual pupil. They are able to make trial decisions or choices about their abilities, interests, preferences and attitudes and to receive a computer printout which records the consequences of these choices as a list of possible jobs. The system operates in the batch mode and is normally offered in the fourth year but may be repeated later to take account of maturing attitudes and changes of mind. For these reasons and because it is basically a tool of careers education, its administration is school-based. It is not a simple 'go/no go' system, but one which finely balances contrary and similar responses and computer weightings, and records the outcome with a graded degree of matching on a ten-point scale. The first essential, therefore, is that adequate preparation time and opportunity be given to pupils in a well-organized and structured programme. The second requirement is that staff who manage the whole programme must have completed a JIIG-CAL administrator's course lasting several days. A local education authority may insist upon the first requirement and the second is a condition of use imposed by the JIIG-CAL researchers.

The decisions to be made were, first, whether or not the JIIG-CAL System should be adopted and, secondly, how and when the system should be incorporated into the existing curriculum, especially in the light of increasing demands for staff and resources in all areas.

Apart from educational considerations, there were several external reasons why the school was under pressure to adopt the JIIG-CAL System. For one thing, the world of computers was rapidly developing and computer-assisted learning in education was becoming established. In addition, the JIIG-CAL System had been given 'trial runs' in several other schools in the same local education authority which was now anxious to make the system available to all schools able to meet the requirements of a satisfactory careers education programme and staff JIIG-CAL training. Several other local schools were also giving consideration to implementing the system which further increased the need for the decision to be made.

The responsibility for assessing the possibilities and submitting recommendations was given to the head of careers education and guidance. Feedback from several of the 'trial runs' schools had given rather inconclusive and conflicting reports, but two major areas of concern were apparent. First, difficulties had arisen because of teething troubles with the County Hall based mainline computer and the consequent chaos resulting from lost, damaged, misread or delayed pupils' guides which had increased the administrative problems within the schools. (It was customary for whole year groups to use the system.) Secondly, the system radically increased the awareness and interest shown by pupils and thus made greater demands upon the careers education staff in particular and most other staff in general.

Initially, primary source information was needed. This resulted in the head of careers education and guidance undertaking the administrator's course, which included going through the same process as the pupils. This enabled him to make a realistic assessment of the timescale necessary for the process to be completed — including the explanations, completion and return of the actual guides. It also presented an opportunity to assess the nature and number of careers education based topics to be covered in the preparatory course work. In the event, he discovered that the school's existing careers education programme adequately covered these topics, but might need retiming. Meanwhile, the initial problems in the mainline computer were being eradicated.

In the school, pressures were building up to adopt the system which would cost the school nothing. The local education authority would meet the cost of all fees and materials. But the major question still remained. The system had the reputation of making excessive demands to the extent that the costs in staffing and timetabling might very easily become disproportionate to the benefits which it could bestow. How successfully could a timetable cope with quite large numbers of pupils needing inputs to be made on an irregular basis over the timescale of the varying lengths of the spring term? Could sudden delays, retakes, extended feedback sessions, and extra demands on the staff time and expertise be incorporated into the curriculum? In principle, the school decided that it would like to adopt the system but wondered how it could be implemented effectively.

A social and personal education (SPE) course had been introduced for fourth and fifth-year pupils. This was timetabled for a whole morning session for each year and careers education had been incorporated into this integrated course from the start. During the intervening period, other SPE staff had become involved in careers education at various levels which meant that not only was a possible flexi-timetable available, but also sympathetic and proven staff. The SPE framework seemed the most logical area of the curriculum to cope with the introduction of the JIIG-CAL System. Some teachers, however, thought it should be included in the pastoral care programme. Each tutor group had a tutor period each week and there were other occasions when some input might be possible. On the face of it, the pastoral care system had much to commend it. The pupils and tutors knew each other well and were in daily contact. The tutors probably knew of other factors concerning the pupils, such as home and family backgrounds, which would enable them to give appropriate counsel.

But there were several factors against using the pastoral care system compared with using the SPE programme:

— every fourth and fifth-year group tutor would be required to undertake the full administrator's course which would be costly in staff commitment, whereas only two or three staff were involved in the SPE programme,

— tutors might change more frequently than SPE personnel,

— not all group tutors might wish to be involved with the JIIG-CAL system,

— the question of control, vital record-keeping and accountability might be acute if many staff were involved compared with two or three only,

— the time available for JIIG-CAL within the pastoral care system might not be as adequate or flexible as that within the SPE programme.

One further factor to be considered before the final decision was taken to adopt the JIIG-CAL System was the attitude of the staff. JIIG-CAL would be more effective if it met with staff support. Up to a point, all staff were involved in careers education. There was a great reservoir of knowledge and expertise within the staffroom which could rightly be tapped by any pupil. It was possible that any member of staff might be approached by pupils seeking help or advice as a result of the JIIG-CAL Programme. It would be unfortunate if staff had inadequate knowledge of JIIG-CAL, were indifferent or even resentful, instead of showing a positive attitude to it. Staff cooperation was vital, therefore, and to this end a half-day course was suggested when careers office staff could present the background, aims, approach and methodology of the JIIG-CAL system. Additionally, understanding the positive approach and value of the system might help the staff towards a more tolerant view of computer-assisted curricular innovations generally.

Consequently, the following recommendations were made and accepted by the senior management team:

— that the JIIG-CAL system be adopted as an additional tool of the careers education programme,

— that the system should be incorporated into the social and personal education timetable,

— that the head of careers and guidance should be responsible for the administration and control of the system,

— that two other members of the SPE staff should undertake the JIIG-CAL administrator's training course,

— that a half day in-service training course should be held for all staff before the introduction of the JIIG-CAL System,

— that the careers education input necessary before the pupils undertook the JIIG-CAL programme should take place in the autumn term of the fourth year. This would involve an increase in time from about 35 double periods for careers education to some 65 double periods during that term out of a total available of some 140 double periods; a major SPE timetable change to accommodate the course would be necessary,

— the pupils would use the JIIG-CAL system during the spring term of the fourth year and the timetable would be structured to allow flexibility.

The following programme was suggested, bearing in mind that there were approximately 150 pupils in the year, divided into five groups for SPE purposes and that the JIIG-CAL system required a ratio of 1 staff member to about 15 pupils.

First Week — three groups plus two careers plus one or two other SPE staff for the whole morning to cover the introduction to the system together with administration and completion of the JIIG-CAL Interest Guides (Sessions I and II).

Second Week — two groups plus two careers plus one other SPE staff for Sessions I and II.

Fifth Week — as week one — return of Interest Guides and the administration and completion of Part 2 — the personal factors questionnaire, etc. (Sessions III and IV).

Sixth Week — as second week — Sessions II and IV.

Ninth Week — as weeks one and five — the feedback of computer printouts with the list of suggested jobs areas — Session V.

Tenth Week — as weeks two and six — Session V.

Committing a whole morning would allow for the desired flexibility in the programme input and for coping with individual variations in response — such as slower pupils. The intervening weeks would allow for the current SPE programme to be maintained. To allow adequate time for the return of material from the computer and delays which might occur, a block timetabling system was used for the rearrangement of the SPE programme.

In the event, trial runs of the system, using fifth-year pupils, proved that the prior appraisal and careful implementation of the JIIG-CAL system were very necessary. Difficulties such as confusion over a pupil's identity, delays in returning material from the computer and the total loss of pupils' guides, were all experienced. On the credit side, however, the use of the system engendered a great deal of interest and enthusiasm among the pupils themselves, together with a more realistic and positive attitude and understanding about their futures.

Commentary

In recent decades many attempts have been made to devise pretested, developed and packaged materials for use in schools. Schools have been exhorted to adopt them, perhaps to adapt them, and to incorporate them with those of their own making. Essentially the school is regarded as the recipient and consumer of research and development work completed elsewhere. This centre — periphery model of dissemination and innovation — has attracted limited support. Either the syllabus material is too coarse for adaptation and use in the particular school, or it is too refined and specific for its purposes.

The computer is a powerful instrument capable of transforming many aspects of school life. It may become an indispensable tool for school management in general. It will certainly facilitate a revolution in the volume and speed of delivery of information. The curriculum, the pupil's means of study, and teaching methods will all be subject to new possibilities through the use of the cheap and easily handled computer. Centrally located resources and information may be instantly accessed by the computer in future.

The particular service which the computer offers in this case is careers guidance. In days of restricted job opportunities for school leavers schools are increasingly interested in providing any means possible to assist their pupils in finding employment. The school's public image may thereby be enriched. It is interesting to note that the school in this case was sensitive to the actions of its neighbouring schools with which it was in competition for pupils from the primary schools.

Finding time in a secondary school's already overcrowded timetable means removing an activity previously preferred. From the pupil's point of view it might be expected that careers guidance was a priority, making school relevant and useful, less insular and introspective, more open to the world in which they live.

From the point of view of other teachers, however, finding time for pupils to use new materials may mean the diminution of an existing subject so that space may be created. Thus, the introduction of new materials or equipment may have a political aspect to it. Their introduction may be resisted because particular interests are threatened. In this case, the understanding and support of the staff were sought through the dissemination of information and offer of explanations in a half-day in-service staff development session. This was doubly necessary because of the likely increased demand which pupils would make of staff generally over careers guidance, as a result of the introduction of the new system into the school.

Too often the introduction and use of new materials and equipment are precipitately managed. The timescale allocated is too short for a feasibility study and for adequate plans and preparations to be made. In this case the entire programme — from the initial idea that the school might have the system to the actual implementation of it at operational standards — seems to have been thought through and competently managed. It is an example of a new readiness of schools to adopt and adapt packages or systems which are highly sophisticated and of necessity must be designed, manufactured, and marketed from elsewhere.

Issues for further discussion

1. Means for finding out what ideas, developments and practices elsewhere might be of use to the school.

2. Mechanisms and procedures for initiating the adoption of an innovation in a secondary school. To what extent should the curriculum of a particular school be determined by the local education authority and/or the Department of Education and Science?

3. The head's role as stimulator of innovation.

4. What consideration should be given to the timescale of making a major innovation in a secondary school?

5. Judging the efficiency of an innovation — costs in time, money, administration and dislocation.

6. The extent of the responsibilities of the school for careers guidance.

7. Criteria for choosing a particular package or system.

8. The value of pilot tests.

9. The art of persuasion in management.

10. The development of computer usage in school:
    (a) for curricular purposes;
    (b) for administrative purposes.

Further reading

Department of Industry (1982) *A Programme for Advanced Information Technology*. The Report of the Alvey Committee. London, HMSO.

McCleary, L.E. and Thomson, S.D. (1979) 'The Future Principal'.

Chapter 5 in *The Senior High School Principalship*, Volume III. The Summary Report, Reston, Va., National Association of Secondary School Principals.

Smith, C. (1982) *Microcomputers in Education*. Chichester, Ellis Horwood.

CHAPTER 12
RELATIONS WITH PARENTS
Case 12.1: Conflicting expectations

Introduction

A pupil of infant age and an only child is admitted in turn to a succession of schools. Each one comes to be regarded as unsatisfactory by the parents, who entertain extremely high expectations of their child's actual and potential ability. Their anxiety becomes acute. It affects the way in which they relate to teaching staff and the lengths to which they are prepared to go to invoke the support of public authorities. Their *a priori* negative attitude towards schools prevails over the strenuous efforts made by teaching staff to accommodate their interests. The head of a junior school knowingly takes on the task of trying to satisfy the parents in admitting the child to her school, but her efforts also end in failure as the child himself shows signs of becoming the chief victim of his parents' behaviour.

Narrative

James Brown was a six-year-old only child, who had been withdrawn from three infant schools because his parents maintained that he was not being educated to the requirements of the 1944 Education Act. The family lived in a detached house on a new estate. Mr. Brown was a professional man and Mrs. Brown was a housewife. The parents were convinced that their child was highly gifted and as such should be given 'special' conditions to enable him to develop. The parents were highly articulate and were prepared to devote all their energies to 'fighting' for the rights of their child. The attitude of the parents is highlighted in the following extract, taken from a letter sent by the parents to the head of a junior school, when James was six years old.

> James was born in January, 1976. When he was two and a half years old he was sent to a playgroup. His work was superb and the playgroup leader, an extremely intelligent woman, was so impressed with him that she wanted to keep in touch and to follow him through life as she felt that he had great potential . . . . It is the specialised teaching that he will need that we wish to discuss with you.

The head of the junior school had been approached by the local education authority to accept him in her school. She responded willingly but with unexpected consequences.

The school was set in an urban environment. It drew its pupils from a mixed social catchment area. Housing was mainly private and the majority of children came from homes where parental expectations were high. The school enjoyed an excellent reputation for being both caring and able to ensure that children achieved their academic potential. The school was open-plan in design but its philosophy and organization reflected a belief in drawing upon both traditional and modern techniques.

The school was organized in four year groups, with a team coordinator responsible for the work of the year and for continuity between years. The children were organized both individually and in groups, the teachers ensuring that the curriculum matched the individual needs of the child. Much effort was made by the staff in developing positive home-school relationships and parents were encouraged to play a full part in the life of the school. The working atmosphere of the school was quiet, orderly and relaxed. The school day was extended by the staff to include a wide variety of clubs and out-of-school activities. A local education authority official who visited the head of the junior school to outline the problem told the head that the case would require a firm but tactful approach. The official said that James' parents were convinced that their child was a genius and that local schools were not prepared to help the child by providing a suitable curriculum. He informed the head that the parents were extremely difficult to interview and that they were likely to criticize the school and the staff. The parents had already criticized the local education authority staff and the staff of James' previous schools. Since James was not yet seven he would have to be enrolled at an infant school for one term before being of an age to transfer to junior school.

The official suggested that the head should discuss the case with relevant members of staff. After these consultations the head agreed to accept James and to try to gain the confidence and respect of the parents. The head suggested that it would be in the boy's interests if he were enrolled in the junior school at once and was not expected to go to yet another infant school. The head was assured by the local education authority that she would be given all possible support. The head also took the precaution of briefing the school's governors concerning the delicacy of the case.

On further reflection the head informed the local education authority that she was concerned about the possible bad effect upon the school that accepting James would have. She had been given information about the Browns which supported the view that they were eccentric in their views and attitudes. Despite the knowledge that troubled waters might lie ahead the head agreed to interview the parents with a view to accepting James in the school.

The parents presented themselves as being extremely tense and anxious. The mother was close to tears and was extremely outspoken in her adverse views of the education service in general and local schools in particular. She said that she wished to see those who had been involved with her son in court because they had 'done James down because they were frightened that he was so bright'.

The head took a firm but concerned approach saying that she was not prepared to hear professional colleagues being criticized but that she would do all in her power to ensure that James would feel happy and secure in her school. The head said that it would not be necessary for James to be placed in an infant school for one term but that he should be allowed to come straight into a junior school. (This might well have been a mistake for the parents were not prepared for James to rejoin his correct age group in the following September.)

The head told the parents that they must allow James to settle and that she would meet them again on parents' evening. The head wrote to the family confirming that she was looking forward to admitting James. She also informed them that she had briefed the child's teacher and the chairman of governors concerning the general nature of James' needs. The head also wrote to the local education authority:

> . . . our most difficult task will be to make the parents have confidence in the school and our ability to provide for James' needs. After an initial honeymoon period I anticipate a difficult period which will require great patience and tact.

A month later the head wrote to the local education authority. The following extract is taken from this letter.

> James has settled down well at school. He has developed positive relationships with both his teachers and peers. However, as he is still of top infant age he has found our curriculum and expectations demanding. Mrs. Pring, his teacher, has been giving him every possible help to enable him to cope with the extra work involved in joining a class of first year juniors, especially now that it is late in the school year.
>
> James has been given the Schonell Word Recognition Test which gave him a Reading Age of 8.3 years. He has also been given the NFER Picture Test A, with the result that he achieved a standardised score of 126.

During parents' evening, Mrs. Pring and the head talked with James' parents. The following is a report of the head's interview which helps to illustrate that the parents were very disturbed about their child and that a definite mismatch existed between the school's and the parents' assessment of James. The parents believed that he was a genius who had been underfunctioning because of the attitudes of teachers and officers of the education service.

The parents were very anxious and Mrs. Brown opened the conversation by stating that she was appalled to think that her child was having to learn his two-times table. If she had realised that schools still taught tables then she would have taught them to her son before he was five.

When the word 'ability' was mentioned, the head considered that it was appropriate to give, as sensitively as possible, her considered assessment of the child's ability. This proved a great mistake for it made Mrs. Brown extremely upset. The head said that James was proving a 'bright' little boy but not a 'genius'. At this Mrs. Brown became close to tears and told the head that she was like the rest, trying to 'do James down', and was like the rest of the teachers, frightened by the prospect of having to deal with a highly gifted child.

By far the most disturbing aspect of the conversation was that both parents referred to remarks that the head had made at previous interviews and then used them out of context. It appeared that they used and internalized remarks to suit their own arguments. Mrs. Brown said that she had often discovered that previous teachers had been liars. They admitted that they were social isolates in the community and if they were not happy with James' progress then they would move away from the area. Without doubt it was clear to the head that the parents had excessive and unrealistic aspirations. The head's fear was that James would show signs of stress because he was unable to 'perform' to the satisfaction of the parents.

The head was anxious to ensure that all possible was being done but she felt that the parents were not going to allow James to settle.

The head continued to ensure that all agencies were briefed concerning the development of the case.

The parents were invited to attend an evening at school for the parents of children transferring from the infants school the following term, but they said that they could not come. They had hinted to the class teacher that they expected James to continue with the present class to which he had been temporarily attached and not to join the new intake from the infants school which he normally would have been with and which was his correct age group.

During the summer holidays the head received a telephone call from a local councillor who reported that the Browns were saying that both James' teacher and the head were not providing for his educational needs. The councillor said that James was a sad child who was not allowed to play with other children and that he was showing signs of stress. He had been taken for assessment to an independent psychologist. The councillor said that he intended to see the family to say that he thought that their allegations were unfair.

The head wrote to the local education authority informing them of developments:

> . . . I am of the opinion that the state educational system will never satisfy this family. I am sure that they will press for James to be placed in an independent school . . . Although I am worried because of the adverse effect that this case may be having upon my school's reputation, I am doubly worried for James. He has shown himself to be a likeable boy who would develop quite normally if not subjected to such unreasonable parental stress.

Three days before the beginning of the autumn term the head received a letter from Mr. Brown stating that although he appreciated her kindness, he would not be allowing James to return to the school. Mr. Brown said that an independent psychologist had tested James and had recommended that the child should be placed in a small class where his individual needs could be helped. Mr. Brown also listed several complaints which he had against James' teacher — 'James said that he only read eight times to his teacher during the term . . . James only found part of his work interesting . . . Wrong answers were not followed up.'

Thus the child was withdrawn from the school but was then kept at home. The local press became involved and a legal case developed. The local education authority took the parents to court for failing to send their child to school. The parents pleaded guilty but pleaded mitigating circumstances and were given a complete discharge. James was given tuition at home by his parents under the guidance of a senior adviser of the local education authority. He was subsequently taken to several other schools with the parents to see if they liked them. An HMI visited the junior school James had left to investigate the case. James was finally enrolled in another junior school but after one term he was again removed by his parents.

Commentary

This case highlights the gulf which can exist between the interests of parents and the interests of professional educators. In essence, the objectives of schooling are at stake. There is a conflict between personal objectives and the exercise of individual rights on the one hand, and the claims of the community and the corporate nature of the school on the other.

Parents have a legal responsibility to ensure that their child receives an education. The local education authority has a legal responsibility to provide an education suited to the child's age, ability and aptitude. The Education Age of 1980 encourages the exercise of the right of parents to select a school in the maintained sector in which the education of their child may proceed to their satisfaction.

The explicit and insistent demands made on the school are greater today than ever before. They may be expressed by individual parents who are informed of their rights and exploit them to the full. In contrast, they may be expressed by way of orchestrated pressures brought to bear by many parents acting in association or through public representatives. Parents and their children might have pronounced personal objectives which they expect the school to serve. These objectives may be unreasonably excessive but they may equally be too superficial and bordering on the non-existent. They can certainly vary to the consternation of the head of school. It is not unknown for a head to receive two different sets of parents within the same morning, one to complain that their child is receiving insufficient academic training, the other to complain of insufficient social education.

Nevertheless, it is the duty of the school to reconcile the multitude of varying and often contradictory personal objectives represented by a large body of pupils. Many pupils have to share inevitably limited resources. All the pupils in a school cannot have the best teacher. All the pupils in a class or teaching group cannot have the undivided attention of the teacher. A pupil or parent who preoccupies the teacher and takes up disproportionate attention and time, distracts the head and staff from other individuals in their care.

Heads of school and teaching staff have become used to accepting heterogeneous intakes of children in infant, junior and primary schools. They pride themselves on being able to cope with children of a wide range of ability and family backgrounds. They depend, however, on the sympathetic and active support of parents, though not without differences of opinion.

Thus, the combination of circumstances which best guarantees the success of a child at school is raised by this case. It is customary to argue that a warm and collaborative relationship between parent and teacher is the best. Friction between the two is held to be detrimental to the pupil. Harmony, however, is inauthentic if based on the required submission of either the teacher to the parent or the parent to the teacher. It is probably more common for parents to feel intimidated by teachers and officials in education than the reverse, but the number of parents who are articulate and confident in their relationships with teachers has grown. A small minority of parents is unreasonably demanding, if not actually aggressive towards teaching staff. It is the latter who lead heads of school into protectionist policies and practices. Such heads limit and regulate the access of parents to teachers and the school premises. Parents play little or no part in the education of their own or other children during the school day as auxiliary helpers.

Clearly, the objectives of a school are primarily to serve the interests of its pupils. The objectives of a school are frequently expressed in words which encourage parents to expect that the educational experience and curricular programme provided will indeed vary with the individual child. For example, a school itself may publicly declare that

by the time the child leaves this school we hope that he or she

(a) will have achieved literacy and numeracy at least to the level of basic competence

(b) will have become a responsible member of the school and local community

(c) will have been motivated to accomplish the best possible performance in all spheres of school life

. . . . we hope to facilitate these results by providing a secure learning environment and by caring for the academic, physical, emotional and social needs of the individual child.

Parents naturally translate such statements to mean that the practical and visible arrangements for their child in the school relate to his or her individual needs and are known to be meeting them. Add to this the fact that some local education authorities afford special help to primary schools which have difficult children. An itinerant or part-time person is employed to relieve the regular teacher of a particularly disruptive or disaffected pupil. The child is given varying amounts of undivided attention by this person perhaps several times a week. Similarly, a handicapped child may be admitted to the regular school. In such a case, special attention is given and extra provisions are made, in deference to the individual's needs. Hence, there is an increasing demand that children who are potentially or actually high achievers — the gifted child — should also receive consideration commensurate with their needs.

Issues for further discussion

1. The criteria parents might use to judge the effectiveness of a school before sending their child to it.

2. The relation between a school's published objectives and its actual performance.

3. The evidence parents might use to judge the school's performance in relation to their own child after entry.

4. What should the individual teacher's policy and performance be in relation to the school's objectives?

5. The individualized curriculum — its feasibility and desirability. What share of resources should an exceptional pupil have?

6. The skills required for consultation, negotiation and counselling with parents.

7. Coping with unscheduled encounters. What skills are needed?

8. Involving parents actively in the school in the education process of their own and other children.

9. The extent of a school's duty to stand up to parents in the perceived interests of the child.

10. Using adverse events to good advantage in the management of the school.

Further reading

Clarke, G. (1983) *Guidelines for the Recognition of Gifted Pupils*. London, Longman.

Congdon, P.J. (1978) *Spot the Gifted Child: A Guide for Parents and Teachers*. Solihull, Gifted Children's Information Centre.

Wilby, P. (1980) *Parents' Rights*. London, Franklin Watts.

Case 12.2: The transforming event

Introduction

An independent girls' boarding school has been established for 100 years. For the last 25 years the school has been under the same head — a woman with a strong personality who remained aloof from the staff and exercised an autocratic style of headship. A new head is appointed. Between being appointed and taking up her appointment she spends an extended period of time in visiting other schools and undertaking some managerial training. On taking over as head she assumes responsibilities for both years of the sixth form.

Within the first year of her appointment there are complaints from parents about deficient pastoral and academic care as well as signs of restiveness among several members of the teaching staff. The deputy head is well established in the school. She is an experienced teacher with qualifications in educational management. As a team the head and deputy head relate seemingly disparate events to one another and devise a solution which proves very effective. The results which accrue from the innovation introduced prove to be far-reaching.

Narrative

An independent secondary school of 300 girls, whose ages ranged from 10 to 18 years, had a long established record for academic achievement. Added to this it had a reputation for high standards in both music and art, both of which were encouraged throughout the school. Entry to the school was by the Common Entrance Examination, a national examination taken at ages 11, 12, or 13 years. The largest entry to the school occurred at 11, with a smaller entry at 12 and the occasional entry at 13.

Recently there had been a considerable increase in the entry to the sixth form. This was probably due to the academic reputation which had been built up by the range, variety and success of A level courses, an extensive extra-curricular programme, and the decline in employment opportunities at 16. The structure of the school had been simple, tending towards the authoritarian. Being a small school there were only limited opportunities for staff career progression. Two separate — and at the time seemingly unrelated — events, however, led to a significant change in the organizational structure within the school.

The first event was the request for a meeting by two sets of parents, whose daughters were respectively members of the first-year sixth form and the second-year sixth form. These meetings revealed parents' concern that there was a lack of information about their daughters' work. They also felt that their work was not properly monitored during term time, and they were concerned about the lack of parent/teacher contact. The head of school acted as form tutor to the sixth form. The parents said that although they understood the head's wish to know her sixth-form girls better by being their form tutor they were not convinced that it worked well in practice. The head was often busy or away at meetings and so was frequently unavailable for consultation by sixth-form pupils. The parents, too, were apprehensive at contacting her for personal consultation about their daughters because of her position as head and because her commitments often resulted in cancelled or postponed appointments.

It was said by the parents of the first-year sixth-form pupil that girls in that year in particular felt isolated in the school, having so recently moved up from the fifth form where a formal structure provided nightly supervision of study and a family atmosphere under a form mistress who was a subject teacher well known to the girls and who had worked with them for several years.

At the meeting with the parents of the second-year sixth form pupil, they were keen to seek help and advice on careers for their daughter but a large part of the conversation turned to the same topics as had been raised by the other parents. They explained that their daughter's reports at the end of the summer term had come as a shock both to them and to their daughter. The girl, who was undoubtedly intelligent and had attained eight grade As and two grade Bs at O level, was criticized by most of her A level teachers for lack of planning and for constantly being late with scheduled work. The staff in their reports had also appeared pessimistic about her A level chances. These parents too were concerned about the monitoring of sixth-form work and felt that there was no parent/staff contact as there had been lower down the school.

Both these meetings with the parents highlighted a problem of communication. Since the problem was occurring at a vital stage of the girls' education, it was important to find a solution to it as soon as possible.

The other event occurred shortly after the meeting with these parents. At an informal discussion amongst the staff it was revealed that there was a general dissatisfaction with the lack of career structure and challenge for the staff. One of the most successful A level teachers was looking for another job. She said that she was reluctant to leave but although she was head of department, the fact that her department consisted of only one other full-time member of staff, plus one part-time member, was not providing sufficient challenge. She spoke at length about how much she enjoyed teaching at the school and how much she would miss both the girls and the friendly atmosphere created by her colleages. She could see no career progression or professional challenge, however, within such a small organization and felt that she had no alternative but to leave.

These two problems at the time seemed unrelated — the first, a lack of communication with pupils and parents, the second, the lack of job satisfaction and career progression for staff within a small organization. Numerous consultations and discussions followed the emergence of these problems, and eventually it was decided that a change of structure and procedure within the organization could solve both problems satisfactorily.

Following discussions between the head and deputy head the latter's ideas were presented to the heads of departments. Some amendments were suggested but an agreed scheme was then placed before all the A level subject teachers. The objectives of the scheme and the procedures to be adopted were fully explained and discussed. It was decided that eight members of staff who taught A level subjects should become tutors, each being responsible for monitoring the work of a group of six sixth-form pupils. They would also provide pastoral care and advice to their tutorial group. They would be the link between the pupils and the head, the pupils and other staff, and the pupils, the school and their parents.

The eight tutors were chosen, some because of their considerable teaching experience, some because they were known to be excellent teachers, and some because they were generally popular with the girls. They were interviewed by the head and given the opportunity to decline if they wished: none refused. To aid the communication procedure it was decided that a special report form would be devised and made available; it would be filled in by each pupil's subject teacher twice per term. This form required an assessment grade A to E plus space for an honest and, if necessary, lengthy comment. The form would be returned to each girl's tutor and would be confidential between subject staff and tutors. However, it was hoped that through these reports a tutor would be able to gain an accurate picture of each pupil's progress.

Once the tutors had been appointed and were fully conversant with their new roles, the scheme was explained fully to the sixth-form pupils. They were encouraged to ask questions and were given 48 hours in which they could indicate to the head those nominated tutors they would prefer not to have as tutor. It was explained to them that because fairly close relationships between tutor and tutees were envisaged, it was important to avoid personality clashes between staff and pupils. Their responsibility in facing this problem at the outset was emphasized and explained.

In the event only seven girls expressed reservations or made specific requests in the time given. Four of them named various staff with whom they felt they would not be able to establish a close relationship. Two did not wish to have any of their particular A level teachers as tutors, and one requested not to be the tutee of the one male member of the group of tutors. Following this, a letter was sent to all the parents explaining the new procedure and its origins, and giving the tutor's name and telephone number and a time when their daughter's tutor would be available for discussions. Rooms were allocated to each tutor and they were asked to set up their own meeting arrangements with their tutees. Most preferred general discussion group meetings once a week over coffee or tea with separate access arranged for individual talks.

This relatively simple change to the procedures within the school resulted in a greatly improved communication system at the top of the school. There was much improved staff/pupil relationships at a vital stage of the girls' education, and improved staff morale — the latter undoubtedly because the staff could all see a possible career progression coupled with widened scope within the new school structure.

The response to the change in procedure was fairly dramatic. A great flow of information in all directions resulted. Staff began readily to discuss problems with colleagues and the girls themselves. They expressed openly how much happier and more secure they felt. All staff mentioned that problems did not seem as insurmountable as they once were. The staff-pupil relationship within A level work became noticeably friendlier and, according to staff, produced much livelier and more productive A level lessons.

The parents' response too was favourable and enthusiastic. Some fears expressed by staff when the idea had first been floated proved groundless. Parents did not telephone tutors indiscriminately and without good reason. The majority who voted to provide their home telephone numbers to enable parents to have even greater access to them felt it had been worthwhile.

Commentary

The new head wanted to be seen to be making a substantial and constructive contribution to the productive work of the school. Like many heads who are newly appointed to headship she probably felt the need to demonstrate her capacity as a teacher to other members of the teaching staff. It was evidently neither a prudent nor a practicable choice to make. As with many heads who undertake to teach regular classes so this head found that the duties of headship constantly interrupted teaching duties or prevented her giving adequate attention to them.

She evidently favoured and wanted to implement a change of regime from that established by her predecessor, who had been a charismatic leader who ruled by directives and personalized methods. Decisions had been taken by the head alone. Communication had been minimal and usually restricted to top down. As the school had grown, it had been found necessary to have senior staff positions. Some of the long-established staff had been replaced by younger, highly qualified and motivated staff. Yet under the previous elderly head, the old ways had lived on. There had been very little contact between head and staff. Staff had been particularly frustrated because they were never told if parents had complained or even if or when they wished to discuss a pupil's progress. All such communication was undertaken solely by the head with no recourse to subject staff. Occasionally, requests for information about a certain pupil were sent by letter from the head. Replies were also expected to be by letter and returned to the head via her secretary.

The new head would have had no difficulty in deciding that a new managerial strategy was needed with herself and a new style of leadership as the centrepiece of it but characterized by more consultation and freer communication among both staff and parents. The invitation to the latter to take advantage of more open access to the school brought its perils but also its rewards.

Parents made use of the offer to express their concerns and staff felt less inhibited in making known their own reservations. Clearly the developments which actually flowed from the fortuitous combination of events had not been part of the prior planning and preparations of the new head and the deputy head in their attempts to introduce a new regime. Yet the attitudes and expectations were pointing in the direction of the changes they wanted to see. When the opportunities came they were quick to use them to advantage. Having decided on a change of objectives it is sometimes necessary to wait on events for the means to achieve them.

Parental complaints became a catalyst for the development of the more participative organization which the head sought. The will was present and the ground had been prepared. It remained to have the imagination to see an opportunity in an ordinary event and the organizational ability and thrust to act quickly. Because of the special importance of parents' attitudes in an independent school, this case has many elements in common with commercial or industrial organizations which need to be sensitive to market conditions and able to respond to market changes with speed and confidence. Schools concerned about providing the best possible educational service in both the maintained and independent sectors, however, would take such action.

Issues for further discussion

1. The length of tenure of headship.

2. The approachability and accessibility of the head of school to pupils, parents and staff.

3. The value, form and content of written reports to parents.

4. The extent of direct access of parents to teachers.

5. Are guidelines governing the relations between head and deputy head feasible? When should a pupil choose his/her teacher? How far is choice of teacher a *de facto* situation in schools?

6. Pragmatism in school management — its benefits and limitations.

7. How can the effectiveness of A level teaching be increased?

8. Alternative ways of providing pastoral care and study guidance for pupils after the age of 16.

9. The respective merits of the open (organismic) and closed (mechanistic) structures in school management.

10. The teaching head: is this an anachronism?

Further reading

Davies, E. (1982) Parental Involvement in School Policy-Making. *School Organization* 2, 4, 341–345.

Hughes, M.G. (1974) *Secondary School Administration.* Oxford, Pergamon.

Vroom, V.H. and Deci, E.L. (editors) (1972) *Management and Motivation.* Harmondsworth, Penguin.

CHAPTER 13
FINANCIAL MANAGEMENT
Case 13.1: Bidding for viability

Introduction

A middle school takes a bold and uncompromising position in the face of constraints imposed by the reductions of public expenditure in education and the decline in its pupil rolls. In order to maintain its educational standards and to introduce new facilities, equipment and materials, the school decides to finance itself. This at first is no more than an effort to raise money for particular items. As time passes, however, and the shortfall between capitation grants and the level of funding the school requires becomes more serious, a conscious effort is made to close the gap by self-funding activities.

The policy adopted proves successful. The volume of income from this source increases to the point when it represents just under 40 per cent of the school's entire budget. With the money a number of projects are completed to modernize the curriculum and provide the best possible facilities. The results are not achieved without some controversy but learning from its experience the school adroitly adjusts its policy as it proceeds along the path to partial financial self-sufficiency.

Narrative

An 8 to 12 middle school had outstanding facilities for a school of its type. Each of the four year groups had its own classrooms and shared the resource areas, including fiction and non-fiction libraries, and quiet rooms for individual study and tuition. Special accommodation included a fully equipped science laboratory, heavy and light craft room, art and pottery room, music and computer studies room, medical room and two smaller areas. One of these catered for pupils with learning difficulties, the other for able pupils, especially in mathematics and science. The school roll had dropped from 730 to 377 in five years, these figures respectively representing the largest and smallest rolls the school had had in its entire existence.

The school was built around a central administrative block with two halls and a stage. One of these was fully equipped for educational and olympic gymnastics, the other for drama and stage productions and had its own specialized lighting equipment. It was used throughout the week as an adult education evening centre, and by many local community organizations. On the school campus were facilities for rugby, cricket, hockey, football and athletics (including jumping and throwing areas). A hard playing surface was provided for tennis, netball and basketball courts.

The school was situated on the edge of a council estate, surrounded by heathland. Traditionally pupils came from four local first schools. One was in the village itself and three were in neighbouring communities. The proportion of parents who were owner occupiers to those who were council tenants was approximately 70:30 and had changed very little during a period of ten years although the population had become more mobile. The parents were keen to support the school and participate actively in its organization.

The interest and support of parents had been a major influence in the development of the school's financial policy. Although the school always used its initiative in raising funds, during the early seventies this only supplemented local authority provision. In the early eighties the budget had become a single entity with inputs from the local education authority, parents and the school. This tripartite conception of the school's finances had developed as a direct consequence of the effects of inflation, successive governments' public expenditure policies and the efforts of the school to respond to the changing climate and circumstances.

When the school had 443 pupils on roll, with a capitation allowance of £2177 the parents' association had not been formed but the school fund had a turnover of £1,666 p.a. with working capital at the end of the year standing at £273 and a sum of £100 in a bank deposit account. This fund was used for coordinating educational visits and the working balance was raised through jumble sales. The parents' association on being formed immediately embarked upon fund-raising activities. The school fund turnover rose to £5267 with £600 working capital and £100 in the bank deposit account. In addition, all parents were expected to make a 'compulsory' yearly contribution to the school fund of £1 per family.

From this beginning the following elements subsequently influenced the financial policy of the school: changes in the school population; school capitation allowance from the local education authority; donations from the parents' association; and contributions by individual families to the school fund.

The changing balance between official funds (i.e. capitation) and unofficial funds (other sources) reflected the changes of attitude and circumstances which took place and showed how the concept of an overall budget was developing. A fifth increasingly important element was the turnover of the school fund. This became capable of generating its own capital as a result of short or longer term investments as well as the more traditional fund-raising activities. Table 1 provides the details of this entire development.

The capitation allowance for the school rose from £6.54 in 1973 to £17.74 per pupil in 1983. Although the trend was upwards this increase did not match the rate of inflation. Based on 1973 figures, the shortfall in the allowance when the school reached its maximum size of 730 was approximately £4000. Although the capitation allowance per pupil since 1979 kept reasonable pace with inflation this loss was never recovered. In addition, items of expenditure previously not included were slowly transferred by the local education authority into the school allowance, e.g. television licences, equipment hire and maintenance agreements, telephone charges and selective teachers' travel expenses.

In the face of such financial constraints the school considered either reducing the resources available for teaching/or modifying its curriculum. The alternative was to devise and launch a new financial policy in which unofficial or non-capitation funding came to play a larger part in the school's budget to compensate for the deficiencies.

The well-established parents' association originally raised money to give the school an independent source of income to manage its daily business. As the association became more active, however, it was able to purchase additional items of equipment not expected to be provided by the local authority, e.g. television sets, football and netball kits for the school teams and later a minibus. In principle and practice the association provided a reference point for debate as the financial realities became significantly more difficult.

A resource centre was needed for the school. This was something the local education authority would not have funded either in the past or in the more recent financial climate. The centre was therefore dependent on a school-based initiative. Although in the initial stages the planned expenditure was intended to be modest, it soon became apparent that a major investment in terms of finance and additional equipment would be required. This resulted in the establishment of a three-way partnership between the school, the parents and the local education authority. The basic provision of furnishings and equipment came from the school budget. Resource-based learning themes were financed by the parents. Short and long-term loans of equipment in addition to individualized learning

	Year	1972	1973	1974	1975	1976	1977	1978	1979	1980	1981	1982	1983
School fund	Special project funds					1 750					1 000	1 000	2 000
	Deposit account at end of financial year	376	700	723	600	730	719	1 243	1 516	1 450	2 010	2 118	2 500
	Annual turnover: income/expenditure	1 666	5 267	4 475	5 354	6 965	6 659	10 331	14 534	20 068	17 128	22 148	29 500
	Family donations	–	186	168	168	168	184	180	185	400	577	700	
Parents Association (year ends in September)	Donations to school for educational projects	–	300	400	550	800	900	1 000	1 200	1 300	1 400	1 700	2 000
	Deposit account	–	100	400	400	400	200	200	100	600	1 000	1 200	–
	Funds raised per year	–	635	925	2 546	1 939	1 807	1 950	1 900	2 100	2 829	3 386	–
	Percentage of unofficial funds to total budget	–	11	12.4	13.4	14.5	15.2	15.9	16.5	16.8	27.3	31.6	39.8
	Total budget	2 177	4 390	4 593	5 345	6 660	7 008	7 339	8 380	8 808	10 254	10 355	11 796
	Unofficial funds (from parents, school fund, special events)	–	486	568	718	968	1 068	1 184	1 380	1 485	2 800	3 277	4 700
	School capitation allowance	2 177	3 904	4 025	4 627	5 692	5 940	6 171	7 000	7 319	7 454	7 078	7 096
	Number on roll	443	597	636	665	675	715	730	572	519	513	409	377

Table 1   Financial trends 1973-1983 for an 8-12 middle school

material from a variety of county projects were provided by the local education authority. In total this represented an investment of approximately £4000. Each of the partners alone could not have supported the venture, but working together the project's first phase was completed within one year. Further expenditure was planned as the curriculum developed. This style of financial management was further refined during subsequent years.

From 1973 to 1979 parents were expected to contribute a 'compulsory' sum of £1 per family each year to the school fund. This was, not surprisingly, resisted by some parents and was a matter of contention within the teaching staff. In 1980 the policy was changed. Parents were given a detailed account of how the school fund was spent and what plans there were for the coming term or year. They were asked to make a donation to the school fund according to their own personal circumstances. The effectiveness of this policy is clearly demonstrated in Figure 11.

Both the parents' association and the school fund have had their own deposit accounts. During a year they have varied considerably from £1,000 to sometimes £15,000. The time from the initiation of a project to its completion and the presentation of accounts have taken between 3 and 12 months. The advice of an accountant and a good working relationship with the local bank manager have enabled these accounts to generate further capital. It has been found that care must be taken not to exceed the limits set for the levy of corporation tax or value added tax. By having these funds always available the school has taken maximum advantage of good commercial offers which can be negotiated with suppliers.

The development of the concept of an overall budget involving the use of official and unofficial funds has enabled the staff to maximize financial resources to the benefit of the school — for example the establishment of a new computer studies centre.

By 1983 a capitation allowance of about £11,500 would have been needed to place the school in the comparable financial position it enjoyed in 1973. The unofficial funding in rising to occupy almost 40 per cent of the overall budget, however, has done much to compensate for the shortfall.

Commentary

A school is accountable for providing an education for its pupils which is of use to them at present and also in the future.

Schools variously claim to be accountable to pupils, parents, governors, the local education authority and other schools. The work that they must do

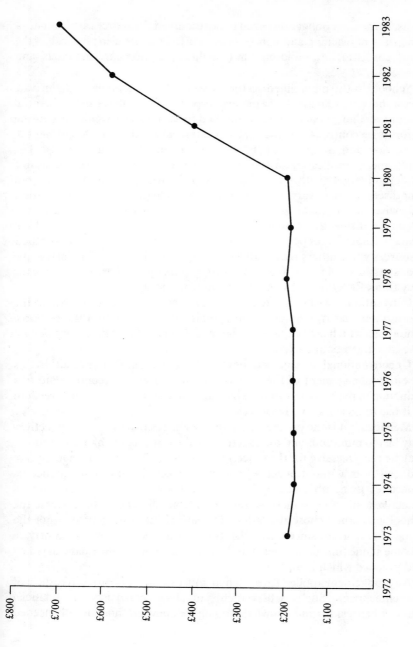

Figure 11 Individual family donations to school fund

to discharge their obligations need to be resourced. Resources are human — consisting of teaching and non-teaching staff. They are also physical — the plant consisting of buildings and facilities, equipment, materials and finance.

Schools in the maintained sector, compared with schools in the private sector, have customarily had a passive responsibility with regard to financial resources. The global resources allocated to a school are decided according to formulae controlled by the local education authority, the Department of Education and Science, and by the agreement of national bodies. The deployment, application, disbursement and use of allocated resources to a school fall largely within the discretion of the head, though the degree of that discretion may vary considerably between local education authorities. Likewise the mechanisms by which the head distributes and uses the resources inside the school varies widely between schools. Some local education authorities permit heads to exercise powers of virement over their resources while others reduce those powers to a minimum. Similarly some heads may accord freedom to staff to appropriate their share of resources as they think fit. Others operate direct control systems.

Conventional wisdom and practice in school management makes the assumption that it is necessary to operate effectively within the resource limitations which are imposed on the school. These limitations vary but are essential given boundaries.

Unconventional management never takes a boundary for granted. In this case the management of the school is not prepared to accommodate to a reduction in the school's resource base and chooses to exercise such freedom as it has to raise its own resources.

Management is the process of relating resources to objectives. Objectives may be too numerous and too exacting for the resources to hand. Resources may be too excessive for the objectives adopted. Thus, when resources are reduced from without, a school has two choices. It may either reduce its objectives in number and/or level of exactitude, or it may maintain its objectives and seek to increase resources from elsewhere. In this case the school concerned chose the latter. The surprising feature of it is not the principle involved, since most schools have embarked on obtaining private income at one time or another, but the scale and scope of the financial policy and practice which it undertook.

Any judgement applied to this school must surely be positive in respect of its enterprise. Such achievement involves expertise in financial management, skills and knowledge going well beyond those usually needed by heads of maintained schools. In the event of greater financial autonomy in schools, a stronger emphasis on financial management would need to be incorporated in training programmes for heads. Many people would deplore such developments, however. Self-financing would be seen by them as a distraction from the essential work of educating and an undesirable preoccupation for the head. Many schools have found, however, that the processes, procedures and activities involved can be used as a realistic educational experience for their pupils.

Issues for further discussion

1 — 6. The implications of a substantial level of self-financing in a school in the maintained sector in respect of
— the pupils,
— the parents,
— the head and teaching staff,
— the curriculum,
— the governors,
— the local education authority,
— the government.

7. The current state of accounting expertise and procedures in schools.

8. A school's information bank — what it should consist of; who should have access to it, and how is it maintained and kept up to date?

9. A school's public relations policy in the light of substantial self-financing.

10. In-service training in respect of school finance.

Further reading

Hinds, T. (1982) Giving Heads and Governors Control of the Purse Strings. *Education*, 26 November, 417.

Knight, B. (1983) *Managing School Finance*. London, Heinemann.

Society of Education Officers (1975) *Management in the Education Service — challenge and response*. London, Routledge and Kegan Paul.

Case 13.2: Economies in examinations

Introduction

A secondary school becomes all things to all parents in respect of its public examinations policy. Its teachers patronize various examination boards. Double entries and the support of high-risk pupils are characteristic practices. Costs gradually grow and reach inordinate levels. The situation is seen as a problem to be tackled. A combination of reduced admissions and direct financial support from parents is attempted. The professional judgement and standing of teachers are thereby given greater visibility but are also made vulnerable by this decision. The solution is tried for three years and subjected to review.

Narrative

A large urban, mixed comprehensive secondary school of 1400 pupils had been in existence for six years. With the full school finally established, a keen interest was shown in each successive year's external examination results. A large examinations programme developed and a senior member of staff was given formal responsibility for managing it year by year. A friendly spirit of rivalry grew up between the faculties and between the departments within each faculty. Attention focused primarily on the school's General Certificate of Education (GCE) results at Ordinary(O) and Advanced (A) levels and the Certificate of Secondary Education (CSE).

The parental body in the school's catchment area generally attached a great deal of importance to external examination results. The school responded positively to their interest and support. Every encouragement was given to pupils to enter for as many subjects as possible at GCE O level and the CSE examinations. In many cases pupils were entered for both these examinations in the same subject. Teaching staff exploited their knowledge and previous experience of different examination boards to the full. At GCE O and A levels a variety of boards were used according to subject staff preferences.

After a further three years the entire programme had assumed substantial business proportions with an annual total expenditure on examination expenses and fees of around £10,000. The local education authority had already issued general guidelines for schools to use in developing their examinations policy. From time to time different aspects of practice and expenditure were raised by the authority for discussion, but essentially a liberal policy was followed by the authority. Each secondary school continued to exercise its customary autonomy in the matter.

Within the school voices were sometimes raised over the length, size and organizational demands of the actual examinations programme itself. It could have a distorting effect on the whole school. Some members of staff also became disquieted about the extent of double entries at GCE O level and the CSE examinations. In addition, concern began to grow over the number of candidates who failed to justify being entered in the GCE O level, the CSE and the GCE A level examinations although the financial implications of the school's examination policy did not enter into consideration in these issues.

With the advent of financial cuts in secondary education, however, one or two senior members of staff began to have serious doubts about the policy adopted by the school. The teacher in charge of the examinations programme was heard to express his opinion openly in the staffroom on several occasions that there was plenty of room for financial economy in the school's examinations programme.

The head of school, who was about to retire, became sensitive of the vested interests of the teaching staff in using a variety of different examination boards and in having duplicate entries for GCE O level and CSE examinations. Parents generally continued to expect an open entry policy for their children for all examinations, including the GCE A level.

On appointment, the new head of school was determined to reshape the school's policy on examinations. It was decided to seek four important changes, as follows:

1. Staff must predict pass levels for all pupils for all external examinations.

2. No pupil was to be entered for any examination at the expense of the school if a minimum pass level could not be predicted.

3. A pupil exempted from entry under 2. above could be entered at the expense of the parent.

4. Simultaneous entries to the GCE O level and CSE examinations in the same subject were to be discouraged — but possible at the expense of the parent.

Reactions from the departments were mixed. There were grumbles about extra chores and some were afraid of the reaction of parents. Many teachers were suspicious of the motives of the head and senior staff. The word 'accountability' was heard mentioned and hostile views about 'management efficiency' were expressed. Even teachers who were generally sympathetic to the proposals had reservations. There was a sincerely held belief that during the substantial time which must elapse between making a prediction for registration purposes and the actual examination, a pupil's progress in a subject might change dramatically — either for the better or for worse. Furthermore, heads of departments warned that the varied experience of staff would inevitably result in different abilities to forecast examination grades.

Parental reactions were similarly mixed. The words 'equality' and 'discrimination' were used on several occasions in discussions with staff. Many parents had previously never entertained the thought of paying directly for educational activities of any kind. Most of them, however, accepted the logic of the situation. They appreciated the fact that they could assert their own wishes and judgement against that of the school and enter their children for examinations for which they were willing to pay the entry fees.

The changes were duly implemented. Predictions by the staff were gathered in by the teacher in charge of examinations. It made a good deal of extra work for him but he anticipated substantial benefits from the investment of his time and effort.

The examination results of that year were of even greater interest than usual. The results were compared with predictions and everyone felt that a new dimension to professional competence and interdepartmental competition had been added. Although accurate predictions by the teaching staff were regarded as the ideal for which to strive, it was recognized that it might take a little time for all departments to reach the optimum performance which could reasonably be expected.

Some departments were very discouraged by the first comparison of predictions with actual results. Others congratulated themselves on their perspicacity.

When predictions and results were subsequently compared in the second year, it was felt that a general pattern of improvement on the first year's efforts had been registered. Some features of the second year's results, however, gave the head some grounds for disquiet. For example, at the GCE O level examinations the mismatch between predictions and results was regarded as excessive in some cases, such as the following:

GCE O level

Pass levels

	Total entered by the school	As predicted	+ or − 1 level	+ or − 2 levels	+ or − 3 or more levels	Index of Variance
English	150	23	61	31	35	1.5
History	45	4	8	10	23	2.2
Mathematics	108	24	46	22	16	1.3

However, the head, in discussion with the teacher responsible for examinations and other senior staff, agreed that staff should be asked to approach the task in the third year as carefully as possible. He thought that the third attempt at it should be the time to make a thorough evaluation of the practice as part of the school's examinations policy.

The results of this third attempt are contained in Tables 2 to 4. The results for the GCE O and A levels are in full; those for the CSE are for selected subjects only. The Index of Variance figure for each subject is the average amount of error incurred in the predictions, corrected to one decimal place. For example, in the case of Commerce at GCE O level, one result was as predicted, counting as O, five were one place in error, counting for five(1 × 5), six were two places in error, counting for twelve(2 × 6), and two were three or more places in error, counting for six(3 × 2). The total of place errors was, therefore, 23. The number of candidates entered for the examination was 14. The average error per pupil entered, or Index of Variance, was, therefore, 1.6 (23 ÷ 14) The entry of pupils who were sponsored and paid for by parents was found in practice to be almost exclusively confined to the GCE O level examination. The number entered by this method and the results obtained are included in Table 2.

Commentary

In the light of the Department of Education and Science's Circular 6/81, the results of public examinations are a subject of considerable importance for secondary schools. To the extent that they believe in the efficacy of public examination passes to govern employment opportunities, occupational interests, and even life chances, parents and/or pupils naturally attach exceptional significance to a school's record of performance. To the extent that the Education Act of 1980 increased the power of choice of school for

Table 2 General Certificate of Education – Ordinary Level
Teacher predictions and actual results

AEB	Total entered by the school	As predicted	Pass levels + or – 1 level	+ or – 2 levels	+ or – 3 or more levels	Index of Variance	Parental entries Total	Results*
Accounts	7	2	3	2	–	1.0	–	–
Commerce	14	1	5	6	2	1.6	3	u × 3
Economics	16	–	2	3	11	2.6	–	–
English	97	37	39	17	4	.9	37	u × 14 E × 13 D × 3 C × 5 B × 2
Latin	6	5	1	–	–	.2	–	–
History	80	16	19	23	22	1.6	8	u × 7 E × 1
Mathematics	84	38	16	22	8	1.0	14	u × 8 E × 5 D × 1
Religious Education	2	–	2	–	–	1.0	–	–
German	33	10	20	3	1	.8	1	E × 1
French	45	22	21	1	1	.6	1	E × 1
Biology	15	7	6	2	–	.7	1	E × 1
Physics	19	6	12	–	1	.8	3	u × 2 E × 1
Integrated Science	52	29	18	5	–	.5	4	u × 4
Integrated Science	52	27	19	6	–	.6	4	u × 3 E × 1

AEB	Total entered by the school	As predicted	Pass levels + or − 1 level	+ or − 2 levels	+ or − 3 or more levels	Index of Variance	Parental entries Total	Results*
Engineering Workshop, Theory & Practice	19	5	5	2	7	1.6	—	—
Woodwork	8	2	4	2	—	1.0	—	—
Cambs.								
Art A	25	7	13	3	2	1.0	—	—
Art B	32	11	14	4	3	1.0	—	—
English Literature	64	24	27	11	2	.9	2	u × 1 / E × 1
Geography	65	20	28	12	5	1.0	21	u × 13 / E × 7 / D × 1
Needlework	2	—	1	—	1	2.0	—	—
Food & Nutrition	39	10	20	7	2	1.0	—	—
Music	7	—	2	2	3	2.0	1	u × 1
Elem. Eng. Design	15	4	10	1	—	.8	—	—
Geometrical & Mechanical Drawing	9	1	6	2	—	1.0	14	u × 1 / E × 6 / D × 4 / C × 2 / B × 1
Technology	4	1	—	2	1	1.8	—	—

*u = unclassified

Table 3 Certificate of Secondary Education
Teacher predictions and acutal results for selected subjects

	Total entered by the school	Pass Levels				Index of Variance
		As predicted	+ or – 1 level	+ or – 2 levels	+ or – 3 or more levels	
English	174	80	88	6	–	.6
Geography	110	35	64	10	1	.8
History	106	37	40	22	7	1.0
Office Practice	45	16	16	11	2	1.0
Mathematics	113	35	54	13	11	1.0
Physics	48	22	22	3	1	.7

Table 4   General Certificate of Education – Advanced Level
Teacher predictions and actual results

Pass Levels

AEB	Total entered by the school	As predicted	+ or – 1 level	+ or – 2 level	+ or – 3 or more levels	Index of Variance
Pure & Applied Maths	9	1	4	.4	—	1.3
Pure Mathematics	3	1	1	—	1	1.3
Applied Mathematics	3	1	1	—	1	1.3
English	13	2	4	4	3	1.6
Physics	9	3	5	2	—	.9
Economics	12	4	2	3	—	.9
Economic History	9	—	2	4	3	2.1
Sociology	7	—	1	—	6	2.7
Geography	4	—	—	1	3	2.8
Cambs.						
English	7	2	3	—	2	1.3
Geometrical & Mechanical Drawing	4	—	—	3	1	2.3
French	8	3	4	1	—	.8
German	6	3	2	1	—	.7
Home Economics	1	—	—	1	—	2.0
Art	4	1	1	2	—	1.3
Art	5	—	1	2	2	2.2
Biology	9	1	3	3	2	1.7
Music	3	1	1	1	—	1.0
Chemistry	4	2	1	1	—	.8

parents and pupils, schools naturally wish to follow a policy which will encourage recruitment and achieve results that appeal to the public. These results are most persuasive when they are seen to be superior to those of other schools in absolute terms. However, most schools by definition need to portray their results in terms which are relative to the many variables of school life, especially the range of pupils admitted and the school's own results for one year compared with those of the previous year.

Unmistakable and reliable measures of a school's productive capability are hard to find. Nevertheless, public examination results form a visible and intelligible index to pupil, parent, employer and institutions of further or higher education. As the best of the imperfect means available therefore, they contribute a basis for choosing or rejecting a school. By implication they comprise a basis of accountability for the school as a whole to the public at large. In turn, within the school, they make a touchstone for comparisons of performance between faculties, departments and individual teachers. teachers.

There is always conflict in education over the extent to which it is possible to create talent as distinct from simply finding it. Schooling may be seen as the process which makes of pupils what could not be predicted of them or which brings out of them what already could be predicted. The attitudes of teachers are a crucial factor. Teachers may continue to encourage pupils in the belief that they have yet more to give, or they may reach a point where they feel the potential is exhausted. The grouping of pupils for teaching purposes can reflect these contrasting attitudes. So too may a school's policy in using the public examination system. Teachers may advise pupils to opt for CSE rather than GCE examinations but not uncommonly direct them to one or the other. Implicit predictions lie behind these practices. Part of the reason why such directive authority can be exercised has been the freedom of the school to pay whatever examination expenses it chose on behalf of its pupils.

In this case a halt had to be called to the runaway expenditure on public examination expenses. This school, in common with many others, found that the use of its discretionary power over its finance had led to indulgence on an excessive scale. Even before the reduction of monies to schools induced compulsory economies, the disproportionate allocation of funds to support its public examination policy in this particular school could have been challenged on grounds of opportunity costs.

The new head evidently found in these circumstances the need for a new departure and a chance to make his mark in the school. Savings can be made by reducing double entries for GCE and CSE, by reducing the number of examining boards involved, and by not entering high risk candidates. Any move to reduce expenditure in such ways, however, incurs a restriction of opportunity for some pupils, giving rise to claims that rights are being infringed. Teachers fall back on the argument that they are the best judges of a pupil's potential and the risk which the school is prepared to take in financial terms. Parents respond with the argument that predictions are patently not always fulfilled. Prejudice may even exist. Public money is there for the benefit of everyone.

Each side gives ground in a sensible compromise. Teachers will take steps to raise the accuracy of their predictions. Parents will support their words with money from their own pockets in cases where the school does not feel justified in spending public money.

Pupils may gain from the closer scrutiny given to their estimated chances by both teachers and parents. Certainly those whose chances are declared low by the teachers may suffer a loss of morale and motivation but this may be corrected by the crusading spirit of the parent and the demonstration of faith of the parent in the child. As in all cases when a child's education depends upon a parent's financial position, it is hoped that the new balance of discretion between school and parent will not disadvantage a deserving pupil.

Issues for further discussion

1. What justification is there for the current multiplicity of examination boards and examinations (a) within the system as a whole and (b) within a particular school?

2. The work and prerogatives of the teacher acting as examinations officer in a secondary school.

3. The validity and reliability of teachers' predictions of pupils' examination results.

4. The school's right to veto a pupil's entry to an examination.

5. A fair way of presenting a school's examination results under the requirements of the 1980 Education Act.

6. How far should a school go in expecting parents' financial support of its examinations policy?

7. Fund-raising schemes initiated by schools.

8. The action to be taken by the head when

(a) a department's predictions of examination result grades are persistently inaccurate, and

(b) its examination results are poor.

9. Steps for initiating a major change in a school's examinations system.

10. Alternative uses for money saved: how a school may formulate and manage an overall financial policy.

Further reading

Beckett, J.T. (1982) Assessment of Departmental Performance in Examinations. *Educational Management and Administration* 10, 3, 233–236.

Hornsby, J. (1983) 'Perceiving the Purpose of Schooling'. Chapter 1 in Paisey, A. (editor) *The Effective Teacher*. London, Ward Lock Educational.

Hough, J.R. (1981) *A Study of School Costs*. Windsor, NFER-Nelson.

CHAPTER 14
EXTERNAL RELATIONS
Case 14.1: Fighting for survival

Introduction

Each of a group of villages has been served by its own school for a hundred years or more. The schools have become cherished as one of the essential and distinguishing features of village life. They are prized for their intrinsic merits as the best institutions for the education of children at the primary stage, though the need for access to secondary education in larger institutions at a distance has long been accepted. As church foundations, they have become an integral part of the culture of the parish concerned.

Falling rolls inevitably draw the attention of the local education authority to the cost of maintaining these schools. An investigation into their future viability is conducted. The suggestion of closures arouses the antagonism of local interests. The church and the government become involved. Yet even after a High Court case the schools are still open.

Narrative

The chief education officer of the local education authority informed the public of the education committee's plan to change the age of transfer from primary to secondary schools from 11 to 12 years of age. At this time a group of parishes had four small church-aided schools between them catering for children aged from 5 to 11 years of age. A joint meeting of the governing bodies was held to consider the future of the schools and how to provide for the children who would now have to spend an extra year in the primary school. The discussion was always focused on the best possible education for the children. It was agreed without one dissenting voice to recommend to the county council that a new aided school should be built as soon as possible to replace the four existing schools which would then close.

It was suggested at this meeting that some parents would not wish their children to be taken from their home villages before the age of eight. To retain first schools would mean a reduction in the numbers attending all schools which would create non-viable units. Many children were already travelling out of their own parishes to school. It was considered better to transport them within their own area, however, than to take them outside it altogether — which would have to be the case if the first school rolls fell below 30, the figure quoted by the county council as the minimum for a viable unit.

A governors' liaison committee, formed to consider the best site for a central school, recommended three sites in order of preference. All four governing bodies approved the preferred site, and this was supported by the education committee, but there were strong objections from the residents of the village concerned. The bishop responsible for the parishes and the local education authority then accepted these objections.

There ensued a whole series of meetings involving parochial church councils, parish councils and village committees with education officers and diocesan representatives in attendance. There was much disagreement among inhabitants as to where the central school should be built. The bishop and clergy appeared to favour the village which was the pastoral centre of the group. Although a landowner offered to make some land adjoining the existing school in this village available, the county's planning committee considered that it would be too costly to develop it to provide a school for the necessary figure of 200 pupils.

When the suggestion was made public there was a great deal of correspondence in the local press. Many meetings were held by all interested parties and it became the main talking point for months. Petitions were organized for and against the proposal, friendships were made and broken as ill feeling was generated between those in favour and those against. It was noticed that views expressed against the building of the new school were often those of people who were not faced with the problem of bringing up a young family. Initially, the request for a public enquiry came from such people. Some quite harmful letters were published which exaggerated the difficulties which might be created by the proposed central school. For instance, one letter suggested that an access road, five metres in width, would have to be built through residents' gardens. This was never mooted at any meeting and was a mischievous statement to make because it sowed seeds of misgivings for those who desired a new school.

A public local inquiry into the proposed siting of the central school was held. Meanwhile the governors of one of the four constituent schools had decided that their school would close. Most of the pupils on its roll had travelled each day from a small town nearby whose own schools were now able to accommodate them. In addition, the head of the school was moving to another county to take charge of a larger school so the governors agreed that to close down would be a reasonable course of action. Six months later, the Department of the Environment wrote to the county council saying that on the advice of their inspector, planning permission would not be granted for the central school on the preferred site. The inspector had recommended that one of the other villages involved was a more suitable and economical site than the one suggested.

Four months after that, the secretary of the diocesan council of education wrote to the chief education officer suggesting that before involving the local education authority, a meeting of school governors and head teachers should take place. A meeting was held within a few weeks at which the head teachers stated that they were satisfied with the standard of education offered to the children in the remaining three schools. The governors hoped that existing arrangements whereby children could remain at these schools until the age of 12 would be continued. If this was found to be impossible the local education authority was asked to consider the acquisition of additional land adjacent to the school in the village in which the Department of the Environment considered the central school should be located. If this proposal were adopted, it was thought, pupils from church schools outside the four parishes could also be accommodated.

A letter from the local education authority in reply stated that the schools' subcommittee of the education committee had considered the reorganization of primary education in the locality and had decided for the time being that the schools should stay as they were. The minutes from this meeting suggested that education for the 9 to 12 year-olds in the longer term should be concentrated in the village proposed by the Department of the Environment. The proposal should also be subject to further review, taking account of the views of the diocesan authorities, the schools' governors and the local community.

The governors and heads of the three schools were subsequently asked to join in discussions with diocesan representatives to propose some kind of revised educational programme which would be suitable for the children in the villages. At this meeting no one felt it necessary to change the existing arrangements. As a result of the decline of the school population, however, the county council created a Falling School Rolls Panel whose function was to visit small schools with a view to amalgamating or closing them. The chief education officer informed the three remaining schools that this panel would visit them in turn. The visits lasted for approximately 30 minutes and a decision was taken that further schools in the area should be visited before any decision was taken. Subsequently, other schools were visited and further meetings of the panel were held, following which it was declared that one of the three schools should close, the second should remain open for children aged five to eight, and the third, which was the proposed site for a central school, should be enlarged to accommodate children aged five to twelve, including children from the second school and another church school from outside the group.

Each school received a set of data showing an analysis of pupil numbers over a period of years, the catchment area, residential development, school sites and buildings, accommodation capacity, transport arrangements, community use and unit costs. From these unit costs, a figure was arrived at showing the average cost per child. From the outset it was difficult to decide whether the panel was trying to justify its proposals on financial or educational grounds.

At a meeting held four months later, the panel invited the teaching and non-teaching staff of all the schools involved in the proposals to attend. The chairman stressed that at that stage all proposals were initial and subject to change as a result of consultation. The chairman and members of the panel had received many letters and it was promised that all would be considered by both the panel and the diocese before any firm proposals were put to the schools' subcommittee. The timetable of future proceedings was outlined and the chairman explained that there would be plenty of opportunity for representations to be made in what was expected to be a very long drawn-out process. If proposals were agreed, it would still take three years to put them into effect.

These remarks were repeated later the same evening when the public were invited to attend and state their views on the panel's proposals. It was inexpedient for the parents and expedient for the panel that this meeting was arranged not only to debate the proposals for the village schools but also to change the age of transfer from first to middle schools in another area nearby. There was much criticism of the way in which this was organized.

The panel identified three major anxieties after visiting the schools: the substantial amount of vertical grouping within the schools; the substantial amount of subsidy that was needed to maintain the teaching staff in the schools; and the total costs of educating children in the three villages.

With reference to the first proposal, vertical grouping, sceptics remarked that it was considered to be an educationally sound principle before it became a necessity in some schools. Vertical grouping had existed in one of the three schools for over 100 years and would still have existed if the panel's proposals were accepted. Indeed, one member of the panel, a retired headmistress, when in service herself, introduced vertical grouping into her school, not because of necessity, but because she considered that the children would benefit from this form of teaching organization.

With regard to the second anxiety, some doubted that there could be a saving in the teacher subsidy. Indeed the projected numbers, supplied by the county council, suggested that the proposals if implemented would save little. One of the local education authority's own advisers at the public meeting said, 'It is my view that a middle school adequately to meet the needs of the children, should have at least six or seven teachers.' To do this for the proposed enlarged school at the third village would have meant employing six teachers to teach 96 children.

The third anxiety of the panel was the high cost of educating children in the villages. The figure for the transport of children at one school alone was given as over £10,000 per annum, no one at the meeting explaining that this figure also included the cost of transporting pupils attending secondary schools. The county has continued the transport system unchanged. In the case of the village school quoted, the number of children entitled to free transport was 12. It seemed, therefore, that a question of management was involved, leaving the impression that the cost of educating a child in these village schools was higher than the average for the county as a whole.

Opposition to the proposals came from the parents, teachers, local clergy, locally elected county councillors and village committees. This took the form of letters written to members of the panel, members of the education committee and Member of Parliament. All opponents of the proposals recognized the importance of maintaining a school in the community. The disastrous effect on a village of closing its school had already been seen in the locality. Although the panel proposed to keep the second school open for five to eight year-olds, many believed that this was only a gesture since the numbers attending would be less than 20. The school's governors rejected the proposal and so did the governors of the school to be enlarged. As the panel's proposals were interdependent, this effectively prevented the public notices to close the other school in the trio from being published.

It was reported in the press that the chief education officer, learning of this new development, wrote to a Member of Parliament saying, 'I do hope that a way can be found of establishing long-term stability without having to ask our members to consider closing even more schools and then possibly establishing others as the only method of ensuring good educational opportunities for the future.'

As a result of the governors' refusal to accept the proposals of the panel, the education committee declared their intention to reduce the number of teachers in the village schools. This decision to reduce the staffing levels in the schools was seen by the governors as a reprisal for non-acceptance of the proposals of the Falling School Rolls Panel. The governors felt that the county council made the decision for improper purposes and spurious reasons.

After seeking legal advice, the governors of one of the village schools made application to the High Court for a judicial inquiry. An injunction to prevent the local authority from altering staffing levels was refused after the county council gave an undertaking that no changes in staffing would be made until an inquiry had taken place. At a judicial review, the judge decided that, in his opinion, the county council had not acted in an improper or unlawful way. At the same time he suggested that the council should reconsider its decision to prune the number of teaching staff so drastically. The impression gained by a governor of one of the schools attending the hearing was that the judge was in sympathy with the schools but was bearing in mind that a decision against the council would have been a precedent with nationwide repercussions. The chairman of the Falling Rolls Panel then said that if nothing was resolved following the High Court decision, the schools would come under review again and again in each succeeding council. The governors of the three schools were inclined to regard this as an acceptable exercise. They reflected on the fact that the council's attempt to close and change the schools has been unsuccessful so far. A whole decade had passed since their first attempt made in 1973. Those fighting for the schools wondered how the schools would fare during the next decade.

Commentary

This is hardly an exceptional case of its kind, marked as it is by the extreme tenacity of the opposition to changes and closures, the long duration of the struggle, and the progress of it to date. The national and local press in many parts of the country are currently reporting intense battles over proposals for reorganization and/or closures but these are understandably more dramatic and noticeable when the number of schools and population involved is large. The decline in the numbers of children of school age has already made its impact on primary education. It is now affecting secondary education and will continue to do so throughout the 1980s.

The effects are felt differently. At one extreme are those schools which are located in areas where the numbers of children are constant or even increasing because of the building of new houses or the particular composition of the population. At the other extreme are those in localities of ageing families or actual depopulation. Such schools may become progressively expensive to maintain. For example, overheads such as rent and loan charges, and some current expenditure, such as fuel and some ancillary staff salaries — the school caretaker, for instance — continue at the same level, irrespective of whether the number of pupils is 200 or 100. This means that the cost per pupil place is rising as the numbers of pupils fall. Even the reduction of teachers is not strictly pro rata. Where transport is involved as in this case, a bus may be needed for 10 pupils which once carried 30. A smaller vehicle may be used as numbers decline but again, it may not be easy to avoid costs rising as they do so.

Multitudes of small village schools have been closed in this as in other countries to provide an improved curriculum and to gain economies of scale. Reliable road transport has developed to make it possible. Even where transport is impossible, however, as in Norwegian mountain villages during winter, the trend has still taken place for curricular and economic reasons — even to the extent of introducing weekly boarding.

This trend implies urban-based education and therefore urban influence. Behind this case, among other factors at work, is a love of village life, the determination to preserve rural English culture and a resistence to bureaucratic penetration from distant towns.

But education costs money. Money is subject to alternative uses — not only between education in schools and other uses, but also between education in one school and another in the same area. The residents throughout a rate-raising area may be charged equally but may receive in return an unequal expenditure on the resources which they need. These villages, however, were not about to be charged differentially high rates to support differentially expensive schools. Being church schools, the diocesan authority could have made funds available to maintain them but did not do so.

Thus, the dilemma of public bodies is acute. They have every sympathy with the interests of the protagonists but must exercise their duty to manage the system of education in an economic way. The worst aspect of their dilemma is the creation, in effect, of specially expensive education in one particular locality as a subsidy borne by ratepayers and taxpayers elsewhere in the same area for which the local education authority is responsible.

Two other aspects of this case are prominent — one explicitly, one implicitly. The governors are seen very much in an active, positive role. Schools' governors are often concerned only with routine business and some people would argue that their work is essentially marginal and successfully restricted by the system to deal only with trivia. In this case they are critically involved as the fulcrum for opposition in events of the utmost importance.

Associated with these events by implication is the internal life of each school and the education being offered throughout a decade of uncertainty and tension. It might be assumed that they would have had a negative effect on the staff of the schools and the education of the pupils. Anxiety may not be the best fuel for happy relations and effective learning. On the other hand people charge village schools with being recondite and out of touch. In this case it is more likely that the reverse was true. The dynamism which brought diverse interests together in opposition may have quickened the life of the schools in many ways. Opposition and fighting spirit over a decade had time to become a way of life.

It may be regretted that many schools are directly and visibly upset in their daily work by contextual events affecting the staff. It is probably true in this case, however, that the education of the pupils went undisturbed, aided if anything by the events which evidently upset the adult community so much. The system is built to facilitate this and the head of school and staff are expected to be detached but in practice this is less so today than formerly. The heads and teachers inevitably became involved and must have taken sides, though torn between the local education authority, the church, the parents and pupils, and residents in their villages at large. This case illustrates the work of the head of school in the fields of diplomacy, negotiation, public relations and communications in addition to the demands of instruction and care.

Issues for further discussion

1. The value of education in a small school. What is the optimum size for first/infant, junior/middle and secondary schools respectively?

2. The efficiency of a curriculum for a single group of pupils aged five to eight in a one-teacher school.

3. What should be the attitude and action of the head and staff in the face of closure or merger with another school?

4. The role of the head in a school's external relations.

5. A head of school's relations with the school's governors.

6. The work of the teacher governor.

7. The parent-teacher association — its purpose, structure and record.

8. Involving the pupils in public affairs — in particular those which affect their school.

9. Management problems in running down a school to the point of closure.

10. Alternative survival strategies for a village school on the withdrawal of support by the local education authority.

Further reading

Baron, G. (editor) (1981) *The Politics of School Government*. Oxford, Pergamon.

Johnson, D. and Ransom, E. (1983) *Family and School*. London, Croom Helm.

Paisey, A. (1982) Participation in School Organization. *Educational Management and Administration* 10, 1, 31–35.

Case 14.2: Strategy for recovery

Introduction

A secondary school finds itself at a particularly difficult stage of development. Its efforts to build up sixth-form work have been successful in terms of numbers of students, the range of subjects offered, and the regular variety of university places secured. In spite of substantial extramural achievements by its pupils which ought to have counterbalanced their negative effects, a series of cases of indiscipline in the school brings unwelcome publicity.

A trend is detected for pupils to leave at the end of their fifth year in favour of studies at local colleges at the same time as secondary school rolls are falling generally and the consequences of greater parental choice of school are being felt. The school takes the initiative to arrest the trend. Spirited efforts are made to solve the problem and to secure the academic standing and viable student population of the school.

Narrative

With the retirement of the head in the offing, an urban comprehensive school decided to take stock of its position. On the positive side there had been notable successes at national level in volleyball, dance and public speaking. The school's good record of gaining university places, including Oxbridge, had been maintained. In addition, fund raising had been very successful. For example, a new ambulance had been purchased for the transport of handicapped people. On the negative side, however, the school had been troubled by indiscipline. There had been a number of serious incidents of assault by pupils on other pupils and on staff. Some of these had led to court cases and bad publicity for the school.

An increasing number of pupils were found to be leaving the school to take places at either a sixth-form college or a college of further education in the locality. They included both those who were looking for vocational courses which the school *could not* offer and those who were looking for GCE A level courses which the school *could* offer. The introduction of the Manpower Services Commission's Youth Training Scheme at the college of further education led to an increased outflow of pupils, which in turn was further accelerated when a financial inducement was subsequently added to the scheme. This situation showed signs of being exacerbated by the Education Act of 1980 which provided that 'every local education authority shall make arrangements for enabling the parent of a child in the area of the authority to express a preference as to the school at which he wishes education to be provided for his child in the exercise of the authority's functions and to give reasons for his preference.' There were two other secondary schools in close proximity with more modern and attractive buildings, and a third at a distance but reasonably accessible.

The school was anxious to retain its sixth form not only to attract more highly qualified staff to teach in the school but to gain in many other ways. For example, the sixth-form play which was produced and cast exclusively from the upper sixth; an efficient prefect system; a wider range of library books; assistance in the running of societies; and at a time of staff cuts, sixth-form classes did not need to have their classes covered by other staff when their normal teachers were absent for a short time. Many pupils found it advantageous to continue their education into the sixth form. It was an opportunity to take responsibility for younger pupils, and to be taught in smaller groups by staff they knew.

Another problem was the common experience of falling rolls. The following figures show past and expected numbers of pupils in each year group year by year, the numbers in brackets indicating actual or revised predictions. The school was required to lose nine members of the teaching staff in the period 1981–1983.

Year	Intake	3rd	4th	5th	L6	U6	Total
1980	208	198	224	191	69	40	930
1981	175	208	198	224	64	41	910
1982	191(151)	175	208	198	76	60	908(868)
1983	231(196)	191(151)	175	208	67	58	930(855)
1984	209(175)	231(196)	191(151)	175	71	51	928(819)
1985	190(170)	209(175)	231(196)	191(151)	59	52	932(803)
1986	197(181)	190(170)	209(175)	231(196)	65	45	937(832)

Thus, taking all these factors together, including negative publicity, it was felt that steps should be taken to correct what threatened to be a substantial decline in the work and size of the school.

These problems were first discussed at the senior management team (SMT) meetings. The SMT consisted of the head, two deputy heads, the senior mistress, the head of upper school, and the director of studies. It was decided to separate the problem into three distinct areas, namely, the sixth form, the intake year and general school morale.

The first of these three areas to be discussed was the sixth form. The second deputy head, as head of the sixth form, was asked to gather information regarding the sixth form curriculum and pupil numbers. The result of his study was as follows in Tables 5 and 6.

It can be seen that in the first-year sixth there were 38 different examination groups covering 29 subjects. Fourteen of these classes contained five or less students. The total number of students in these 14 classes was 43 and yet 79 lessons during the week were used for these small classes. The sixth form were provided with a very wide range of subjects and in fact a good range of possible combinations of subjects. However, the very small class size in some subject areas was clearly a cause for concern. There was a need to investigate which pupils in the rest of the school were suffering because of it. Altogether there were 109 students in the sixth form, as follows:

	A level only	A and O levels	O level/CSE	Total
First Year Sixth	6	36	27	69
Second Year Sixth	28	5	2	35
Third Year Sixth	5			5
Total	39	41	29	109

Table 5 First year sixth form programme analysis

In columns (a) the subject of study
(b) the number of students
(c) the number of groups
(d) the number of periods per week
(e) the examination level A, O, CSE or non-exam (NE)
(f) the examination board where applicable
(g) details of combined classes

(a)	(b)	(c)	(d)	(e)	(f)	(g)
Art	1	1	8	A	London	Taught with O & CSE
Biology	7	1	8	A	London	
Chemistry	16	1	8	A	London	
Classical Civilisation	3	1	6	A	London	
Computer Studies	2	1	8	A	Oxford	
Economics	10	1	6	A	Oxford	All follow O course in L6 and then A in U6
English	7	1	8	A	London	
French	8	1	6	A	London	
Geography	4	1	8	A	London	
Geology	3	1	8	A	London	Taught with O
History	5	1	8	A	London	
Maths: Pure & Applied (P & M)	23	3	8	A	London	15 of these candidates are also studying for Add. Maths
Maths: Pure & Stats.	2	1	8	A	London	5 lessons are with one of the P&A groups as the PM is same
Further Maths	8	1	8	A	London	This is one of the P&A groups members of which have Add. Maths and are studying for Further Maths too
Physics	16	1	8	A	London	
Religious Studies	1	1	5	A	London	
Textiles & Dress	2	1	8	A	London	Taught with U6 and O
Art	7	1	8	O/CSE	Lon/S	Taught with A
Biology	9	1	4	O	London	
British Constitution	7	1	2	O	London	
Class. Civilisation	2	1	4	O	Cambridge	Taught with 4th year
Computer Studies	19	1	5	O	Oxford	
English	23	1	6	O	London	
Food & Nutrition	1	1	4	O	London	Taught with 4th and 5th years

(a)	(b)	(c)	(d)	(e)	(f)	(g)
French	4	1	4	O	London	
Geology	5	1	8	O	London	Taught with A
German	4	1	5	O	London	
History	4	1	5	O	London	
Human Biology	7	1	5	O	London	
Mathematics	32	1	8	O	London	
Music	2	1	2	O	AEB	
Needlecraft & Dress	1	1	5	O	London	Taught with A
Physics	10	1	4	O	London	One group member probably CSE
Sociology	6	1	4	O	Oxford	
Technical Drawing	2	1	4	O	AEB	
Typewriting	11	1	6	I,II,III	RSA	Taught with U6
Bus. Communication	11	1	6	CSE	Southern	Taught with Typewriting
Shorthand	4	1	5	–	Pitman	
Art	2	1	3	NE		
English	5	1	2	NE		
Games	45	10	3	NE		Combined with 5th and U6

Table 6   Second-year sixth form programme analysis

In columns (a) the subject of study
(b) the number of students
(c) the number of groups
(d) the number of periods per week
(e) the examination level A, O, CSE or non-exam (NE)
(f) the examination board where applicable
(g) details of combined classes

(a)	(b)	(c)	(d)	(e)	(f)	(g)
Biology	13	1	8	A	London	
Chemistry	12	1	8	A	London	
Economics	8	1	8	A	Oxford	
English	8	1	8	A	London	
French	3	1	8	A	London	
Geography	4	1	8	A	London	
Geology	6	1	8	A	London	
History	7	1	8	A	London	

(a)	(b)	(c)	(d)	(e)	(f)	(g)
Mathematics:						
Pure & Applied	12	1	8	A	London	
Pure & Stats.	7	1	8	A	London	
Further Maths	4	1	6	A	London	
Music	1	1	8	A	London	
Physics	14	1	8	A	London	
Spanish	2	1	8	A	London	
Textiles & Dress	1	1	10	A	London	Taught with L6
British Constitution	1	1	2	O	London	Taught with L6
Computer Studies	2	1	5	O	Oxford	Taught with L6
Economics	1	1	6	O	Oxford	Taught with L6
Mathematics (Additional)	3	1	5	O	London	Taught with L6
Religious Studies	1	1	1	O	London	
Sociology	3	1	4	O	Oxford	Taught with L6
Typewriting	5	1	6	I,II,III	RSA	Taught with L6
Games	20	10	3	NE	–	Taught with 5th and L6

These details were discussed at length at the next SMT meeting and the following decisions were reached. First, it was decided to retain the same number of subjects offered. A reduction in the small-sized subject classes would only create less choice and consequently fewer sixth-formers. Secondly, it was decided to investigate the sizes of the other sixth forms in the area. Thirdly, it was decided to look at schools with sixth forms which had combined with other schools. Of the three other schools in the area, one had a large sixth form, a second had a small sixth form, and the third had a sixth form of similar size. It happened that this third school was also nearby. Because visits to other schools which had combined their sixth forms had proved encouraging, the head began to explore the possibility of creating a joint sixth form with this third school.

The next step was a meeting of the heads, deputies and directors of studies of the two schools. This was a valuable meeting and although most of those present were very much in favour of the proposed project it was thought that there could be a great deal of opposition from heads of departments. The proposal was to categorize the teaching subjects into 'A', 'B', or 'C'. 'A' subjects would be those which would be offered by each school as at present, 'B' subjects would consist of those being offered on an alternate-year basis and 'C' subjects would consist of those being offered in one school only. This proposal meant that some staff would lose some or all of their sixth-form teaching.

Staff meetings were held in both schools and after a great deal of discussion in the schools a combined heads of department meeting was held. The main purpose was to talk about the various syllabuses leading to the start of the A level courses. Not only did this stimulate some staff to become more aware of developments in their subjects but it was also a pleasant social occasion. A joint academic board was established to discuss the many implications of such a venture.

This type of cooperation needed the support of other bodies outside the school. It was necessary to obtain the support of the local education authority, the governing bodies of the two schools and a new committee in the area which had just been set up to coordinate and advise on education in the 16 to 18 age group. The heads took responsibility for these negotiations and after a few months the project was able to proceed as planned.

During this time the joint academic board had met on a number of occasions and had come to the following conclusions. The advantages of the scheme were that even more subjects could be offered with greater option flexibility. The opportunity of more choice meant more students would enter the sixth forms. The merging of some subjects and the ability to offer other subjects at different times in both schools should mean larger groups and more efficient staffing. This would mean that politically the sixth forms in the schools would be less vulnerable. The logistical implications were the need to block off sixth-form options to timetable the sixth form before the rest of the school, to harmonize the class times of the two schools, and to cooperate on reports, assessments, and parents' evenings.

The final outcome was that each school offered a core of nine A levels, leaving the more esoteric subjects to be offered in either one school or the other, as shown in Table 7.

The cooperative scheme started in a small way but promised to be a growing venture. Already the cooperation between the schools led to the setting-up of plans for a Business Education Council general course although this idea was held up by the reluctance of the college of further education to provide the necessary sponsorship.

The second area of concern for the SMT was the intake year. The head of the second year was invited to join the SMT meetings and a very rushed course of action was embarked upon. In the normal way it would have looked with routine interest at the numbers of pupils expected to join the

Table 7   A summary of the subject options at two schools for the first-year sixth form

School X Option List

Level	A	B	C	D
A level	Physics Economics Geography Computer Science	Mathematics Biology French Sociology Classical Civilisation	Mathematics with Statistics Further Mathematics English Geology Textiles & Dress	Chemistry History German Art
O level (and in some cases CEE or CSE)	Physics Economcis Technical Drawing	Mathematics French Sociology	English Computer Studies Geology Needlecraft & Dress	Chemistry Human Biology Art
Other				Typing & Business Communication

Other subjects
A level: Religious Studies, Embroidery
O level: German, Latin, Greek, Music, Religious Studies

School Y Option list

Level	A	B	C	D
A level	Chemistry Sociology French	Physics Geography Spanish Mathematics Art	Biology History Ancient History Further Mathematics	English Mathematics
Other	Office Practice	Shorthand	Typing	
O level/ CEE	Science & Technology Sociology	Law Commerce Mathematics	European Studies Ancient History	Mathematics English

Other subjects
A level: Engineering Drawing, Ceramics, Design & Technology, Religious Studies
O level: Religious Studies

following year. During the summer term visits to the middle schools with brochures and information would have been made. New pupils would have been invited to the school. The erosion of numbers, however, meant taking different action. It was decided to bring forward the publication of the school brochure to November. The implications of the 1980 Education Act meant that it needed to be rewritten and extended. Most of the team felt the need to make the brochure much more attractive with photographs, a glossy cover and a good binding. The school wondered if it would be criticized at a time of cutbacks for spending so much money on non-educational material. The final decision was a compromise. It would have an attractive cover produced by a printer but the inside would be produced on the Gestetner, printing each section on paper of different colour. By delegating responsibility for various parts of it, a very presentable brochure was quickly produced at a reasonable cost.

There was then the question of distribution. In the November the school did not yet know the names of the intake pupils. The aim was to attract more pupils to the school. An Arts Week was planned for the end of November so it was decided to send out invitations to all the parents in the final year of the feeder middle schools to come to the various activities during the week. On the Thursday night before the performance, a special display of some of the school's work was to be shown. The brochures were sent in advance with the invitations and others were available for distribution during the evening itself. The intake parents made their final choices in the following January. Plans were made for follow-up meetings of intake parents at the beginning of the summer term.

It was found that people in the locality needed to be made more aware of what the school could do. This was the subject of continuing discussions and gave rise to the possibility of several community projects. One proposal was for developing a leaflet giving details of a walk around the area. The town trail leaflet would highlight places of historical and natural interest; it would be made available in local shops and libraries. Another possible project was the clearing of some unsightly waste areas.

The problem of improving school morale was one in which it was more difficult to come to any firm and clear-cut plans. The first staff meeting of the following school year saw an agreement by all staff to enforce the school rules so that the pupils had a calm and well-ordered atmosphere in which to work. Most of the group of badly-behaved and disruptive pupils had left the school during that summer and this enabled the school to get off to a good start in the autumn term. The Arts Week clearly helped to raise the morale of the pupils and in general the school enjoyed a much calmer and happier atmosphere. There was clearly a need for staff to discover and publicize some of the positive out-of-school activities of the pupils — for example, gaining the Queen's Guide Award, and sporting successes not linked to the school.

Staff morale at a time of falling rolls and staff reductions created difficulties. The internal promotion of four staff brought new life into some subject areas and the possibility of further promotions in the following year helped to maintain the drive of some staff. Nevertheless, it was expected that despite a drop in pupil numbers of only about 50 the school would have to lose a further six staff. Some of the six would have to come from natural wastage and promotions to other schools but redeployment for some seemed to be inevitable. The SMT felt that the only approach to this problem was to encourage staff to be positive and for senior staff to generate confidence in the school's future.

Commentary

This case offers a vivid example of the change of conditions in which schools have recently found themselves. Within the working lives of most serving teachers expansion has been characteristic of schools in general. Contraction, however, has replaced the growth which many schools formerly experienced. In this more unfamiliar state of affairs it may take a little time for individuals to adjust their thinking and adopt new practices.

Good management may be demonstrated — and may be needed more — in adverse contexts as in propitious ones. The essential tasks of management are to set objectives for the organization or to see that they are set; to marshal the resources necessary to reach those objectives; and to guarantee continuity — making sure that all functions have back-up staff and that the organization survives.

In this case the senior staff are seen dealing with problems of fundamental proportions. It was decided that corrective action needed to be taken on three fronts. The school was losing students by premature withdrawal in favour of another institution. This outward flow had to be stemmed at once or reversed if possible. The amalgamation of their sixth-form work with that of another school was intended to form a more attractive basis for study for students and logistically a more viable basis for the two organizations concerned. The second front on which action was needed was taken at the point of recruitment. This was a longer-term but more substantial matter since recruiting enough pupils into the school in the first place obviously determined whether there could be a school at all. The fall in recruitment had to be stemmed and if possible turned into a net increase. This the school tried to do by a vigorous publicity campaign consisting of the circulation of literature, holding events to show the school to good effect, and embarking on a series of community activities.

The third front on which action was taken was that of school morale. In the narrative this is represented as a negative factor. Morale must be sustained in adverse circumstances. The absence of morale may lead to the further degeneration of the school. High morale is the product and sign of effective management. It is easier to achieve when everything is going well for the school. It is a difficult and a severe test of leadership to sustain it when adverse conditions abound. Usually the work itself, achievement, recognition, advancement and responsibility are factors which enable management to build and maintain a high morale. When employment is shrinking and even internal job mobility is limited or non-existent, some or all of these variables become inoperative or unavailable.

The experience of the school in this case is familiar to managers in commercial and manufacturing in the private sector. It is interesting to note the similarity of response made to similar circumstances and pressures. If survival is threatened, a merger may be the answer. The presence of competition may encourage amalgamations and, as explicitly stated in this case, can sharpen and increase effort. Competition may be an antidote for stagnation. Teachers in the school were alerted to wider perspectives and encouraged to find out 'what was going on in their subjects' outside their own school. The increased visibility which schools now have and the keener scrutiny which goes with it, allied to more freedom of choice of school for parents and their children, suggest that a new and constant awareness of the school's public image is needed. It may be worthwhile for a school to assign publicity and public relations duties to one of its senior staff as is the practice in many other organizations.

Issues for further discussion

1. The relation between sixth forms and the Burnham points system. Is it time for reform?

2. Uneconomic sixth-form teaching: is it justifiable?

3. The composition and functions of the senior management team in a comprehensive school.

4. Links and relations between a secondary school and its feeder schools.

5. Which institutional and curricular provision for the 16 to 19 age range is to be preferred, and why?

6. Competition and cooperation between schools — some possible trends.

7. Staff morale and organizational climate of the school — the main variables involved. What can be done to ensure continuity in the discharge of all tasks throughout a school, by having 'back-up' or 'understudy' staff?

8. Community activities a school might undertake.

9. The basis and guarantees of staff job satisfaction.

10. The duties of a school's publicity officer.

Further reading

Cooper, R. (1977) *Job Motivation and Job Design*. London, Institute of Personnel Management.

Department of Education and Science (1983) *Curriculum 11 – 16: Towards a Statement of Entitlement, Curriculum Re–Appraisal in Action*, London, HMSO.

Jackson, K.F. (1983) *The Art of Solving Problems*. Reading, Bulmershe College of Higher Education.

CHAPTER 15
SCHOOL MERGERS
Case 15.1: First and middle schools combine

Introduction

Adjacent first and middle schools serve an unusually mobile population. Falling rolls affect them to the point when it is decided to merge the two schools. The steps by which the merger is accomplished are recounted, together with the implications which staff began to discern in the proposals being made. Reservations about the merger are mostly generated by hints that there might be a loss of jobs. These are increased when mistakes are made in the formal public procedures which need to be followed. Parents also express their preferences and everyone involved anticipates the eventually agreed merger with mixed feelings, not least because most of the important operational arrangements remain undecided with little more than one term left in the school year before the new school opens.

Narrative

The local education authority in this particular case had already set up an educational development subcommittee which had proposed to the county council that a new development plan should be prepared, based on the low variant of the possible birth rate projection of the population census survey. This proposal had been approved and a new development plan was to determine the likely number of school places to be provided, the accommodation likely to be required and the extent of land and buildings surplus to requirements in each area.

Relevant information was to be gathered to produce tentative proposals for each primary school. Each school was to be subsequently examined to assess its capacity. Originally the views of the governors of each school were to have been sought before findings were reported to the subcommittee but it had been requested that the procedure be varied to enable the subcommittee to see and to note the tentative proposals for each district before they were submitted to the governors of the schools concerned. The governing bodies were informed of subsequent general developments through the area offices of the local education authority at their regular meetings. The area inspectorate began conducting their feasibility studies and the two schools in this case, a first school and a middle school on adjacent sites, were duly inspected.

The numbers in the middle school had fallen and the staff had remained static until a point had been reached when the pupil-teacher ratio was comparable with sixth-form ratios. The first school numbers had fallen but were still within acceptable limits. The two schools had always been generously staffed above the normal county figures because of their particular problems arising from high pupil turnover rates. The questions to be resolved were the redeployment of surplus staff to reach acceptable pupil-teacher ratios and a viable size for a middle school from the point of view of providing an adequate curriculum.

Another matter to be considered was the first school building. It had been built in the 1930s and taken over by the county council after 1945. It was still in need of attention even though some extensive repairs had already been completed. The middle school building had been built by the county council in the late 1960s and had more playing area than the first school. The cost of maintenance was subsequently investigated by the county architects' department.

These facts were conveyed to the subcommittee whose decision was to propose combining the two schools in the middle school building. Full consultations with governors, divisional officers and head teachers were held, beginning with a meeting between the area education officer and the governors to explain the proposals on both economic and educational grounds, followed by a meeting between the area education officer, governors, head teachers and the subcommittee itself at County Hall. At this meeting the case was presented for additional accommodation to cater for the varying needs of the wider age range. The transfer of a demountable classroom on the first school site would answer that need. Additional hard play areas were also requested. The problem of providing an adequate curriculum was discussed. There was agreement that combining the two schools would allow greater flexibility in the use of staff resources, whilst at the same time maintaining classes of a reasonable size.

The question of implementing the reorganization was raised and the first unforeseen objection to the proposals was revealed. Up to that point there had been no mention of how the merger was to be achieved. The subcommittee chairman explained that the normal procedures under section 13 of the 1944 Education Act would be for the first school to close and the middle school to be reorganized and enlarged as a combined first/middle school. The committee would have to decide whether this procedure should be adopted in this case. The first school head teacher queried this since the school was still a viable unit as far as staffing was concerned. The governors were invited to submit their formal comments after the deliberations of the meeting had been reported back to the full education subcommittee.

The first-school staff were very concerned at the news of the implementation procedure. The school was only slightly overstaffed. It was doing a very satisfactory job according to the inspectorate and yet the existing teachers would lose their jobs and possibly not find a place in the combined school where the middle-school staff would already be employed. Since it was necessary for their anxieties to be considered the head teacher invited the area education officer to come to talk to them. This meeting took place with reassurances being given that by the time the merger occurred natural staff wastage would have solved the problem. Several of the middle-school staff were approaching retirement age. However, no guarantees could be given that it would be so. The position of permanent full-time teachers involved in reorganization was that wherever possible it was the county education committee's intention to offer continued employment to all teachers within their own part of the county with a safeguarding of salary and of status: 'Wherever a reorganization proposal affects a school an opportunity for personal interviews with inspectors and administrators will be made available to all teachers involved.' However, redeployment was an option which had never been exercised up to that point.

The teachers were still not convinced of the justice of the merger procedure although they accepted that it was a sensible idea to combine the schools. They decided to present their case to the governing body, which was a joint governing body for the two schools. The governors finally recommended that the fairest solution would be to close both schools and open a reorganized first and middle school in the middle-school building. This seemed at first sight to be a retrograde step. The first-school staff, however, accepted this recommendation since it placed the staff of both schools in the same position.

The governors' suggestions were formally presented to the subcommittee. The county council, on the recommendations of the education committee, adopted the proposed development plan for a first and middle school, subject to the approval of the Secretary of State. The plan would be implemented by the closure of both existing schools and the opening of a new combined school. Consultations took place with the parents, who were invited to a meeting. The education subcommittee, the area education officer and the county inspectorate were represented and available to answer questions. This was potentially the most difficult stage in the procedures. The locality, however, was not typical of the county as a whole. The meeting was sparsely attended and no objections were raised. The mobility of the families had always been an inhibiting factor in parental involvement in the schools and the head teachers had not anticipated much interest in a proposal which would affect the existing population less than their successors. The subcommittee expressed their 'gratitude to the parents for their understanding of the education committee's plans to make the most effective arrangements for the education of their children.

All the interested parties having been consulted and given opportunities to raise objections, the stage was set for the official notices to be made. Under section 12(1) of the Education Act 1944 the local education authority was required to publish formal notice of their intentions. This was duly done. All objections were to be submitted in writing within two months. Two months later, the notice was withdrawn and reissued because someone had forgotten to state the details of admission to the combined school. This delay increased the frustrations of the staffs of both schools who were still awaiting confirmation of their positions when the schools merged. No one in the local education authority was able to do more than state that no decisions could be made until final confirmation was received from the Secretary of State for Education.

The uncertainty had been with the teaching staffs since the inspections carried out two years previously. The teachers knew that their salaries were safeguarded but their future careers were not. Non-teaching staff did not have the same protection. The governors had been reassured by the subcommittee that should key posts in either school fall vacant in the interim period they would be filled on a temporary basis. This in fact had already happened when the deputy head of the first school secured a headship. Internal temporary promotions were made and a full-time temporary replacement was provided, though this was subsequently lost when the pupil-teacher ratio was worsened six months later. The temporary teacher was transferred to the middle school to replace a permanent full-time teacher who retired. Both staffs were being effectively reduced.

The non-teaching staffs were in a similar position but only one temporary appointment had been made (the first-school helper) leaving a potential surplus of clerical, cleaning and school meals staff, most of whom were part-time employees. All their hours had been steadily reduced as the county cut its expenditure over all areas. The teachers' frustrations centred around the fact that their roles in the new school organization could not be settled; there were no opportunities to participate in decision making for the new school as the head teacher had not been appointed from the two contenders for the post; the promotion structure in the reorganized school could not be defined; and teachers who had been given temporary posts of responsibility would soon have to revert to their former positions.

As the time for the merger grew closer, parents who had more recently arrived were seeking reassurances about the future. This was left to the head teachers to explain as each new family appeared. One parent who had been present throughout the procedures and had not raised any objections up to that point was aware of rumours concerning the possible appointment of one of the two existing head teachers and decided to lodge a personal objection to the local education officer and subsequently to the governors. The threats to organize a petition among the parents were taken seriously and complaints procedures were set in motion. This did little to ease the concerns experienced by both head teachers at that time.

It required specific requests from the first school head to the inspectorate and area education officer before personal interviews with all members of the staffs were arranged to discuss their futures and to receive advice. The general opinion expressed afterwards was that teachers knew no more after the interviews than they had before.

The agenda of the governors' meeting for the spring term did not include an item on the merger but a request was made that a representative from the area education office should be present at the meeting to explain the final procedures in relation to the duties of the governors and the appointment of the new head. This was arranged. The heads were requested to leave during the discussions. When they were invited back they were given an outline of what had been discussed. Both were of the opinion that they were told that the existing governors would continue in office to carry through the merger procedures (this was not to be the case according to later information). Once the Secretary of State for Education had approved the proposals, the procedures for the appointment of the head would be that one of the existing heads would be selected. There would be no external candidates. It was then revealed that the middle-school head was entering into discussions on the possibility of redundancy and early retirement and had expressed willingness to accept if the conditions were suitable. If this happened the position would automatically be offered to the first-school head who had expressed a willingness to accept. The existing full-time teaching staff would be offered new appointments in the new school. The middle-school head then told his staff that he was planning to retire at the end of the summer term.

The area education officer wrote to both head teachers to inform them that as there had been no objections, the subcommittee had formally approved the implementation of the proposals. This would be reported officially to the governors at their next meeting.

The way was now clear to formalize all teaching staff appointments but some problems still had to be resolved for the non-teaching staff. All except the school meals staff received their redundancy notices and were requested to complete forms to assist the administrators to effect their redeployment. The school meals staff had their own set of procedures and an adviser was sent to discuss their position. It required a specific request from the first-school head to arrange this. It appeared likely that they would adopt the same pattern as in the case of the teaching staff. Posts in both schools were to be terminated and the available hours rearranged fairly.

Both schools had to wait until the local government elections had taken place and the governing body of the new school constituted before staff could be selected, according to a letter sent to the non-teaching staff announcing redundancy. Whether this also applied to the teachers was unclear as it had been assumed that the existing governors would make the appointments.

The first-school head, in expectation of being appointed, took stock of the situation and found that with less than one term remaining the following decisions still had to be made:

—how the school was to be organized,

—the final teaching establishment,

—the final non-teaching establishment,

—how the full range of subjects could be covered,

—planning of timetables,
—individual consultations between the staff and the new head,

—arrangements for school meals,

—school hours,

—joint staff meetings,

—ordering of equipment,

—effecting the move,

—assessing furniture requirements.

Commentary

Circular 5/77 issued by the Department of Education and Science in June 1977 entitled *Falling Numbers and School Closures* made clear the central government's policy on the need to reduce public spending in education, as a result of lower numbers of children in the population. It outlined the national projection of the school population and against this background local education authorities were asked

> to make the most realistic assessment possible of future school population trends in their own areas and then in consultation with the managers or governors of voluntary schools, to examine systematically the educational opportunities offered to children in their schools and to consider how the premises, both buildings and sites, might best be used, either for primary or secondary education (including nursery education) or for some other educational purpose.

Mergers bring sharply into focus the possible divergence between the constant need for a rationalization of the larger system and the short and longer-term interests of individuals who are members of it. Institutions must have an economic basis. Those who manage the larger system must observe the costs of an institution to public funds. Individuals naturally wish to safeguard their personal interests which as often as not lead to a wish to support the status quo.

Normally the anxieties and even anger of the parental body are added to fears which staff may have. Unusually in this case, the interests of parents were governed by a high incidence of geographical mobility, as may be experienced by schools serving the families of servicemen, some businessmen, diplomats and others whose job locations are constantly changing.

It is to be noted that in small schools such as the first school in this case, the number of non-teaching staff may equal or even exceed the teaching staff. They too enter into the equation with the teaching staff since any merger implies a possible loss of jobs for both groups.

With only just over one term of the school year remaining, the head of the new school had not been appointed, the new school's governing body had not been appointed, pending local elections, and staff jobs had not been confirmed. Against such a background, the first-school head, who had good reason to expect the headship of the new school, grew anxious and frustrated over her inability to plan and prepare for an effective school to be operating in the new school year. Such extreme uncertainties are not normally the conditions in which schools are managed. Formerly, with high staff turnover, uncertainties were considerable. Recently, with the decline in pupil numbers and the increase in parental choice, uncertainty is present on very different grounds.

The circumstances were certainly unpropitious. The anxieties of both the teaching and the ancillary staffs could have seriously disturbed the orderly conduct of teaching and learning in the schools. It must have been tempting to delay and defer arrangements of every kind as long as possible — which in turn creates even more anxiety about the timescale in which to complete them eventually. The use of good management skills by the head was still possible. Leadership could be given to maintain morale and expectations. In addition, by the use of contingency planning, the head would have been able to provide for several sets of eventualities. This is commonly the lot of managers in organizations of many kinds where uncertainties are legion and constant. Operating in uncertain conditions is the opportunity for the demonstration of management skills of a high order.

Issues for further discussion

1. The merits of having combined schools for the primary age range
   (a) for teaching staff;
   (b) for the education of the pupils.

2. A timescale for merging two schools in the primary sector compared with the secondary sector.

3. The tasks of two heads during the final term with respect to their existing schools which are being merged.

4. Why should the appointment of a first-school head to the headship of a combined school be less likely than the appointment of a middle or junior-school head?

5. Staff deployment policy for merging the teaching staffs of a first school and a middle school.

6. The task of new governors of a new school formed by a merger.

7. Redeployment — finding the teacher to go and receiving a redeployed teacher in the school.

8. The curriculum, teaching methods and teaching organization for a pupil population with a high turnover rate.

9. How can parental support and interest be secured when families are transitory?

10. The contingency theory of management: should teachers know about it and apply it? How far is it already applied?

Further reading

Department of Education and Science (1978) *Primary Education in England*. London, HMSO.

Paisey, A. (1981) *Small Organizations — the management of primary and middle schools*. Windsor, NFER – Nelson.

Hargreaves, A. and Tickle, L. (1980) *Middle Schools — origins, ideology and practice*. London, Harper & Row.

Case 15.2: Combining two secondary schools

Introduction

With the number of pupils falling steadily in the locality, it was decided to merge two secondary schools. By the time that action was taken, the curricula in the schools had become difficult to sustain and morale among the teaching staff of one of the schools had declined. An agenda for discussion was drawn up and a systematic programme of action unfolded.

Latent and manifest difficulties and rivalries appear as the two schools raise and solve a succession of problems which lie in the path of their intended merger.

Narrative

The case for merging two particular secondary schools in this instance rested mainly on the following evidence of declining rolls. Pupils were drawn from middle schools with an 8 to 12 years age range. A grammar school recruited the most able pupils in the locality each year and also accepted transfers at 16 plus.

Pupil Numbers (actual or forecast)

	1976-77	1977-78	1978-79	1979-80	1983-84	1988-89
School A	654	620	564	540	430	350
School B	525	460	441	390	244	171

By 1980 both schools were operating well below capacity. Music and religious education had almost disappeared from their curricula as it became difficult to appoint specialist teachers. Morale in School B was particularly low, since for several years every solution for solving the problem of falling rolls including these two schools and others in the vicinity had resulted in the proposed closure of School B or its merger with another school.

Once the decision was made to merge Schools A and B the first step taken was to call a meeting of all six heads of secondary schools in the locality. The discussion paper used at their first meeting with an assistant education officer and several advisers was as follows:

Secondary School Mergers — Curriculum: Agenda for Discussion

Aims of exercise:

1. To achieve reasonable identity of practice in 1981–1982.
2. To achieve merged curriculum by 1982–1983 even if all pupils not yet on one site.

Topics to consider:

1. Aims and objectives:

   (a) Interim
   (b) Long term

2. Curriculum

   (a) General — what will be offered in (i) 1981–1982; (ii) 1982–1983; presence or absence of . . . (e.g. Mod. Lang.); no. of periods per subject; no. of pupils per subject (present and future distribution of pupils across curriculum); non-examination courses.

   (b) By subject — type of course (to be delegated to subject teachers?) integration with other subjects; textbooks and other resources; equipment.

3. Examination boards:

   current position; steps towards merger.

4. Options
   4th Year Option Process — for 1981–1982; 1982–1983

   Information and Consultation: parents; pupils; role of career service.

5. Organisation
   Mixed ability/streaming/banding/setting; by year; core subjects and option pools.

6. Pupils
   Intelligence range; background — social, schools of origin, mix or not? on what basis?

7. Pastoral

Relationship with academic/organisation; tutor/form groups; pastoral 'time'; horizontal or vertical division.

8. Accommodation

Type and amount (by subject); constraints and opportunities.

9. Staffing

Subject needs/availability; location — mobility (1981–1982: 1982–1983); continuity; horizontal or vertical division for split site (interim)?

10. Pupil Deployment

By building; by year group or other basis; in phases — 1981–1982, 1982–1983, etc.

11. Timetable.

During negotiations, the head of School A abandoned his preference for a 40 minutes x 7 working day in favour of the timing practised in School B. It was agreed that from September 1981 both schools would operate a 35 minutes x 40 period week, with the following timing:

Registration/assembly	9 00 — 9 20
Periods 1, 2	9 20 — 10 30
Periods 3, 4	10 50 — 12 00
Periods 5, 6	1 10 — 2 20
Periods 7, 8	2 35 — 3 45

The meeting reconvened one month later to receive progress reports. Reactions were also received from a second-tier meeting of deputy heads, senior teachers and advisers of the merging schools which had been held in the interim.

Many subsequent meetings took place between the heads of Schools A and B and various members of their staffs, especially heads of departments. Detailed differences and similarities of attitude and policy began to be accommodated.

Speculation developed about the headship of the new school to be formed by the merger. Declarations of loyalty were made by the staff of School A to their head, who took pride in his good relationship with senior staff. He had formed a management team of eight among whom he claimed there were 'no rigid lines of demarcation as to who did what.'

In a further meeting between second-tier staff of the merging schools, some important operational matters were agreed, resulting in the following series of proposals to the local education authority.

1. That for September 1982
   (a) the fifth-year pupils should remain in their respective schools
   (b) all third and fourth-year pupils to be housed in School A buildings.
   (c) all second-year pupils to be housed in School B buildings.

2. That in September 1983 all pupils be housed in School A buildings.

3. That the outline curriculum for September 1981 in both schools should be:

Year 2 (E_5 Hu_5) (M_5 S_5) (F_5) (Dr_1 Mu_2 $ReGen_2$) (Cr_4 A_2 Pe_4)

Year 3 (E_5 Hu_5) (M_5 S_5) (F_5) (Dr_1 Mu_2 $ReGen_2$) (Cr_6 A_2 Pe_2)

The reduction in Pe should be compensated for by an insistence on 'Pe skills' taught by qualified teachers, and by the incorporation of some Pe in the Dr Mu ReGen box.

Year 4 School A: E_6 M_6 Ga/Gen_4 / OPA_4 OPB_4 OPC_4 / Hu_6 S_6

School B: E_6 M_6 Ga/Gen_4 / OPA_6 OPB_6 / OPC_6 OPD_6

Some interchange would be possible in the options as shown.

The following progress reports were also made at that meeting:

1. English: good agreement on syllabus; book stocks to be compared; library provision to be considered.

2. Humanities: good progress, further meetings planned particularly to look at community studies.

3. Mathematics: initial meeting held between staff and relevant advisers.

4. Building: £234,000 approved and a brief required.

In addition the following courses of action were decided:

1. Senior education officer to be asked by adviser for information on group size, points and ancillary hours for the new school.

2. Staff to convene meetings for art/craft and science.

3. Staff to convene meeting for mathematics and to involve the adviser.

4. Staff to convene meeting for French.

5. Heads to continue detailed discussion on options.

6. Meeting to be arranged to discuss pastoral care.

7. Walkabout in School A to be arranged in preparation for building brief.

At a third meeting of the second-tier staff with the two heads, agreement was reached on the curriculum for the lower school. A persistent point of contention, however, proved to be the option programme for fourth and fifth-year pupils. School A insisted on maintaining science as a required subject. They preferred a strong core with only three options.

It was decided that the plans for the curriculum of the newly merged schools could be published for the guidance of the feeder middle schools. The outstanding issues at that point were the relationships between pastoral care, social education and humanities, the proportion of physical education in the curriculum, and the need to develop the mathematics programme.

The two heads discussed impending staff appointments, giving preference to staff from each other's school whenever possible. A large social function for staff from both schools and their partners was arranged, supported by the local education authority.

It was also decided to design the staff structure for 1982–1983. Meanwhile departmental meetings were to continue. Extraordinary meetings of the governors of each school were held to report progress and to discuss the issues. A building brief was drawn up for the sum of £234,000 which had been allocated. It was alleged that the architects took 'a very uneducational view' of the expenditure of the money on School A, although the brief was clearly intended to meet the needs of the newly planned curriculum. Final decisions on the building alterations and the staff structure were still pending the appointment of the new head.

Commentary

The opening of a new secondary school will be a rare occasion during the next few years. The mergers of two or more existing secondary schools, however, will be common. The opening of a new school heralds opportunities for everyone concerned whereas a merger inevitably suggests less opportunity for some. When primarily based on the contraction of pupil numbers, a merger can generate suspicion and create fear among both teaching and non-teaching staff with regard to either their positions or even their jobs.

Often a merger can be accomplished without loss of jobs, leaving everyone reasonably happy about their positions. The negative aspects of a merger, however, may run deeper than a concern for status. A sense of grief may be experienced as cherished practices are lost, preferences in values, conduct and relationships are foregone and years of hard work seem to be terminated. This applies not only to staff. Former pupils may lose a sense of continuity as the identity of their former school is obscured or removed. The community itself may feel that a part of its own corporate identity and continuity had disappeared. Schools in the primary sector which have become used to relating to a foreclosed secondary school may also experience dislocation.

In such circumstances excitement may be the diet of some of the participants who anticipate large changes and new chances. Heightened competition for some individuals is stimulating. Sometimes the circumstances are conducive enough to avoid the worst excesses which aroused emotions can bring — as when a head and other senior staff are retiring or are prepared to take early retirement, thus smoothing the way for a new staff structure to be established.

Nevertheless, the stress factor for everyone is a potential danger. For some a merger leaves permanent scars, damaging their personal as well as their professional lives. As occurred during the establishment of comprehensive schools in the 1960s, there can be real casualties in mergers. Care, sensitivity and time are needed to minimize these effects.

The positive side to a merger, however, must not be forgotten. Old practices are not necessarily the right ones. There is a new opportunity to establish adaptive measures. It is a time for designing a new curriculum. The occasion may attract new investment by the local education authority. Although old loyalties and prejudices die hard, a merger is the time to establish a dynamic basis for unity with different values that will inspire the new institution.

Issues for further discussion

1. The prominence and part which objectives play in the merging of two schools.

2. Guarantees of educational continuity for pupils involved in a merger.

3. Protection of employment for teachers.

4. The leadership task of incumbent heads of schools prior to a merger.

5. Job design, job definition and job delegation.

6. The use of two sites: management problems involved in working with split sites.

7. Communication before and after a merger.

8. Policy and practice for the selection of middle management staff in schools.

9. Policy and practice for the selection of senior management staff in schools.

10. The leadership task of the head of newly merged schools.

Further reading

Morgan, C. and Hall, V. (1982) What is the Job of the Secondary School Head? *Education* 18, June Supplement.

Neale, D.C., Bailey, W.J. and Ross, B.E. (1981) *Strategies for School Improvement*. Boston, Allyn and Bacon.

Nicholls, A. (1983) *Managing Educational Innovations*. London, George Allen & Unwin.

244

BIBLIOGRAPHY

Adams, N. (1983) *Teachers and the Law Today*. London, Heinemann.

Barnes, A. (editor) (1977) *Management and Headship in the Secondary School*. London, Ward Lock.

Baron, G. and Howell, D.A. (1974) *The Government and Management of Schools*. London, Athlone Press.

Baron, G. (editor) (1981) *The Politics of School Government*. Oxford, Pergamon.

Barrell, G. (1983) 'Knowing the Law'. Chapter 2 in Paisey, A. (editor) *The Effective Teacher*. London, Ward Lock Educational.

Barrell, G. (1970) *Legal Cases for Teachers*. London, Methuen.

Barrell, G. (1984) *Teachers and the Law*. London, Methuen.

Beckett, J. T. (1982) Assessment of Departmental Performance in Examinations. *Educational Management and Administration* 10,3, 233–236

Belbin, R.M. (1983) *Management Teams — why they succeed or fail*. London, Heinemann.

Bennett, N. (editor) (1980) *Open Plan Schools: Teaching, Curriculum, Design*. Windsor, NFER.

Bennett, N., Andreae, J., Hegarty, P. and Wade, B. (1980) *Open Plan Schools*. Windsor, NFER.

Bennett, N. and McNamara, D. (1979) *Focus on Teaching*. London, Longman

Best, R.E., Jarvis, C.B. Oddy, D. and Ribbins, P.M. (1980) *Perspectives on Pastoral Care*. London, Heinemann.

Blake, R. and Mouton, J.S. (1978) *The New Managerial Grid*. Houston, Gulf.

Borich, G.D. and Madden, S.K. (1977) *Evaluating Classroom Instruction: A Sourcebook of Instruments*. Reading Mass., Addison-Wesley.

Braddick, W.A.G. and Smith, P.J. (1977) *The Design of Appraisal Systems*. Berkhampstead, Ashridge Management College.

Brodie, M. and Bennett, R. (editors) (1979) *Managerial Effectiveness*. Slough, Thames Valley Regional Management Centre.

Brown, W.B. (1965) *Exploration in Management*. Harmondsworth, Penguin.

Bush, T., Goodey, J. and Riches, C. (editors) (1980) *Approaches to School Management*. London, Harper and Row.

Cahen, L.S. and Filby, N.N. (1979) The Class Size /Achievement Issue — New Evidence and a Research Plan. *Phi Delta Kappan* 60,7, 492–495, 538.

Castaldi, B. (1982) *Educational Facilities — Planning, Modernization and Management*. Boston, Allyn and Bacon.

Clark, D.L. and McKibbin, S. (1982) From Orthodoxy to Pluralism: New Views of School Administration. *Phi Delta Kappan* 63,10, 669–672.

Clarke, G. (1983) *Guidelines for the Recognition of Gifted Pupils*. London, Longman.

College of Preceptors (1969) The Prentice Affair. *Education Today* 19,4, July/ August.

Congdon, P.J. (1978) *Spot the Gifted Child: a Guide for Parents and Teachers.* Solihull, Gifted Children's Information Centre

Cooper, R. (1977) *Job Motivation and Job Design.* London, Institute of Personnel Management.

Coventry, W.F. (1970) *Management Made Simple.* London, George Allen and Unwin.

Cyster, R., Clift, P.S. and Battle, S. (1980) *Parental Involvement in Primary Schools.* Windsor, NFER.

Davies, E. (1982) Parental Involvement in School Policy-Making. *School Organization.* 2,4, 341–345.

Davis, J. and Loveless, E.E. (1981) *The Administrator and Educational Facilities.* Washington DC, University of America.

Davis, S.A. (1974) 'Building more effective teams'. 119–133 in Gellerman, S.W. *Behavioural Science in Management.* Harmondsworth, Penguin.

Dean, J. (1983) *Organizing Learning in the Primary School Classroom.* London. Croom Helm.

Department of Education and Science (1977) *A New Partnership for Our Schools.* Report of the Committee of Enquiry Chairman Mr Tom Taylor, London, HMSO.

Department of Education and Science (1978) *Primary Education in England: a survey by HM Inspectors of Schools.* London, HMSO.

Department of Education and Science (1979) *Aspects of Secondary Education in England: a survey by HM Inspectors of Schools.* London HMSO.

Department of Education and Science (1981) *The School Curriculum.* Circular 6/81, London, HMSO.

Department of Education and Science (1983) *Curriculum 11–16: Towards a Statement of Entitlement Curriculum.* Re–Appraisal in Action. London, HMSO.

Department of Industry (1982) *A Programme for Advanced Information Technology.* Report of the Alvey Committee, London, HMSO.

Dunham, J. (1983) 'Coping with Organizational Stress'. Chapter 10 in Paisey, A. (editor) *The Effective Teacher.* London, Ward Lock Educational.

Dunkin, M.J. and Biddle, B.J. (1974) *The Study of Teaching.* New York, Holt Rinehart and Winston.

Fullan, M., Miles, M.B. and Taylor, G. (1981) *Organization Development in Schools: the State of the Art.* Washington DC, National Institute of Education.

Garland, R. (editor) (1982) *Microcomputers and Children in the Primary School.* Lewes, Falmer Press.

Glass, G.V. (1982) *School Class Size: Research and Policy.* London, Sage.

Glatter, R. (1972) *Management Development for the Teaching Profession.* Institute of Education, University of London.

Goodlad, J.I. (1983) A Study of Schooling: Some Implications for School Improvement. *Phi Delta Kappan.* 64,8, 552–558.

Great Britain Consultative Committee of the Board of Education (1931) *The Primary School.* London, HMSO.

Hargreaves, A. and Tickle, L. (1980) *Middle Schools — origins, ideology and practice*. London, Harper and Row.

Harlen, W. (1983) 'Evaluating the Curriculum'. Chapter 7 in Paisey, A. (editor) *The Effective Teacher*. London, Ward Lock Educational.

Harrison, G. and Bloy, D. (1980) *Essential Law for Teachers*. London, Oyez.

Hinds, T. (1982) Giving Heads and Governors Control of the Purse-Strings. *Education*, 26 November, 417.

Hornsby, J. (1983) 'Perceiving the Purpose of Schooling'. Chapter 1 in Paisey, A. (editor) *The Effective Teacher*. London, Ward Lock Educational.

Horton, T. and Raggatt, P. (1982) *Challenge and Change in the Curriculum*. London, Hodder and Stoughton.

Hough, J.R. (1981) *A Study of School Costs*. Windsor, NFER-Nelson.

Hughes, M.G. (1974) *Secondary School Administration*. Oxford, Pergamon.

Jackson, K.F. (1983) *The Art of Solving Problems*. Reading, Bulmershe College of Higher Education.

Johnson, D. and Ransom, E. (1983) *Family and School*. London, Croom Helm.

Jones, R. (1980) *Primary School Management*. Newton Abbott, David & Charles.

Knight, B. (1983) *Managing School Finance*. London, Heinemann.

Knipe, H. and Maclay, G. (1973) *The Dominant Man*. London, Fontana.

Lavender, A.M. and Megarry, J. (1979) *Management of Resource Centres: Design and Layout*. Glasgow, Jordanhill College of Education.

Lorenz, C. (1982) Strategic Doctrine Under Fire. *Financial Times*, October 15.

Lyons, G. (1976) *Heads' Tasks*. Windsor, NFER.

Marland, M. (1971) *Head of Department*. London, Heinemann.

Marland, M. (1980) *Pastoral Care*. London, Heinemann.

Matthew, R. and Tong, S. (1982) *The Role of the Deputy Head in the Comprehensive School*. London, Ward Lock Educational.

McCleary, L.E. and Thomson, S.D. (1979) 'The Future Principal'. Chapter 5 in *The Senior High School Principalship*, Volume III, The Summary Report, Reston, Va., National Association of Secondary School Principals.

Michael, P. (1967) *The Idea of a Staff College*. London, Head Masters' Association.

Miles, R.E. (1975) *Theories of Management*. London, McGraw Hill Kogakusha.

Morgan, C. and Hall, V. (1982) What is the Job of the Secondary School Head? *Education*, 18 June, Supplement.

Morris, T. and Dennison, W.F. (1982) The Role of the Comprehensive Head of Department Analysed *Research in Education* 28, 37–48.

Napier, R.W. and Gershenfeld, M.K. (1973) *Groups: Theory and Experience*. New York, Houghton Mifflin.

Neale, D.C., Bailey, W.J. and Ross, B.E. (1981) *Strategies for School Improvement*. Boston, Allyn and Bacon.

Nicholls, A. (1983) *Managing Educational Innovations*. London, George Allen & Unwin.

OECD (1975) *Programme in Educational Building: School Building and Educational Change*. Paris, OECD.

OECD (1981) *Programme on Educational Building: School Furniture*. Paris, OECD.

Open Systems Group (1981) *Systems Behaviour 3/e*. London, Harper and Row.

Paisey, A. (1975) *The Behavioural Strategy of Teachers in Britain and the United States*. Windsor, NFER.

Paisey, A. (1981) *Organization and Management in Schools*. London, Longman.

Paisey, A. (1981) *Small Organizations — the management of primary and middle schools*. Windsor, NFER-Nelson.

Paisey, A. (1981) The Pupil's Experience of School Organization. *School Organization* 1,3, 267–270.

Paisey, A. (1982) Change and Innovation in Educational Organization. *School Organization* 2,2, 179–183.

Paisey, A. (1982) Participation in School Organization. *Educational Management and Administration* 10,1, 31–35.

Paisey, A. (1984) 'Trends in Educational Leadership Thought'. Chapter 1 in Harling, P. (editor) *New Directions in Educational Leadership*. Lewes, Falmer Press.

Paisey, A. and Paisey, T. (1980) The Question of Style in Educational Management. *Educational Administration* 9,1, 95–106.

Paisey, T. (1983) 'Adjusting to Work, Pupils and Colleagues'. Chapter 6 in Paisey, A. (editor) *The Effective Teacher*. London, Ward Lock Educational.

Phi Delta Kappa (1980) On Mixing and Matching of Teaching and Learning Styles. *Practical Applications of Research, Phi Delta Kappa* 3,2.

Pollard, H. (1974) *Developments in Management Thought*. London, Heinemann.

Pollard, H. (1978) *Further Developments in Management Thought*. London, Heinemann.

Poster, C. (1976) *School Decision-making*. London, Heinemann.

Poster, C. (1982) *Community Education — its Development and Management*. London, Heinemann.

Putnam, S. (1981) The 'Reality' of School Organization. *School Organization* 1,3, 255–266.

Randell, G., Shaw, R., Packard, P. and Slater, J. (1979) *Staff Appraisal*. London, Institute of Personnel Management.

Richardson, E. (1973) *The Teacher, the School and the Task of Management*. London, Heinemann.

Richmond, W.K. (1969) *The Education Industry*. London, Methuen.

Rushby, T. and Richards, C. (1982) Staff Development in Primary Schools. *Educational Management and Administration* 10,3, 223–231.

Secondary Heads' Association (1983) *The Selection of Secondary Heads*. Occasional Paper No. 2, London, Secondary Heads' Association.

Shipman, M. (1983) *Assessment in Primary and Middle Schools*. London, Croom Helm.

Smith, C. (1982) *Microcomputers in Education*. Chichester, Ellis Horwood.

Society of Education Officers (1975) *Management in the Education Service — challenge and response*. London, Routledge and Kegan Paul.

Stenhouse, L. (1975) *An Introduction to Curriculum Research and Development*. London, Heinemann.

Stillman, A. (1984) *School to School – LEA and Teacher Involvement in Educational Continuity*. Windor, NFER – Nelson.

St. John, W. (1983) How to Plan an Effective School Communications Program. *National Association of Secondary School Principals Bulletin* 67, 459, January, 21–27.

Taylor, G. (1970) *The Teacher as Manager*, London, Council for Educational Technology.

Urwick, L. (1963) *The Elements of Administration*. London, Pitman.

Vroom, V.H. and Deci, E.L. (editors) (1972) *Management and Motivation*. Harmondsworth, Penguin.

Ward, C. (editor) (1976) *British School Buildings: Designs and Appraisals 1964–1974*. London, Architectural Press.

Waters, D. (1979) *Management and Headship in the Primary School*. London, Ward Lock Educational.

Waters, D. (1982) *Primary School Projects*. London, Heinemann.

Waters, D. (1983) *Responsibility and Promotion in the Primary School*. London, Heinemann.

Whitaker, P. (1983) *The Primary Head*. London, Heinemann.

Wilby, P. (1980) *Parents' Rights*. London, Franklin Watts.

Woodward, S. (1982) The Headteacher as Manager: A Personal View. *School Organization* 2,2, 123–126.

Woolcott, L. (1983) 'Achieving Administrative Efficiency'. Chapter 8 in Paisey, A. (editor) *The Effective Teacher*. London, Ward Lock Educational.

INDEX